FIGHTING SEASON

FIGHTING SEASON

Tales of a British Officer
in Afghanistan

Graham Lee

Duckworth Overlook

First published in the UK in 2012 by
Duckworth Overlook
90-93 Cowcross Street, London EC1M 6BF
www.ducknet.co.uk
info@duckworth-publishers.co.uk
www.ducknet.co.uk

A catalogue record for this book is available
from the British Library
Cataloging-in-Publication Data is available
from the Library of Congress

ISBN 978 0 7156 4297 9 (UK)

Typeset by Ray Davies
Printed and bound in the UK by the
MPG Books Group, Bodmin, Cornwall

For the pieces of us which we left behind

1

My war started like many others, with a man in a uniform standing alone at the break of dawn.

I was in a corridor in an officers' mess in Colchester, and the winter air was sharp with cold. Something mysterious was happening. The first page of my story was being written, in very small script, into the annals of human history.

Had I known what was going on I would have felt angry, because we all know that stories start as they mean to continue. They have twists and turns but they never deviate from their basic theme, and my story was already going badly.

I was about to go to war in a barbaric cleft of desert in a god-forsaken patch of Asia. Lots of good war stories start like that. The thing was, I'd never heard of a good war story starting quite like mine before.

It was four in the morning, I had half an hour until the car for the airfield arrived, and I'd just locked myself out of my room. All my military kit, and my rifle, were locked on the inside.

Bollocks.

Why did things like this always happen to me?

It wasn't as if I didn't *try* to stop these things from happening to me. I planned things carefully. I liked to think things through, and prepare for contingencies, and this morning my idea had seemed foolproof. I was going to get up at 4 a.m., shave, put on my uniform, pick up my bags and my rifle, take them downstairs to the lobby, steal a bowl of cornflakes from the mess kitchen and *still* have time to see about making a cup of tea before the car arrived. My problem was that no sooner had I planned something than I was on to the next plan, and the old one got forgotten about.

I can't remember what I was thinking when the door clicked shut behind me. When I heard the noise I rotated slowly under the huge holdall of sports kit, books and DVDs I had on my shoulder, and stood staring at the locked door. *You bastard,* I thought. I put my bag down in the corridor and trudged off resignedly to find the night porter, who had the spare key.

I went down two flights of stairs, desert boots clunking on metal, and got to the front desk. There was no one there. Instead there was a single scrap of paper, with a handwritten note on it.

NIGHT PORTER ON HOLIDAY, it said.

This was getting ridiculous. Whoever had heard of night porters just going on holiday and not having replacements? Fucking civvy contractors.

IN CASE OF EMERGENCY, the note went on, CONTACT THE DAY RECEPTIONIST. After that it gave a mobile phone number.

I stood there for a moment and thought things through. I didn't want to trouble anyone, but deploying to Afghanistan without a rifle did indeed seem like a bona fide emergency, so I reached for the mess phone and gave her a call.

A sleepy voice answered.

'Hello?'

'Hello. Look, I'm sorry about this, but I'm locked out of my room in the mess. I need the keys.'

'What? Hello?'

'Hello? Hello?'

'Hello? … Hello?'

The line went dead.

Bollocks bollocks bollocks.

I called again. No answer.

CHAPTER 1

I looked at my watch. 4.20 a.m. The car was going to arrive in twenty minutes. My staff sergeant, Roachy, was going to be in it, because the two of us were flying to Afghanistan together, and I could picture his face already. He would be standing by the car wearing a bored look, glancing pointedly at his watch and then at me, as I dashed around trying to extract my rifle from my room. I could almost taste his disappointment in me. What was I going to do?

I stood there, searching for ideas for a minute or two. Then I decided I was going to try running around the outside of mess. Maybe, by some miracle, I would find an insomniac cleaner who'd arrived at work five hours early with a set of master keys. I set off at a jog through the twilight.

By half way around the building I still hadn't seen a soul. *Come on, come on,* I thought.

I got three quarters of the way round. Still nothing.

Then I completed my loop and – wait – there was a car out at the front of the mess!

I ran up to it, and a young soldier stuck his head out of the window. 'Morning, sir,' he said.

'Morning,' I replied, slowing to a nervous walk. It was the lad who was supposed to be taking us to the airfield. Roachy wasn't with him, thank fuck.

'You know we're not leaving until 0440 hrs, right?' I said, using all the officerly dignity and disdain that I could muster. 'I'll see you out here in ten minutes.'

Perhaps he thought it was odd that I'd taken an early morning run around the mess in full desert kit, and that I'd come outside to tell him that I would be coming outside in ten minutes, but if he did then he had the good manners not to say so. I turned my back on him and walked calmly to the front entrance of the mess. As soon as I was through it I sprinted upstairs to my door. I stood in the corridor and stared at it frantically. Eight minutes to go. I needed a plan. Please, God, give me a plan.

I could think of two options, and both were bad. The first was to wake up my next-door neighbour, Tom. He was a lumbering giant of a man and between the two of us, with some sort of synchronised shoulder barging technique, I was sure that we could break my door down. Then again, the mess charged twenty quid for using unauthorised Blu-tac on the walls. What were they going to say about a smashed-in door?

The other option was to break in to the glass cabinet behind the reception desk with all the keys in it. The advantage was that it was probably cheaper. The disadvantage was that every single person in the mess would see my stupidity writ large in shattered wood and glass when they came through the lobby for breakfast.

Fuck it, I thought. *Let's go smash the cabinet.*

I sprinted back down the stairs. There it was in front of me. I was trying to remember which bit of smoked glass my key was behind when I had an idea – the lock looked a bit flimsy and I wondered if … could I just … yes!

I got a good grip on the handle and flexed from the shoulder. The mechanism bent and gave as if it was butter. God bless the corner-cutting contractors who'd built the mess the year before.

Grabbing my key I bolted upstairs, opened my room, picked up my rifle and kit bag and careered downstairs again. I spilled out into the lobby and saw someone standing there, staring at the smashed cabinet. It was the day receptionist.

'Hello,' I said sheepishly.

'Hello. I got out of bed as soon as I got your message. I cycled in from home. Sorry I took so long, it was dark and it was really icy,' she said, in a tone which was ever so slightly reproachful.

I looked at the mangled lock and doors in front of us.

'Sorry about the cabinet,' I said. 'You know, I think … well … it should bend back, shouldn't it?'

'… Yeah.'

CHAPTER 1

'Yeah. Well, anyway, I'm afraid I need to be going.'

'Right.'

'Right.'

With a strange mix of guilt, embarrassment and pride, and with a whole minute to spare, I walked nonchalantly out to my car.

'OK,' I said to the lad at the wheel, 'Ready to go. Where's Roachy? Not here yet?' Then a knowing sigh. 'Well, let's go and see if we can find him.'

We found him, I slept all the way around the M25 and we arrived at Brize Norton Airfield ready for war.

2

Mel Gibson is staring across the parade square, and the oily black night is cowering from the steadfast might of his rough-hewn jaw. After several moments' quiet reflection, and some stirring music, another man joins him. Not quite a friend, not quite a colleague. A brother in arms. The two men face each other. They are both as unshakable as slabs of granite. Mel Gibson nods to the second man, and that man understands him. No words need to pass between them.

What is there to say? They are going to war, and a nod is all they need to communicate their shared nobility, to acknowledge with dignity the enormity of what they are about to do. As the music builds in sombre intensity more men appear from the shadows, marching lock-step in a show of profound unity. In perfect order they climb aboard the olive drab troop transports. It is the beginning of their stirring quest to meet and kill their enemies.

The film is *We Were Soldiers* and, as anyone knows who has actually been to war, the scene I have described is complete and utter bullshit.

They weren't soldiers. They were film stars. *We* were soldiers, Roachy and I, and *we* were going to war.

I'd just run myself ragged around the mess, trying to get my rifle out of my room. I couldn't give Roachy a manly and dignified nod, because I was in a secret stew of embarrassment.

Roachy couldn't give a shit about manly nods. He'd been to war plenty of times before, and now he was thoroughly bored with the whole idea. Had I tried to nod at him he would have said something polite and encouraging, and his eyes would have said 'Sir, you are a *fucking* bell end.'

Dignified we were not. Steeled for war we were not. In need of breakfast we were. That's what Mel would have got, with a nod thrown in for good measure – a nod from the chef as he set our breakfasts silently down in front of us two brave bloody boys!

We'd arrived at Brize Norton, and we pulled up outside the cookhouse. Roachy inclined his bison head towards the door and contemplated it.

'Time for some fucking scoff, eh?' he opined in a broad and rhythmic Lincolnshire lilt. He was the quintessential staff sergeant: an inexhaustible source of good advice for the young officer entrusted to his care.

We climbed out of our car with a cursory 'Come on, then' to our driver, who fell in behind us. Then we mounted a short flight of steps and pushed aside the door to the cookhouse. It was deserted.

Well, almost deserted. One ancient man pottered between the tables in the cheap polo shirt uniform of the civilian catering contractors. His employer was a dark and sinister conglomerate whose tentacles wrapped around every tender spot the army presented to it, and sucked its service supply budgets while offering the meagrest possible service in return. We weren't fooled by the cheapness of his uniform. We knew that he was powerful. We proceeded with caution.

'All right, mate,' ventured Roachy, 'sorry we're late for breakfast. We're flying to Afghan in a couple of hours. Could we get some food?'

'This cookhouse is for soldiers stationed on camp,' was his nasal reply. 'You can't eat here. You come under a different *budget*.'

The last word was spat through clenched teeth, like an incantation of dark and powerful magic.

Roachy, like me, had been trained to kill, to take life in open battle, but we both knew that some adversaries could only be defeated by stealth. Roachy knew this even better than I did, for he was an old soldier: a grizzled fighter of sixteen years' service, who had seen many campaigns.

He was a veteran of a long war of attrition against the Manning and Careers Division, who directed soldiers' career paths with a Kafkaesque zeal for doling out misery. He had fought bravely in the short but bloody action waged against the quartermasters when they gave us water bottles without lids, and told us that lids came from a different department. He had even been wounded in combat, in an unpleasant insurgency campaign to soften up the rigid authority of the squadron second in command. Now, faced with a brief sally from the catering contractors, Roachy repulsed it with ease.

'We've already been to the other cookhouse. They said they were closing early and told us we had to come here instead,' he lied.

'Well they shouldn't have said that,' replied our adversary. His words carried the tone of defeat. 'We've cleared away the hot plates, but since it's a one-off you can have some cereal. I'm going to have to mop up around you.'

'Mucker,' said Roachy, turning to our gangly young driver, 'get us some brews in, eh?'

'Aye, Staff,' he replied, fully resigned to his place in the world.

Roachy and I took our bowls of cereal and sat in silence at one of the Formica tables.

'Nice fucking send-off,' he mused.

Our driver returned.

'Here's the brews,' he said. 'That fucking civvy'd cleared away the milk by the time I got to it, so the tea's not got any in it.'

And so we spooned some of the milk from our cereal into our cups, and drank our tea with bits of cornflake floating in them. Then we thanked the fucking civvy for his kindness, and left for the airfield.

Three hours later we were in an RAF TriStar, Afghanistan bound.

CHAPTER 2

The plane was essentially a passenger jet. There'd been a last minute cancellation from a colonel and his sergeant major, so Roachy and I had been bumped up to business class, where we were luxuriating in the extra leg room. We were minor executives in a side branch of our chosen line of business, which was the dealing of death. Our side branch was the working of radios, and we were low down the corporate ladder.

Nevertheless, the RAF treated us well, in a half-hearted sort of way. They knew what made a good airline and they'd had a go at emulating it. Middle-aged men in drab uniforms pushed their drinks trolleys up and down the aisles, and we said 'Thanks, Corporal,' as they handed us our orange juices. The paint on the fuselage was peeling, and the wings had been patched up in the places where they'd corroded over the years. The RAF did value our custom, but they realised that we had no choice whatsoever in our business airline.

Roachy sat beside me. As we spoke, I got the first ever acknowledgement from him that we were going to war. He started on a theme, which I realised he'd been planning for some time.

'Never volunteer for anything,' he said. 'That's when you fucking spank in, when you volunteer for stuff.'

'Spanking in' meant dying. It also meant falling off an obstacle course, or something equally inept, because dying was a form of ineptitude – a failure to navigate your way effectively through The System.

I was impressed with Roachy's insight. He had me down to a tee. He knew that I was a brain-dead young troop commander who thought that life was a game and lusted for action. He knew that I knew nothing about loving a wife and a child, as he did, and about trying to keep myself safe for them.

Safe we would stay, if we played our cards right, for looking after radios was not traditionally a dangerous pursuit. We were a troop commander and a staff sergeant in the Royal Corps of Signals, and we had a comfortable war ahead of us. I hated that idea. I didn't even like the Corps that much. The name was shit. The Royal Signals – it conjured up images of men in tweed battledress and moustaches who waved flags and flashed enormous lights at each other.

Of course the Corps wasn't like that any more, and plenty of Signals soldiers would see action over the coming summer. It just didn't look likely that I would be one of them. Roachy and I ran a troop of nearly forty men, who were following on behind us. We knew that most of them would be in the thick of it, but we were too high up the chain to be getting our hands dirty. We knew that the lower down our soldiers were, and of course the younger they were, the rougher they would have it.

In war it's always been the most junior soldiers who've got it the worst – 'Wilkins, go and charge that machine gun nest.' 'Right-oh, sir!' – but by recompense the commanders, the NCOs and the officers, shouldered the burden of responsibility for their lives. They had to live with young Wilkins' blood on their hands. That's how it was supposed to happen, and that's how it would have happened, had the Taliban not thrown a spanner in the works.

The British Army was structured to fight a conventional force, and the bastard Taliban had dragged us into a counter-insurgency war which, as it turned out, could be fought without my help. Roachy and I were having our soldiers taken off us to be given to infantry and armoured commanders, and they would take on the responsibility for their young lives:

'Young radio operators from the Signals? Well, none of our lads know how to work all this new crypto fill shit, so that sounds like a great idea, let's have a couple to go on patrols with us,' they might say.

'A troop commander without a troop? Fuck that,' they would definitely say. 'We're not running warzone tours for superfluous REMFs.'

And an REMF I was in danger of becoming. A Rear Echelon Mother Fucker.

I was largely surplus to requirements, but I was going to Afghanistan anyway, because a huge wheel was turning and I was a tiny little wheel inside it.

CHAPTER 2

I wanted out. I wanted adventure and action, and once we were in Helmand I planned to break free of the machine and rattle around inside it. I had all sorts of schemes in my head but I kept them secret from Roachy because he would have poured cold water all over them. Mine would be a game of stealth. He played his hand more openly, and he was warming to his theme.

'It's always the cunts who volunteer for stuff that get killed. Guys from the Signals, or whatever, who get themselves on foot patrol and reckon they're off on a fucking jolly. Then something kicks off and everyone forgets about you. If you get shot, no one's coming to evacuate you, 'cos no one knows you there. It's only when they get back to camp that they say, "hang on, didn't we have that Signals fella tagging along with us, what happened to him?" '

I nodded sagely.

'By which point you're fucked,' added Roachy, in case I hadn't yet taken his point.

I had taken his point but I was disregarding it, because I didn't want to hear it. What did he know anyway, the silly old sod. I would go along with him because it made my life easier. Then, when the time was right, I'd show him I'd been ignoring him all along and bugger off on a jolly. Ha! That'd show him.

'I guess we'll just see what happens when we get there,' I said, non-committally.

That was my campaign strategy – keep things obscure. Deny the enemy all knowledge of your inner workings, your Order of Battle. Then, at some crucial point in the future … strike!

Now was not that point, so I withdrew into my book. I was reading *Dracula,* and I wanted to finish it off. Roachy followed suit, producing a small, glossy book with a picture of a woman wearing latex on its cover.

'Are you reading *filth*?' I asked.

'Yeah,' he replied, smiling broadly. 'I'm up to a bit where this house-wife gets off from being covered head-to-toe in roofing tar.'

I said that I thought it was a bad idea to get over-stimulated on the first day of a tour, but he just shrugged his shoulders and immersed himself in his smut. He chuckled from time to time then fell asleep, open-mouthed.

If we were going to be working together in Helmand, surely I had a vested interest in his mental state, I reasoned. I reached across him, surreptitiously, and plucked the book from his chest. I opened it at random, and read a few paragraphs. The heroine was having an alter-cation with her gardener. She was a middle-class social climber, straight out of a 1970s sitcom, and her 'lowly gardener' was ordering her to wet her knickers in public.

I'd thought that the army was the only place in England where the class system was still alive and well. Now it seemed that it lived on in erotic fiction too. Roachy was a man and I was a boy, but he called me 'sir' because inside the army my class ruled his. Housewives ruled gardeners but men ruled women, because sex was violence and vio-lence was sex.

The gardener knew as much, because he was a man of the soil, and he had the power to make a woman urinate at will. The housewife knew it because she was being humiliated, but couldn't stop herself from being turned on. Roachy and I knew it because the army had taught us it was so.

'Smash her in,' was the phrase we'd been taught. It replaced 'make love to her.' It was a good phrase because it removed the necessity of being desired. If we stopped making love to women, if we smashed them in instead, then they could never reject us. Every man in the army knew how to dominate and be dominated. Power and violence were our bread and butter. Sex and adoration were what we craved. Power. Domination. Violence. Sex. Why not make them all the same, and solve man's problems for good? I read to the end of the page, then put the book back in Roachy's lap and settled down in my chair, to sleep and to dream dreams of Afghanistan.

CHAPTER 2

Eight hours later our plane touched down in Kandahar, the Taliban's spiritual home.

There had been around three hundred of us on the flight. Those of us who were heading onwards to Camp Bastion, in Helmand Province, were shepherded into a transit hangar, where we sat under bright fluorescent lights, sipped lukewarm cups of tea and waited for someone to tell us what to do next. After two hours or so, a gruff and portly RAF flight sergeant walked into the room. He announced in a shout that it was time for us to depart. The first sixty of us stood up and lugged our kit towards the double doors, outside which we were corralled onto a coach and driven quickly and quietly to a waiting Hercules, which sat on a blacked-out runway. As we were directed aboard the squat, propeller-driven aircraft, I felt a small degree of comfort in this herding process, in constantly being told where to go and what to do when I got there. It relieved me of the need to think for myself.

We pressed into our small canvas seats, shoulder-to-shoulder in long rows running up and down the fuselage. I'd parachuted from a Hercules, and as I looked down at the exit doors I was glad I wouldn't be jumping from this one. It wasn't a pleasant experience.

We sat facing each other. The familiar high-pitched whine of the props began, with the rumbling harmony of their gas turbine engines, and then the forward thrust kicked in with a jolt, making every man slant to the diagonal and lean into the shoulders of the man next to him for support. We gathered speed, the nose reared up and the staccato vibrations from the tarmac fell away from us. We were aloft again, gliding through a hundred miles of blackness towards Bastion.

It was 2008. The tenth of March. Had the war started yet? No one had announced it. Below our feet, in the darkness, were the killers, the jihadists, the rapists and the torturers. They were waiting for us. If they wanted to, they could reach out and touch us, with a rocket, and bring the war right to us. But it didn't *seem* like we were at war.

There's something irresistibly sleep-inducing about the back compartment of a Hercules. You have the gentle rocking of the fuselage, the vibration of the propellers and the steady white noise of the engines coupled with the almost total darkness, which sits thickly on you like a blanket. Your helmet enwraps and cushions your head. What little oxygen there is in the air is muscled out by aviation-gas fumes, or hoovered up by the sixty other occupants of the plane.

After fifteen minutes of trying to come to terms with the jihadists beneath us, I began to lose interest. Every man in the cabin was now asleep, and I joined them.

Before a British soldier is released into Helmand to fight for his country, he must be processed. He must be briefed by PowerPoint for two whole days before he is deemed ready to kill his enemies. He sleeps in a hangar with two hundred of his comrades, on the same green mattress the army's given him to sleep on all over the world. Thin, plastic and resistant to every fluid a soldier's body can produce. Roachy and I went through this process, along with seven thousand of our comrades, give or take, then everyone went to their assigned camps and bases around Helmand. Roachy and I moved to a homely tent and stayed in Camp Bastion. 16 Air Assault Brigade, the British Army's spearhead force, was going to war. Our places had been assigned to us and we were steadying ourselves. Ready to charge.

The Taliban knew that we were coming. Not far from us, across the desert, they were making ready for the impending storm. They were a mystery. A phantom. We wondered what they were up to.

Perhaps, in some mud-brick hovel, a young Taliban fighter was sitting with his rifle. Perhaps he had been bought from his father on the Afghan-Pakistan border about two months earlier. $300 was the going rate for a son of fighting age. I tried to imagine his situation by piecing together what scraps I had learned of the Taliban's modus operandi.

I imagined the young fighter thus: he understands almost nothing of the world outside his village, but the Taliban have told him all he needs to know. To the north there are men that have offended God, and it is his duty to fight and die repelling them. Across from him, in the hovel, a family might be sitting. The children look at him with fear, because he arrived in the night demanding shelter. He told their father he would kill them if they did not take him in. It was a dishonourable thing to do, but he needed food and a place to rest. Also, he was afraid. He needed somewhere to escape from his fear. He needed somewhere to take the opium that would make the fear go away.

And perhaps he was right and we were wrong, and God really was on his side. Then, as the needle clattered to the ground, his hand slipped from his rifle and the opium fantasies took him, maybe God would grant him a vision of his enemies. The infidels. Us.

His spirit would soar like a bird, up above the desert. Beneath him he would see a vast square of blast walls, shipping containers, tents and sheet metal buildings, thirty miles out in the wasteland. Camp Bastion. The sprawling powerhouse of the infidels' incursion into his homeland. The place where the foreign soldiers go to take it easy. The Barbados of Afghanistan. REMF-tastic Bas-bados. Now he drops like a stone. The desert flies past him and all of a sudden he's inside a tent, and that tent is a filthy sanctuary from the rest of the world. Roachy and I have been processed, and it's where we've moved in to.

There are six camp beds for sleeping on, and two more made into sofas, with plywood backs and mattresses for cushions. The sofas face a television, and either side of the television there are book cases, made from tubes which used to hold heat-seeking missiles. The Taliban got the missiles, and we got the tubes.

On the sofas, watching *Bargain Hunt*, are Roachy and I. Next to us is Chucker, the cryptography expert, whose mind is as cryptic as the codes from which he earns his living. Express an opinion and 'That's absolutely right' is all you will ever hear him say.

Next to him is the bald and genteel Brian, the radio technician, who soldiers and solders in equal measure. On the end of the sofa is Paul, our veteran of special forces communications, known to all as the Cunt from Blah – everyone who's worked in special forces signals is a Cunt from Blah, because all their stories start 'When I was working with the SAS, blah blah blah.'

Finally, in the corner, is the sergeant from the mapping cell. No one knows why he's here. He's got nothing to do with comms, but he's allowed to stay because he's brought a woman with him: Paris. Lovely Paris Hilton, reproduced life-size by the printer in the mapping cell. She stares at us with sultry eyes, always wanting us. She watches us sitting there in our stinking desert combats. She hears the profanity, the whining and the casual racism, but she wants us all the same. Standing there in her panties, as Roachy says, 'We're going to have to punch a fucking glory hole in her soon.'

'No you're not,' says Paul, 'her crotch is right over my head where I sleep.'

'Poor old Paul,' says Roachy. 'We'll be screwing Paris and jabbing him in the head while he's trying to sleep.'

'Ah! Ah!' says Roachy, waving his arms and mimicking Paul's voice. 'Why's my face all sticky?'

This is what God's warrior would have seen of his mortal enemies, as he slipped into his hungry heroin sleep.

I was not the only frustrated REMF in Camp Bastion. The place was full of us. We even had our own shop, with soft drinks, pies in foil wrapping and a karaoke machine, which was usually hogged by an overweight female corporal from the post room trying to sing 'Eternal Flame'.

Jim, technically my boss, was also a frustrated REMF. He was our squadron's operations officer, and he was two years my senior. A short, thin man, with a shock of white-blond hair, who was staring down the barrel of a second operational tour stuck in headquarters. I found him

infuriating, because he knew exactly how to infuriate me and he enjoyed doing so, but I also liked him. It was to our mutual dismay, but
the fact was that we had a lot in common. So, when we weren't winding
each other up, we enjoyed each other's company. We had a strange
relationship.

We met each other in the shop and sat down with a tepid cup of coffee
to discuss my role for the next seven months.

'You'll have to stay in Bastion for a while, mate,' he said. 'Probably
about six weeks. That'll be useful for me though, because you'll be here
to make sure all the lads get out to the FOBs OK. Then we'll look at firing
you out on some comms reccies around the place.'

He went on to explain some technical details of what he wanted me
to look at, while I tried to appear pensive but enthusiastic. The idea was
that I would deploy to the FOBs, the Forward Operating Bases, with a
small team. These were the outlying camps where the real soldiering
took place, and I was to look into the state of the communications
systems I found there. There were dozens of different systems in Helmand, all complicated and eccentric in their own way. They'd been
cobbled together haphazardly over the previous two years, and they
did not integrate particularly well with each other. Jim unfurled a series
of diagrams and flow charts and explained his ideas for improvement
to me, speaking energetically about the good work that could be done.
His plan was richly detailed, and it had clearly been a labour of love
between him and our squadron commander. Still, I had difficulty visu-
alising how it would work in practice. I couldn't shake the notion that
it would live best as a paper plan that would never have to be followed
though. I suspected that it had been dreamed up – at least in part – to
compensate for my lack of a job.

Nevertheless, it would mean travel around Helmand, and variety,
and I was in no mood to complain.

The next day Jim left for Lashkar Gah, the provincial capital, and six
months behind a desk. I did not envy him. He'd rather have done almost

anything else, but he knew he couldn't avoid it. He was the operations officer, and Lashkar Gah held the British headquarters for the whole of Helmand. That, inescapably, was where he belonged. I tried not to seem too smug as he said his goodbyes.

Alas, I wasn't much better off than he was. I had a vague promise of an interesting job at some point in the future, but for now I was waiting in the wings as the whole brigade flowed past me. Coming through Bastion, and going out again to fill up the little bases dotted through Helmand. Taking over from the last lot, as happened every spring and every autumn. Their march to war continued, and I marched back to the tent to open welfare parcels.

We had a near-infinite supply of these bastards. They were shoe boxes, filled with goodies by the well-meaning folks back home. They got sent out to Our Brave Boys in the field, but stopped in Camp Bastion because most of our boys in the field didn't want what was in them, so now it fell to Roachy and me to open them up, sort their contents and stash them in one of the shipping containers at our disposal. We were being crushed under tiny, identical pots of strawberry jam, and short-cake, and books of crossword puzzles.

One lady, who must have been concerned that an excess of fine living might soften us up, had sent us a jar of economy fish paste, a cross-stitch kit and nothing else. Someone else went to the opposite extreme and posted out boxes and boxes of Harrods' tea bags. They were just as unpalatable as the fish paste, and we needed two bags in every cup to make them taste of anything but grit.

Some of the boxes came with letters, which we pored over for hints of sexual deviancy. We recognised the senders. They were the house-wives from Roachy's library of filth, and we knew their secrets.

Our existence continued in this way for a week. Then, one morning, I was handed a message by a runner. It was from the garrison sergeant major, who wanted to know why I had not yet come to see him. He'd been expecting me to appear in his office two hours ago, apparently, so that I could take over the role of Camp Bastion duty officer for the day.

Sergeant majors are strange beasts. They salute young officers, and call you 'sir', but everyone knows who's really in charge. They are the army's old guard who tell tales of brawls with Combat 18 skinheads and of turf wars over drinking rights at grimy Aldershot pubs, back in the beer-soaked glory days of the 1980s. Always the same stories, and never wholly believable, but entertaining nonetheless.

I wasn't sure how the garrison sergeant major knew I was in Afghanistan, but it seemed that he did, and that he had a menial job for me, and that I was late for it. Not exactly a promising turn of events.

I presented myself at his office and made a half-hearted attempt at apologising, but he shrugged it off with a resigned look. I got the impression that being two hours late was better than average.

'Go down to the quartermaster's, sir,' he said, 'and do the day's serial number checks. Then you need to inspect one of the guard towers.'

I dutifully found the quartermaster's, and discovered that the relevant equipment was all accounted for. Then I walked out to the perimeter of camp, past the thick lines of HESCO blast walls – dumpy, bomb-proof wire cages filled with stone and gravel scooped up from the desert, which surround every camp in Afghanistan.

I chose a guard tower at random and made a beeline for it. It lived up to its name. It *towered*. A square concrete base and high, rectangular concrete walls. Cold, grey and impassive, like an oversized gravestone. I knocked at the blank steel door at its base and it was opened by a semi-naked Middle-Eastern man. He was thin, dirty and incredibly pleased to see me. I walked inside. He had clearly just scrambled down from the lookout position. A second man, flabbier and equally dirty but more reserved, lay on a metal bunk under a nylon rug and looked at me as though I was invading his privacy. I managed to establish that they were Jordanians.

Jordan had been the first Arab nation to provide troops for the international coalition, and was still the only one with soldiers in Helmand, but they were not playing a very active role. While Danish, Czech and Estonian troops were all in the thick of the action – some of the Estonian soldiers having fought in the country twenty years earlier under the Soviet flag – the Jordanians were providing security for Camp Bastion. These two seemed to be taking a particularly sedentary approach to their duties. An enemy attempt to assault Camp Bastion – with not a scrap of cover for tens of kilometres – would have been suicidal. The threat was so low that it was almost non-existent, and this fact was not wasted on the guard force. Their part in the war against the Taliban seemed to be to try and sleep through the whole thing.

The air was filled with raspy Arabic singing from a radio which was suspended by a nail in the wall. The thin soldier bobbed around in front of me, delightedly. God knows how long he and his comrade had spent together in this squalid concrete box, or for how long, day and night, they had taken it in turns to lie on the bunk and to alternate it with staring out into the empty desert. Visits were clearly not a frequent occurrence, and he was determined to milk this one for all it was worth.

'Do you want cup of coffee?' he asked me, beaming.

'No, thank you,' I said, trying to impress upon him that this was an official visit. 'I'm the duty officer. I need to inspect your sentry position.'

'Ah, yes, yes. You come up.'

I followed him up the thin ladder to the sentry platform. The idea was to ensure that the men were ready for action and that the position was well maintained. If the former was in doubt, the latter wasn't. The machine gun was tolerably clean and well oiled, and one of the guards had pinned a range card on the wall. This was a laminated template on which one marks the distances and bearings of features in front of a given position. If you are attacked, it can then be used to help pinpoint the location of the enemy. The card was completely blank, but the desert was also completely blank, so I could not fault their accuracy.

CHAPTER 2

I stared out into the yellow distance. At the horizon, mountains rose out of the desert into a pale blue sky, in which hung a burning hot sun.

Everything was in order, so I descended the ladder and prepared to leave. My host wasn't going to let me go that easily. He gave me a hearty handshake, congratulating me on an inspection well carried out, and renewed his offer of hospitality.

'So now you take coffee!'

'I'm sorry,' I said, 'I need to be going.'

'Why, where you go?'

'I've got more inspections to do.'

'What inspections?'

'More inspections, round camp.'

'No. You stay here for coffee. You want tea instead?'

I eventually extracted myself from the Jordanians' lonely guard tower and hitched a lift back into the centre of camp. As I passed the phone cabins I saw that Op Minimise was in force. The ominous words were scrawled on a wooden board, hung on a metal railing, which was barring our way to communication with the outside world.

It meant that all access to phones and the internet had been shut off for British forces in Afghanistan and this, in turn, meant that someone had been killed or seriously injured. Minimise was designed so that no one could contact the UK until a casualty's next of kin had been informed. The lockdown had only just been lifted after an incident the night before, so this was the second in twenty-four hours.

I walked towards my new office, which was a shipping container tucked behind a forest of tents. On the way I bumped into a friend.

'What's going on?' I asked.

'Suicide bombing in Gereshk,' he said. 'Two Danes and a Czech killed.'

He walked on. The fact that my squadron had radio operators with the Danes did not register with me just then. I carried on to the office. When I got there, Roachy met me. He looked subdued.

'Have you heard about Signaller O'Hagan?' he said.

'No,' I replied. 'What about him?'

'He got blown up in Gereshk.'

3

There are three categories of medical priority, or triage, and Priority 1, T1, is the worst. It is used for casualties whose lives are hanging on a thread: those who will go home different and those who will never go home at all.

O'Hagan was a T1 casualty.

He was a private soldier, one of the youngest members of the squadron, and he'd only been in Afghanistan a few days. When he'd been assigned as a radio operator to the Czech company in Gereshk people had remarked, in a slightly jealous tone, on what a good job he'd got.

I sat on the metal chair outside our office and thought about him quietly. As well as his youth, I was struck by the suddenness of it. It was as if he should have been allowed a bit more of a go at patrolling before this happened.

I felt for his family back home, probably still unaware of the incident, and I thought about O'Hagan. Was he conscious at that moment? Was he screaming in pain, or shaking with fear?

I was ashamed of myself. Ashamed that I'd been excited about coming to Afghanistan, and that I'd looked upon it as some sort of adventure. I was ashamed of all the times I'd thought about the terrible things that could happen and shrugged my shoulders and thought, *Fuck it.*

We spent the rest of the morning quietly, with the little jobs we had to do. We didn't avoid talking about O'Hagan, we just had nothing to say.

T1. Triage 1. Priority 1. What could possibly be added to that? In an instant he had been removed from normal life and replaced with a single letter and a single number. Signaller O'Hagan: T1.

A good bloke: completely fucked.

We worked until about midday, when an unfamiliar soldier rounded the corner towards our little office. He had a message from the field hospital. 'I've got some news on O'Hagan,' he said. All heads turned in his direction.

Through several different sources, over a period of days, we would patch together what had happened on that morning of the bombing. What we discovered was this.

The night beforehand, Signaller O'Hagan had arrived by helicopter in FOB Price, which was a coalition base that lay in the desert on the outskirts of Gereshk. His job was to provide communications for the Czech company on patrol, back to the British and Danish headquarters at Price. As soon as he arrived – in true military fashion – he was told that he had twelve hours until his first patrol. In that time he would have to meet the Czechs with whom he would be working for the next six months, get to grips with the communications plan, prepare his kit and snatch a few hours' sleep.

Sure enough, as the sun began to creep over the desert the next day, he was striking out into the unknown vastness of Helmand. He was barely out of his teens, in a war zone, with men he didn't know from an unfamiliar country, handling the comms which might save – or lose – all of their lives.

The mixed patrol of Danes, Czechs and one lone Brit had travelled by vehicle through the desert until they reached the first scattered mud dwellings and fields of the town. Here they had dismounted, proceeding on foot into the close and busy streets, towards their objective for the day – the Provincial Coordination Centre.

Life in the town had seemed normal; the locals were relaxed and willing to talk to them. They even saw an old white man in the street, selling trinkets laid out on the sun-baked ground. Perhaps he was a relic of the Afghan hippy trail, a visitor from before the wars who had never gone home.

The patrol walked through the streets for two minutes, before a local man came up to one of the Danish soldiers and asked him where he had come from.

'We are from Denmark,' he had replied.

The man had smiled innocuously and walked back into the crowd, before halting calmly by a vehicle in the street ahead of the patrol. When the soldiers drew level with him, he had detonated his bomb. The men either side of Signaller O'Hagan were killed instantly by the blast. Another soldier and two local civilians died as well. By sheer chance a vehicle was passing between O'Hagan and the bomber as he detonated, shielding him and probably saving his life. He had got away with a piece of shrapnel the size of a cricket ball in his thigh.

Lying injured in the road, O'Hagan then sent a situation report on his radio.

Later that day, I spoke to the man he had reported to. He told me that he'd thought O'Hagan 'quite well composed' for a young man in his first contact situation. He did not realise, as he heard the report of 'at least three dead', that the signaller he spoke to was looking down at a tangle of his own flesh and bone.

Someone had tied a tourniquet above the wound in his thigh and given him morphine, and he'd kept on talking into his radio. Minutes later, the Quick Reaction Force arrived. He was slung into an armoured carrier for evacuation to FOB Price, and to the helicopters which waited there for him and the others. He shared the transport with a young Danish girl who had also been on the patrol. She had a small wound in her face from a piece of shrapnel.

'We must talk,' she said, desperate to keep him from passing out. 'Let's talk about football.'

'No thanks,' he had said. 'I don't really like football.'

Back in Camp Bastion on the morning of the incident, the unfamiliar soldier was about to give us news on O'Hagan from the hospital.

'He's got a messy compound fracture in his femur from a piece of shrapnel, but the doctors say he'll keep his leg. Other than that, it's just cuts and bruises.'

Relief.

Barely even a T1. O'Hagan was going to be OK.

I picked up the phone and spoke via satellite to Jim in Lashkar Gah, and I could feel the tension unwinding in his voice as I spoke. *O'Hagan was going to be OK.*

He was brought back to Bastion and held in the field hospital. The following day I paid him a visit with two of his friends, who were passing through Bastion for their onward journeys into Helmand. We walked across the dusty camp and up the metal stairs towards reception, and were shown into the bright, clean ward where he lay, shattered, on a pristine white bed. His coarse hair looked strangely hazy and his strong features somehow thinner. His skin was grey and his voice was weak, but he was conscious and coherent. We stood over him, and I wondered how many more of the lads I would see like this before we went home.

In surgery the night before, a doctor had removed the shrapnel from his thigh and put his broken leg into traction. I'd never seen a leg in traction before, and I thought it looked primitive, almost barbaric. A steel cord gripped his ankle, sliding upwards, over a pulley, and down beyond the edge of his bed. On its far end, several heavy weights hung in the air.

He was still being given morphine but the dose had been reduced from the previous day, lest his body grow too accustomed to it. He was in pain and begged for the weight on his leg to be eased a little, but his wish was not granted. We talked together, and the conversation flowed well for a while. He often coasted along happily for two or three sentences before suddenly stopping. Then he would close his eyes and it would be as though he'd left the room. His body would still be in front of us but his mind would be somewhere else, doing battle with his pain. After perhaps twenty minutes our supplies of conversation began to dwindle.

'Well then, lads,' he said weakly. 'Shall we go outside for a fag?'

We smiled in appreciation. What a good bloke he was! What a great spirit he was showing, making light of all this.

'No,' he said. 'I'm serious. Watch.'

He called the nurse over and told her he would like to go outside. Without a word she hooked his catheter, his saline drip and his pulse rate monitor to the side of his bed. Removing the brakes from his wheels she opened the double doors and the harsh sunlight poured into the ward. I was astonished, and I stooped low in front of him and began to steady the weights hanging from his leg; perhaps I would be able to save him a little pain as we travelled. The nurse pushed him out into the blinding day, and within seconds someone had placed a smouldering cigarette between his lips. Somebody lent O'Hagan a desert hat to keep the worst of the sun off his face, and we resumed our chatting.

We were joined by the Czech soldier who had treated him as he sent his report on the radio. The man had a dead comrade to grieve for, but he had come to make sure that O'Hagan was OK. Which he would be, given time. He had a hole in his thigh that a man could put his fist into, but one day he would walk again.

There was another British radio operator assigned to the Czech company in Gereshk – Corporal Bagshaw. He had been resting in FOB Price at the time of the bombing, but the blast had cast its long shadow over him as well. He was part of the Quick Reaction Force which deployed into Gereshk to deal with the casualties. He had treated O'Hagan, along with many others, and it seemed that all the flesh and blood had filled his senses up. When we spoke on the phone afterwards he sounded detached, far away, stepping groggily over his words.

Before coming to Afghanistan I had been through a rudimentary course in recognising trauma. I wanted to see Corporal Bagshaw, talk to him, assess him and help him if I could, so I asked Jim in Lashkar Gah if I could fly to Gereshk. He assented, and I booked myself onto the next day's helicopter.

The next morning I walked alone towards the precise grey squares of the Camp Bastion helicopter flight line. The journey would take me across about thirty kilometres of Helmand Province – ten minutes on the motorway, but here the distance felt like a vast ocean between two tiny, lost little islands. One double booking, or one helicopter redirected, and you could be stuck on your chosen island for weeks, patiently awaiting your onward flight.

The Chinook – a mighty, screeching bathtub of a helicopter – sat in front of me, its twin rotors turning idly. A single file of people hurried down its rear ramp and away to the nearby vehicles while fifteen of us waited to board, mustering ourselves into a sort of line, patiently waiting for the loadmaster's command. The drone of the engines drowned out his shouted words, and he beckoned us forward with his arms through the short and unpleasant blast of the helicopter's gas turbine exhaust. It's two seconds of paradise when you're wet and cold on Salisbury Plain. Here, close to midday in Helmand, it was a wall of new heat on top of old.

I sat down inside, next to the rear ramp, facing towards the door-mounted machine gun. If we were engaged in the air, it would be the loadmaster's job to respond to the enemy with it. The ammunition belt bristled angrily at the weapon's side, disappearing into its innards. I strapped myself into the seat. Unexpectedly, I felt a little cold tickle of fear. Perhaps it was the lack of control; it was like a high-stakes roller-coaster ride on which I could do nothing but hope. I'd bought my ticket. There was no walking away.

CHAPTER 3

Wham!

We pulled off the launch pad as if plucked upward by an unseen giant, and rose high above the desert. The wire of Bastion retreated and the ground crawled slowly along beneath us. A lone hut sailed past, a hollowed-out pile of stones and mud surrounded by a brief green tinge of vegetation. How could this place sustain life?

But soon the yellowy desert was replaced by fields and then we swung, as if on a giant pendulum, and plunged earthwards. At about fifty feet we levelled out, still hammering forward over trees and rooftops. Fly high in the desert, fly low over towns. That was the rule. You're less vulnerable when you're lower. Fewer people can see you.

The fear was gone now; dear God, this was a rush.

Little mud huts. Walls, paths, trees, fields and irrigation ditches.

The pilot weaved back and forth, making it harder for rocket-propelled grenades to find their mark. The door gunner waved over his sights at the children below; dressed in rags, they ran barefoot to see the metal monster scream over their homes.

'This,' I thought to myself, 'is almost worth dying for.'

Just then, flares popped and whizzed from the outside of the chopper.

Automatic countermeasures.

It might mean nothing, but it could mean that someone, down below, had a lock on us with a heat-seeking missile.

I gripped the butt of my rifle, forcing the blood out of my fingers until the joints turned white.

'I didn't mean it,' I screamed inside my head. 'I want to live! I definitely want to live!'

The flares sank down onto the plains below and behind us, and no missiles ripped through our lurching fuselage.

FOB Price came into view below us. It signalled not safety but the most vulnerable part of the flight. We slowed and yawed, offering a tempting target, hung up in the air, but within seconds we were at a gentle rest on the ungroomed desert inside the FOB.

It was like Camp Bastion in miniature; another square of tents and shipping containers laid down neatly in the sand, and again it was a muddled patchwork of uniforms and nationalities. There was one central cookhouse at the heart of camp – the best food in Helmand, or so I was told – with real scrambled eggs for breakfast and three types of fruit juice. Brits, Danes and Czechs ate here side by side; the Americans kept themselves aloof, burning steaks on their barbecues and letting the smell drift tantalisingly over the rest of camp.

Corporal Bagshaw was a gentle, earnest man with dark hair and a sallow face, and he was standing at the helipad when I arrived. We shook hands and walked slowly to the shop for a can of something cold. We spent a couple of hours chatting, and he seemed well recovered from the trauma of the bombing – stronger, calmer and a hundred times more composed than he'd been when we'd last spoken.

After doing what he could for O'Hagan and the other casualties, he'd returned from Gereshk and been seized by a gang from the Coldstream Guards who were on camp. They'd sat him down, talked to him, joked with him and washed him through with endless cups of tea until it was impossible for him to retreat into himself. Assessing him for trauma that afternoon, I realised that he had been shaken badly, but was unlikely to suffer any long-term problems.

In fact, the only permanent damage would be to his brand new Oakley shades.

When the Quick Reaction Force was called, Bagshaw had put the sunglasses down and jumped into a vehicle. An Afghan soldier had picked them up and put them on. Shortly afterwards, the Afghan, too, had been called out to the incident. When the Afghan detachment arrived at the site of the bombing, this soldier inexplicably ran out on his own, crashing straight through the cordon. He was shot dead on the spot. Bagshaw never recovered his sunglasses.

CHAPTER 3

As the midday heat bled away into the afternoon, I walked to the air cell to book my return flight to Camp Bastion for the following day.

They assigned me a space on the noon flight, and for the rest of the afternoon I occupied my time in FOB Price in whatever way I could. I talked to friends and acquaintances around the camp and to the soldiers from the comms detachment to the Danish battlegroup. We sat in their small office amid a jumble of wires and cables, quietly drinking tea until it was time for the evening briefing.

The brief was an undramatic affair, with Danish officers going through their intelligence reports and discussing past and future actions. Towards the end, a thick-set American stood up.

'I'd just like to ask if anyone with medical training could come down to our clinic tomorrow morning,' he said. 'We have a bunch of locals from Gereshk arriving at 1000 hrs and we'd be real grateful for any help we can get.'

This was a hearts and minds tactic which the Taliban could not possibly hope to emulate.

Like everyone in the British Army, I had combat medical training. I decided that the least I could do was to offer my skills. I was also curious to see the clinic first hand.

The call for assistance had not been met with rabid enthusiasm.

In fact, no one else had turned up.

There was a pair of American military doctors in the clinic, which comprised two weary-looking concrete rooms with shelves stacked high with basic medical supplies. On the wall there was a painting of a sinister-looking animal of uncertain species. It may have been a sort of blue koala bear in flying goggles, and was obviously intended to comfort children by glaring at them malevolently.

Both doctors were wearing shorts and flip-flops and baseball caps turned backwards; rock music drifted through the room from a little CD player on the medicine shelf.

I proudly announced my combat medic status.

'OK, so what can you actually do?' one of them asked, with a genial smile.

'Well … I know how to stop someone bleeding,' I said, trying to think of anything else I knew that might be relevant. Treatment for nerve agent poisoning? Unlikely to be needed. Mouth-to-mouth resuscitation? Probably not, given that anyone who turned up would have walked three miles across the desert to get here. 'And … yeah, that's basically it.'

Suddenly my medical skills seemed rather lame.

Still, the two doctors there made me feel as welcome as possible. For the next two hours, I fetched and carried and cleaned up blood.

We saw five patients, all children.

The first two were shrapnel injuries – one, a boy of about twelve with a hole straight through his calf, and the other, a girl of eight or nine with a great chunk of flesh missing from her thigh. We cleaned and dressed their wounds and sent them on their way. No one enquired – or seemed to care – as to how they had received their injuries. Two random shards of steel through two random bodies – just the normal pattern of daily life.

The next was a boy in his mid-teens, almost a man. He had stepped on an anti-personnel mine, a sleeping legacy of the Soviet invasion in the 1980s. He had been extremely lucky; he'd lost the tip of his big toe, sheared off at half-length in a clean cross-section, and that was it.

He would need surgery, though. One of the doctors summoned an interpreter.

'Tell him we're going to operate on him,' he said. 'He needs to lie down. We're going to send him to sleep.'

With that, he turned away and busied himself with something else. There was no further explanation, or any words of comfort; what bedside manner these medics had once possessed, they'd left outside the war.

The Afghan interpreter passed on the message to the wide-eyed boy, and he lay down as directed. One of the doctors walked across with three syringes and administered the various anaesthetic drugs. The boy lay patiently in the heat, waiting for sleep to take him, a look of calm but long-suffering resignation on his face. Once he was out, the Americans went to work, while the rest of the patients looked on, uninterested. They cut away the remains of the toe and removed the bone, closing the skin back over his exposed joint. It was an interesting procedure for them: a bit of a break from the norm.

Once the young man's foot was sealed up, they turned their attention to another boy, perhaps eleven years old. He had been shot through the abdomen a fortnight ago and treated the same day. A ten-inch scar ran across his stomach where the surgeon had opened him up to get at the destroyed intestines within.

The operation had been a success, it seemed, but the patient was not recovering. The scar from his operation now leaked pus around every stitch and his wounds, still open, were like two windows into his interior: obscene, pungent and yellowing.

'Not good, man,' said one of the doctors. 'He either wasn't given antibiotics, or sold them, or just didn't take them. Either way, not good.'

I looked at the lad, who was standing stoically before us. He showed little sign of the terrible pain he must have been in, and he had walked all the way here wearing no dressings or bandages. All he had was a single, filthy rag which he held against the bullet's yawning exit hole.

The doctor took the rag off him and threw it on the floor. 'No good,' he said sternly, in English, wagging his finger at the boy. 'This no good.'

'That's 7.62mm calibre, right?' I asked, pointing at the entry wound.

He turned to me and smiled.

'Good *eye*,' he replied, as if we were discussing a car engine back home.

'Not one of ours,' he said, eyeball to exit wound. 'This is Taliban, a stray round I guess, AK-47. You can tell because it's shit quality – if he'd been shot by a Brit, the exit wound would have been much bigger.'

As it was, the hole was the same size as a saucer.

The boy bent down, wincing, to retrieve his rag, and held it against the gaping hole as if it was a security blanket. It was indescribably grimy. It was probably a useful staging post for the bacteria, before they jumped into his insides. It was probably killing him. It was the doctors' job to tell him this, and they did, in English. It was a much more difficult task to make sure that he understood, so they did not. There was already a lot of awfulness for them to deal with, and they could not get bogged down in such points of subtlety. The boy kept clinging on to his rag and the doctors got back to their surgery.

The last patient was a girl of four or five years old. She had the drooping cheeks, distended belly and wide, sad eyes of chronic malnutrition. Her father, wizened, bearded and hopeful, had brought her in. He had sat with his little girl on his knee, smiling at her and patiently waiting his turn, waiting to see if the foreigners could save her life. The doctor had seen her once before, three weeks ago.

'We gave her some protein pills then,' he said, 'but it doesn't seem to have had much effect.'

'But now she's coming in to the clinic she'll be OK, won't she?' I asked. 'Is it a question of finding the right combination of supplements?'

'Not really, man,' he said. 'Once they get this bad their livers are pretty much screwed. I don't think she'll see her tenth birthday.'

Her father could not understand, and the interpreter did not translate.

My flight was due, and I left the two doctors, happily flip-flopping around their charges. Slicing, injecting and chatting. I returned to Camp Bastion.

The vast, sprawling maze of tents and containers was starting to become familiar to me. The view was monotonous and strangely symmetrical:

north, south, east, west, it didn't matter which way you looked. You would always see a couple of Portaloos, a drainage ditch, four tents in a row, three satellite antennas and an overweight female corporal from the post room.

One week in Afghanistan down, twenty-seven to go. Two Danes and a Czech killed. O'Hagan smashed to pieces and flown home. Four Afghan children maimed – one by the Taliban, one by the Soviets, the other two a mystery. One small girl dying of malnutrition.

The poppy harvest was in full swing, and the Taliban were keeping quiet. Our young and opium-addled adversary was probably lying low in his mud hut, waiting for June, and I was doing the same. Playing the waiting game.

Jim, my partner in frustrated REMF-dom, was not succeeding in finding excitement for me. I would call him occasionally at squadron headquarters in Lashkar Gah, and ask him if there might be some reconnaissance tasks on the cards.

'Well … Look mate, I don't really want to send you off half-cocked; we need to get our heads around what's going on overall before we know where to send you,' was one of the least nebulous answers I received.

Like it or not, I was stuck in Camp Bastion. Roachy was too, and he loved it. He was getting to go down the gym every afternoon, watch DVDs in the evening and speak to his wife and child twice a week, as regular as clockwork. Plus no one was trying to kill him. He was quite happy sitting out his war in the rear echelon while I dreamed of action.

Roachy was not a coward. He was a brave man. He was brave enough to stay safe and ensure that he came home to his wife and child.

I was a coward because I lusted for adventure. I yearned to escape Camp Bastion, not to win a war, or even to stand alongside my soldiers, but because I was afraid.

I began to feel hot and awkward when I thought about going home, and answering the volley of questions that would tip from my friends' lips.

'So, did you get in any firefights then?'

'Did you get mortared much?'

'Did you see any dead bodies?'

'Did you shit yourself?'

'No,' I'd have to reply, 'I stayed in Camp Bastion.'

A fraud. A pretend soldier. A thief of their respect.

Where had I gone wrong?

Maybe I shouldn't have joined the Royal Signals. I liked the people, particularly those in the Parachute Squadron, and I could even summon up a bit of enthusiasm for comms if I was pressed hard. But sitting in Bastion without a job was absurd. Maybe I should have joined the infantry and been on patrol every day.

Then again, I wasn't really sure how I felt about killing. I knew I could do it, in the heat of the moment, if it was my life or theirs. But to make death my profession? That was different. Perhaps I was squeamish, or just an idiot.

Either way, I realised that if I was going to get anywhere near the Taliban I was going to have to fight my way past the British Army first.

I had signed up for a role, and it was turning out to be rear echelon. But now I was discovering that the army *actually wanted me to stay in the role I had chosen*! What an unreasonable, inflexible bastard. No problem though; the British Army was just another adversary to conquer.

I had made a grave strategic error. I had played my hand, committed my forces and found myself in an unfavourable position. But I was not defeated yet. Consolidate, I thought. Bide your time. Wait until the right moment to strike.

One afternoon I met a friend of mine from Sandhurst days, who was now also in the Royal Signals. His name was Benji. The army had tried to trap him too, to crush him, to tie him down. But he'd defeated it.

Like me, he'd arrived in Helmand as a Signals troop commander without a troop. Like me, there was no real job for him, but he could have been useful in some mundane administrative capacity. That's what he should have done. He didn't have the right to do anything else. But then, after a well-fought campaign of persuasion, his squadron commander had agreed to release him to mentor the Afghan National Army, the ANA, in an infantry role. Victory! Goodbye radios, hello soldiering – the lucky bastard!

I met Benji in the gravel yard outside his tent, and he was different to how I remembered him. He stood in front of me, staring vaguely at some unseen point in the distance, as he told me of his five-month deployment to Patrol Base Oscar Four-Four. It was a tiny outpost on the edge of the green zone – the strip of dense vegetation flanking the Helmand River.

'There were seven or eight Brits, and about fifty Afghans,' he told me. 'When the Taliban got kicked out of Musa Qal'eh they all withdrew past Oscar Four-Four, and they all had a pop at us as they came past.'

Benji didn't seem like he was basking in his luck. He seemed more like a machine that had broken down.

'What was it like working with the Afghans?' I asked.

'Fucking ridiculous. We'd go on patrol and get contacted and there'd be two or three Brits returning fire. All the Afghans just lay on the ground and fired their rifles into the air, shitting themselves.

'You try to mentor them, but they just go and do their own thing. We captured a Taliban fighter a few weeks ago and got him back to camp, and we left him alone for about five minutes with the Afghans while we went to radio back to the battlegroup that we had a POW. As soon as we turned our back on them they just unloaded into him on automatic. Just executed him.'

'You didn't do very well on mentoring them the Geneva Convention, mate,' I said. I was shocked, but I was trying to act hard, trying to come across as dispassionate and cynical. Benji had changed. At Sandhurst he had brimmed with energy, and now he seemed to be speaking to me from far away. His words came out with an emotionless lilt, as if he was stoned. I actually preferred him this way, but I wondered what was below the surface of this new persona.

'Was it a good experience, all in all?' I asked.

'Fucking horrible at the time. I was just counting the days till I could get out of there. But, yeah, since I've got back in one piece, I guess it has been a good experience.'

Benji had survived, but the Taliban had taken a chunk out of him. Now he was going home, but that chunk would stay behind in Helmand with his enemies. He had been a victim of his own success. He had catapulted himself from the rear echelon straight into one of the worst patrol bases in Helmand and that, of course, was always the danger.

There are four types of people in the army. You get thrown into a type like a piece of equipment being thrown into the kit bins in the quartermasters' department. First, there is the bin for people who have peaceful jobs and are happy with them, like Roachy. Second, there is the bin for people like me, who have peaceful jobs and are embarrassed by them. Third are those who have action-packed jobs and love the rush of them. These people last in their bin until something truly unpleasant happens to them, which it always does eventually. Then they are thrown into the fourth bin, of damaged goods. This was Benji's bin.

He had wanted to move from bin two to bin three, but he'd overshot and landed in bin four. It was a common mistake. So many people wanted to be in bin three, but hardly anyone managed to stay there for long. It was like the bucking bronco at the fairground.

If I escaped from bin two, I wondered where I would land.

Quite unexpectedly, one day, Jim threw me a bone from Lashkar Gah.

'We need a comms recce doing of Camp Jupiter,' he said. 'After that, maybe Musa Qal'eh, but see how you get on with Jupiter first.'

This was what I had been waiting for – a couple of trips to the outlying FOBs! It was ideal. I wouldn't be stuck in a miserable little fort, besieged and scared for months, as Benji had been. We'd deploy out, see the province (maybe get shot at) and be home in time for tea.

I didn't believe in Jim's grand scheme of comms reccies – fleet of foot, sharp of mind, garnering information like a slightly geeky elite strike force. No, I was in it for the war tourism. Plain and simple.

I walked back to our tent to tell Roachy that I'd been given a deployment. He grunted with disapproval.

'Just don't get fucking killed,' he said, and went back to watching *Ready Steady Cook*.

4

The British contingent at Camp Jupiter had asked to be paid a visit by the Parachute Signal Squadron. They needed us to set up a new piece of satellite kit and to see what help we could give with comms in the future.

There were three young soldiers in the team we hastily formed – each fairly junior but a technical specialist in his own field. There was also Charlie, an officer a few years my senior and another veteran of special forces communications – another Cunt from Blah – making five of us in total.

We were going to hitch a ride with the Camp Jupiter company group across the desert. I'd not yet been outside Bastion's walls, apart from my brief flit to FOB Price and one excursion on foot, to fire my rifle and check the accuracy of the sights. Thirty of us had walked out one day to the firing ranges in the desert and shot at the featureless horizon. We knew that the Taliban were out there somewhere, too far away to be seen, but the desert ranges weren't part of the war. You could tell by the way that people milled around at them, not really caring where they left their rifles. No one seriously expected the Taliban to come charging over the horizon.

Getting out to Jupiter would be different. We'd be cast adrift in two small vehicles, forging our own tracks through the desert. Maybe we'd even find the war. It had been proving elusive so far.

On the morning of our deployment I walked to the company group's quartermaster's department to find out what time we were expected.

We'd been told 1400 hrs, but then over breakfast someone casually mentioned that the departure time had changed to 0930 hrs. After a last-minute panic with kit I went to find out the truth.

The compound was surrounded by high walls, cramped and overflowing with messy disorder. Weapons lay around with no particular heed paid to them, and piles of equipment filled every vacant crevice. I found the company quartermaster sergeant, the CQMS; he was a balding, thick-set man relaxing on a threadbare sofa behind his desk. The first thing I noticed, as I leaned on the plywood counter, was the topless poster pinned to the wall. Someone had carefully crafted a swimsuit top from green gaffer tape for the pouting blonde girl in the picture, and plastered it over her breasts.

There may be four types of man in the British Army, but there are only two types of tape: the soft, cloth-like Green Friendly and the hard, plastic Black and Nasty. This swimsuit was made with Green Friendly, and the precision of the curves made me think that it had been a labour of love.

The CQMS followed my gaze. 'We covered her up so as not to offend the Afghans we're mentoring,' he said, by way of an explanation.

I remembered Roachy's stories from his time teaching comms to the Afghan National Army during his last deployment to Helmand. Contrary to their briefs about Afghan sensibilities, he'd said, their soldiers could not get enough of Western porn; in fact, they'd refused to work unless bribed with nude magazines, and so the mentors had walked to lessons with notes in one hand and *Readers' Wives* in the other.

The CQMS was just as clueless as me about our transport for Camp Jupiter. The vehicles were doing a round trip, and as we spoke they were somewhere on the 40km route. 'I'll try to find out where,' he said. To talk to Jupiter securely, it was necessary to go through the Ministry of Defence operator in Whitehall. The CQMS rang through to establish the connection, but it broke before he'd got half a dozen words out. He tried twice more, and both times the link failed; Camp Jupiter's comms were clearly in need of attention. He gave up in exasperation and pulled a locally bought mobile phone from his pocket.

Personal phones were banned in Afghanistan to prevent the enemy from listening in to our calls – not only could the signal be intercepted, but there was also no guarantee of the allegiance of local telecoms company staff. Nonetheless, they were available for certain 'duty' reasons. The CQMS dialled Jupiter, and simply said, 'Hello, mate. Just answer "yes" or "no." Have they left yet?'

The answer was not a yes or a no. The man on the phone had no idea who 'they' were supposed to be, or where it was that they should have left.

I stood in front of the CQMS. He launched into a party game where he tried to explain something without using any words that related to it. He fought for a few minutes but then wearily slipped further and further into unveiled speech. Finally the game ended when the unknown voice at Jupiter told him everything he needed to know in plain English.

'OK,' the CQMS said, hanging up his phone and turning to me. 'Come back here in thirty minutes.'

I returned to our accommodation to pass on my intelligence to Charlie and the lads. Charlie was a tall, gentle, rounded man with hair that was thinning early. I found him standing outside our tents with the three soldiers.

'We've got twenty minutes,' I said.

'I reckon that gives me enough time for a shower,' Charlie said, with a conviction borne of his tough special forces training. He marched towards the ablutions block and I was left with the three soldiers. None of them had ever ventured out of camp either, and they were as restless as I was. I had everyone busy themselves with oiling their rifles and preparing them for firing.

'Should be a good trip out, this,' someone said.

'It will be,' I replied, 'if we all come back in one piece.'

I was apprehensive, and I was laying it on a bit thick. When Charlie returned he wasn't concerned with such melodrama. His skin was flushed pink from the shower and he made for his patrol sack with a determined look on his face. Up went a quick-release Velcro flap and out came a small vanity mirror. Charlie squatted in the sand and studied himself. Seconds later he opened more pouches. Out came a little tin of hair clay and then an expensive-looking tube of moisturiser. Each was applied with military precision, in the sand, in front of the little mirror. This was my first experience of special forces pre-deployment preparation, and it was strangely reassuring.

We drove to Camp Jupiter in two unarmoured Toyota pickup trucks – the five of us, plus two drivers and two 'top-cover' riflemen making up a team of nine. It wasn't usual to go out in so small or so lightly armed a force, but the featureless desert through which we were to travel made ambush by the Taliban all-but impossible. Our top covers sat on boxes on the rear beds of the vehicles, scanning the horizon for movement.

Through the bumpy desert, at 40mph, this was a painful duty. They had softened the ride a bit with packing foam, taped down by yards and yards of Black and Nasty, to create makeshift padded seats.

Bastion grew smaller behind us, and finally disappeared into the haze. The desert was not quite moonscape – occasionally thin rushes would poke up between the stones – but whichever way we looked it stretched out endlessly until it met the sky. We were two specks in an ocean of sand.

After twenty minutes, another speck appeared off to our left. As it drew closer it resolved itself into a white civilian pickup truck. It was unusual for the locals to travel through the desert like this, where breaking down could easily mean death, so it was possible that they were Taliban, smuggling arms or drugs and hoping to avoid attention. We stopped, positioned ourselves to give good arcs of fire, and waited.

The top-cover riflemen trained their weapons on the front cab, and the driver understood the message. He slowed and stopped.

We dismounted and fanned out across the ground, and the convoy commander, a sergeant major, went forward to speak to the Afghan men who had emerged from the vehicle.

I eased myself into a kneeling position on the hard ground, the muzzle of my rifle steadied by my raised right knee and the Afghans framed comfortably in my sights.

I tried to think through every possible eventuality, craning my neck to scan the horizon for signs of other vehicles. A possible ambush? No, nothing there.

The sergeant major reached the Afghans.

Their body language seemed relaxed. They shook his hand. I watched them talking through my optics – it was like watching a film with the sound turned down.

They were around a hundred metres from me. Even though they were side by side I could easily have shot the Afghans and left the sergeant major unharmed.

They walked towards the back of the pickup so that their cargo could be searched. If anything was found then the shooting would probably start. I clicked the safety catch off and rested my finger lightly on the trigger, assessing body language, trying to see the things they were pulling out of the truck, aiming 'off' for wind, wondering where, under their flowing robes, would be the best place to target.

It's strange how one's inhibitions about killing a human being can melt away. How quickly it can become a problem of technique and skill.

Relax.

Several more handshakes, and smiling assurances of friendship. Then they were sent on their way.

The search had uncovered nothing; it turned out they were travelling to their cousin's wedding.

We eased our safety catches back on, mounted up and continued to

CHAPTER 4

Camp Jupiter. Within ten minutes it had appeared on the horizon, and soon we were driving past its HESCO guard towers.

We did what we could for their comms, setting up some new satellite equipment, checking their cabling and taking notes for future projects. I climbed up onto the roof of the operations room, partly to look at their antennas and mostly to admire the view. From where I stood I saw that we had emerged from the desert close to Highway 1, which snaked away to the horizon. It was constructed in the 1960s by the Soviets, who were then vying with the Americans for influence in the region, and it was the only main road through southern Afghanistan. It connected Kandahar to Herat and sliced Helmand Province in two.

Two years previously it had been the nearest thing the province had ever had to a boundary between war and peace; a man on the south side could only be shot in self-defence, whereas on the north side he could be shot simply for being our enemy, according to the coalition rules of engagement. Turn left and you live, turn right and you die. Killed by a line on a map.

Travel on Highway 1 was still fraught with danger. The Taliban knew that most of the trucks on the road were transporting supplies to their enemies, and attacks on drivers were frequent. Nevertheless, vehicles carried on making the journey.

There was a truck drivers' rest stop nearby, under an escarpment. A small group of men sat listlessly in the shade. As I looked at them, another soldier clambered up the ladder and joined me on the roof. The drivers were about two hundred metres distant, and neither of us was wearing body armour or helmets. The only weapon we had between us was the Browning pistol I'd stuffed in my trouser pocket.

'If there's a pissed-off trucker down there with a rifle, we're fucked,' I observed.

A slight pause as my companion looked round. 'Yes,' he agreed.

We shrugged our shoulders and carried on.

Within a few hours we had done all that we could at Camp Jupiter and we got ready to leave. I put my head into the operations room and noticed a printout hanging above the intelligence desk. It was a series of mug shots of all the powerful men in the region, perhaps twenty in total. Someone had decided to cut through the intricacies of tribal loyalties and power dynamics, and had simply written 'GOOD' or 'BAD' under each face. Happily, one of the 'BAD' mug shots had a pencil line through it. Underneath, in shaky infant print, someone had written 'DEAD'.

We drove back across the desert without incident and arrived in Camp Bastion in time for dinner.

I wondered if I had succeeded in taking a day trip to the war. I didn't think that pointing my rifle at wedding-goers really counted.

That night I sat with Roachy and Brian in our tent, appreciating their company as always. Roachy was explaining the workings of a sex aid he'd seen on the internet, revelling in the details. It was a rubber tube which you fastened around your scrotum, and your partner tugged sharply on it in order to delay the moment of ejaculation. Painful and unpleasant it may have been, but on the plus side it came with a lifetime guarantee. Roachy didn't mention whether he had bought one or not, which I suspected meant that he had.

Before we turned in for the night we heard some news from the Kajaki Dam, in the far north of Helmand Province; two Royal Marines had just been killed when their vehicle rolled over an IED, an Improvised Explosive Device. Or a bomb, if you like.

* * * * *

The Royal Marines who had died were barely two weeks from returning home.

Initially we received a report that one marine had been killed and one had lost his legs, but after a few hours it was amended to 'both dead'. The signaller on the casualty evacuation helicopter told me that one of the marines had been conscious when they picked him up. He'd even talked with the lads in the back of the Chinook, with two tourniquets applied above his mangled legs. Slowly, over the course of the flight, the blood loss had taken its toll. He slipped into unconsciousness and died in the Camp Bastion field hospital.

It struck a nasty chord; they'd kept safe through six months of hard fighting that winter, and had died with the finishing line in sight.

A few days later, the whole of Camp Bastion turned out for their repatriation ceremony at the airstrip on the very edge of camp, half an hour's walk from the quiet grid of offices and tents at the centre. I travelled there in one of many open-topped trucks, with soldiers packed in shoulder to shoulder on the metal benches inside. Others walked at either side of the road as the trucks crawled slowly past. It gave the impression of a vast column on the march, like an exodus of refugees.

We dismounted from our wagon and took our places in the three-sided square forming on the tarmac, which then filled out to hold a thousand bodies.

Once the last stragglers had slotted in to their places a hush fell over the crowd. We were called to attention, but the regimental sergeant major's shout was taken by the wind. Those nearest to him, in the centre, performed the movement, and from there it spread out to the wings like a Mexican wave. The padre was closer, and when he launched into his service the words began to peel from his lips with a solemn and measured regularity. We were told a little about how the men had lived and how they had died.

As we listened, a rainstorm blew in – the first and only one I'd see during my months in Afghanistan. Gradually, the most distant objects disappeared from sight, swallowed by the swirling dust. Then the sentry towers, standing isolated in the desert, vanished. Finally the air traffic control tower followed suit. Every point of reference was rubbed out and replaced by a blank and featureless canvas. Nothing was left of the world but a hollow square of a thousand soldiers on an endless tarmac plane, silently staring at two coffins draped in the Union Flag.

As the service drew to a close, the rain-soaked coffins were carried towards the waiting Hercules. Its engines idled with a drone of suppressed power as the band played farewell to our comrades and the wind whipped rain that was as warm as blood into our faces. I was wet to the skin, but I could barely feel it; it was as if I was watching the storm from behind plate glass.

The Hercules' great back ramp drew slowly closed and it sloped off down the runway, as if it was ashamed of its cargo. Soon it was aloft and describing a circle around us, thundering over our heads. It dipped its wings once in salute and then headed off. Once its roar had faded from the sky we broke apart our hollow square; it was time to leave the dead behind, for the memory of this sombre day to be quietly shelved and left dormant, a store of grief laid down for the months and years ahead.

Our thoughts turned to the line of trucks waiting to transport us back to camp. Within a few breaths life returned to the assembled masses. People pushed and shoved and laughed and joked, anxious to find a space on a truck and be near the front of the queue for dinner.

* * * * *

A few days later, another of Jim's allusions to 'deployment' began to take a definite shape. I was to go on a comms recce to the British base in Musa Qal'eh, in the north of Helmand.

The town had been captured from the Taliban three months previously, but that wasn't the start of the story of Musa Qal'eh. The story started in 2006, when we occupied the town to shore up the ailing power base of the district governor's office. The force of reassurance, deployed at the governor of Helmand's behest, was transformed within weeks into a beleaguered garrison under siege in the district centre, battered by the onslaught of a Taliban offensive. Several British soldiers and dozens of Taliban fighters died in the intense conflict which ensued, before both sides reached a state of exhaustion. At that point a three-way agreement between the British, the local tribal elders and the Taliban prescribed an uneasy truce – both warring forces would evacuate the town, leaving the elders to govern it in peace.

Shamefully, the British garrison didn't have enough vehicles to evacuate itself from Musa Qal'eh. Instead, the soldiers and officers were escorted from the town on the backs of local trucks, which were probably owned by the Taliban themselves. Apache helicopters hovered feet from the trucks as they travelled across the desert, watching for betrayal.

The truce had held until February of 2007, when the Taliban reneged on their commitment and reoccupied the town. It became their only real holding in Helmand, although we maintained the myth that it was 'under local administration'.

The Taliban walked the streets unchallenged and administered their own brand of justice to the population. They beat men in public when they refused to grow their beards and did the same to women who would not wear the burqa. Then, all of a sudden, one of their local commanders – Mullah Abdul Salaam – defected. He had been a big man in the Taliban before 2001, the governor of Uruzgan Province, and now he was on our side. According to intelligence, he had defected because of an argument over the use of irrigation ditches on his property. And, while this was not quite the deep ideological rift that we would have liked, it was good enough.

About a third of Musa Qal'eh's Taliban forces defected with him, and this gave the coalition the chance they needed. They invaded the town in December and wrested it from Taliban control. The defecting Taliban fighters, with their considerable experience of law enforcement in Musa Qal'eh, were duly appointed as the town's new police force. Mullah Abdul Salaam became its governor.

In one fell swoop we had won the hearts and minds of Musa Qal'eh. The ordinary people's hearts and minds were won by their new police force, because they knew that if they didn't hand over their hearts and minds they'd be beaten unconscious in the street.

The police's hearts and minds went to Mullah Abdul Salaam because he gave them power, and power is what they craved. And Mullah Abdul Salaam's heart and mind belonged to us, because we gave him a better deal on his irrigation ditches than the Taliban did. Hooray, the war was being won.

There was a new British base in the Musa Qal'eh District Centre, and its comms were in a shit state. It was just the job for a young Signals officer with time on his hands who could fly up there to write a report about the situation. Would anyone read the report? Probably not, but that wasn't the point. For a war tourist, Musa Qal'eh was a *must see*. A comms recce was the perfect excuse to go there. Like I say, it was just the job.

Jim said I'd be taking Sergeant Powell to Musa Qal'eh with me. The squadron's thick-set, olive-skinned technical repair expert, with a rich, lethargic sense of humour. While I wrote my report on the problems with comms in Musa Qal'eh, he was actually going to try fixing some of them.

Sergeant Powell didn't like me. He didn't *get* me, but it wasn't his fault. Sometimes I wasn't an easy man to get. Roachy had been the same with me. It had taken half a year for us to click, but I'd won him over eventually.

With our deployment to Musa Qal'eh I'd beaten the army in a conventional war, and got what I wanted, and now *I* was faced with a hearts-and-minds battle. Sergeant Powell would come round to me in time, I just had to play my cards right.

For now he was using a tactic which had been handed down from NCO to NCO for generations: when you have to deal with an officer you don't like, get on with the job and *shut the fuck up*. No one can call you insubordinate just because you're monosyllabic. It was a good insurgent strategy. Demoralise your enemy. Keep sapping his will to carry on, but never commit to open battle. Never give him a target to strike.

CHAPTER 4

On the appointed morning Sergeant Powell and I walked to the flight line in silence, grunting under heavy Bergen back packs, helmets, body armour, camelback water pouches, rifles, pistols, bullets and grenades. We stood on the gravel, uncomfortable under the weight of our kit, and watched the rotor blades of our Chinook turn in front of us as the fuel line was dragged away from it. We were going to fly over Taliban territory. They wanted to kill us. I was afraid.

It wasn't worth it. What a stupid risk. What a childish, irresponsible thing to do, to volunteer to go on a recce to Musa Qal'eh, just because I was bored in camp. I didn't even think we'd be any use up there anyway. But I was here now, and so was everyone else, and I was just going to have to get on with it.

The loadmaster called us to board. Goggles on. Step forward. All apprehension forgotten.

We flew high over the desert for fifteen minutes, enjoying the strange peace of military flight: the howl of the engines, the constant vibration, the hard encasement of body armour. Every sense was numbed behind a constant background blare. Then we dropped and swooped low into a dried-up river bed with walls fifty feet high. We were below the horizon now. Solid rock drew close by our rotor blades on either side as the Chinook banked and turned, following the weaving course of the wadi. Then the mighty beast leapt out into the open.

The landing marker whirled in the portholes as we danced through a hundred and eighty degrees. We touched down. Out on the ground I ran until the helicopter lifted off behind me. The downwash and engine noise faded and peace returned to the desert.

We had arrived in FOB Edinburgh, a bleak camp a few kilometres out of Musa Qal'eh itself. It was hollow on the other side; half a dozen of us came through a small gap in the blast walls and saw a great expanse of desert in front of us, penned in by a square of HESCO, with a few tents and shipping containers huddled around the walls. Someone had been over-enthusiastic when he was planning the size of the camp, but it wasn't as if anyone else was using that patch of desert.

FOB Edinburgh was our home for the next twenty-four hours while we waited for a convoy to Musa Qal'eh, and in this time I made no progress whatsoever with Sergeant Powell. He didn't want to talk to me and that was that. I gave up and went to see what entertainment could be found in the camp.

The dining tent had some hard wooden benches in front of a DVD player which did not work, and a dart board with a single flightless dart. Other than that, facilities were nil. I chatted for a while with the camp's tactical air controller, who was a friend of mine from parachute training. We soon exhausted all our news.

Sergeant Powell and I retreated to the tent that we'd been assigned for the night. We whiled away the hours by lying on our camp beds in silence. Our tent had no electricity or lighting, and whoever had put it up had been lazy with the sand flaps. Great plumes of dust got in under them and settled on every surface, so that we had to tip our beds sideways and beat them with our hands – causing a small brown avalanche – before we got onto them.

There was an Afghan interpreter who shared our tent with us. He was sleeping when we arrived, mid-afternoon, and he rolled over and looked at us crossly when we pushed back the greasy canvas flap and stepped inside. We were to discover that he did not like to be disturbed. From that first mid-afternoon meeting to when we left for Musa Qal'eh at 0800 hrs the next morning, rolling over once was the only movement we ever saw him make.

The next day Sergeant Powell and I walked to the marshalling point and met the rest of the convoy for our brief. A weather-beaten sergeant took the stage.

'Actions on contact by the enemy: we're a lightly armed group, so we're to return fire, suppress the enemy and drive through the ambush. We don't have enough firepower to take the Taliban on properly.'

He paused, and reconsidered.

'Well, actually we *do* have quite a lot of firepower this morning, but we'll drive through anyway.'

I looked up and down the line of vehicles. We *did* have a lot of firepower. A WMIK at the front and a WMIK at the back. Weapons Mounted Installation Kits; cut-down Land Rovers with swivel turrets, mounted with monstrous 50-calibre machine guns and grenade machine guns. Then, on the bonnet in front of each passenger, a general purpose machine gun (GPMG).

'General purpose' machine guns were a misnomer, because all they could do was kill people. You couldn't open a tin or paint a picture with them. But they were good at what they did. They had been in service since the 1960s, and were still one of the British Army's best loved guns. We were well armed.

In between the two WMIKs were two lorries and a diesel tanker. I got into the passenger seat of the front lorry and Sergeant Powell took the tanker. I couldn't say that I envied him. It was large and unwieldy and highly flammable; it would certainly be the Taliban's target of choice, and I'd always had a bit of a thing about the prospect of burning alive.

We mounted up and rumbled out of camp, just as the sun was creeping into the sky. I drew back the mechanism on my rifle to chamber a round. It slid smoothly, but then when I let the spring fly forward it jammed, wedging the round half-in the chamber. Too much dust in the mechanism. I fumbled for a screwdriver in the foot well and tried to extract the bullet. What if we got ambushed while I was still messing around with my rifle like an idiot? What a way to die – killed by grit!

As we crested a ridgeline we saw a beautiful valley laid out below us. There was a scattering of flat-roofed mud huts, enclosed by little compound walls, and a few fields of irrigated crops. Other than that, there was nothing but desert.

The valley was clean. No filth and plastic detritus like in Africa and India. This wasn't the arse end of global consumerism. The valley looked like it could have been transported here from biblical times.

Appearances, however, could be deceptive. The Taliban knew we drove this road every day, and they knew at roughly what time we drove it. The threat from roadside bombs was high.

We got to the valley floor and passed a couple of families squatting in the sun by their compound walls. We waved to them, and the men waved cheerily back to us. They had been at war for thirty years and they'd clearly learned the value of a wave and a smile to the side which seemed to be winning that year, or that month, or that week, or that morning. 'Hearts and minds' was a game, and they knew how to play it just as well as we did.

The children hadn't learned to play the game yet. They stared at us with fire in their eyes. It was a look that I came to know as quintessentially Afghan. A sort of infinite calmness, coexisting with an infinite, raging storm. Eyes that you could look into and feel like you were standing on the edge of a cliff in front of a vast and mysterious ocean.

On the far side of the valley I noticed a pair of men on a motorbike. They eyed us up and then turned and accelerated, losing themselves in the fields. They may have been 'dickers' – lookout men – watching us as we drove towards a roadside bomb. But, then again, maybe they were just bored and watching us for entertainment. We *were* quite a sight, after all. Five huge metal behemoths, full of strangely dressed men with pale white faces.

We crossed the valley floor and ascended to its far side. At the top of this second ridgeline the Musa Qal'eh valley came into view beneath us: a thin strip of green, a wide and shingled flood plain, then a sprawling mass of huts and compounds which constituted the town itself.

We arrived at a small observation post to unload supplies and three local men watched us curiously. They were infinitely remote to me. Helmand was a synonym for bloodshed, not a place where people actually *lived*. The men seemed as exotic as alien beings, but really they represented three local hearts and three local minds. This was our battleground, here in front of us.

After a few minutes one of them got up and walked slowly towards our vehicle. He was old and frail, with a coarse grey beard and long white robes, under which he looked unnaturally thin. I didn't think he could be concealing a weapon or a bomb. Nevertheless, O'Hagan's experience in Gereshk had taught me how quickly a situation could change. I leant my head out of the window to greet him and, out of sight, tightened a hand around my pistol. One shot to the heart, one shot to the mind; that was how the old joke went.

What was the man thinking?

Our top-cover gunner acted first. When the man was about ten yards away he let off a mini-flare. It's a signalling light which is supposed to launch with a whoosh and a bang and say 'come no closer'.

Unfortunately, they are not the army's best piece of equipment. The flare popped out of its tube and dropped forlornly onto the ground, like a cheap Roman candle. It smoked and fizzed in front of the old man. He looked at it, bemusedly, and then he slowly rocked through a hundred and eighty degrees and shuffled arthritically away from us with a sad look on his face. He had probably only come over for some company. Now he returned to the roadside and squatted with his friends.

Our engines rumbled into life and we descended a steep scree slope towards Musa Qal'eh. We made slow progress. The convoy stopped every five minutes or so for the crew of the lead WMIK to dismount and probe the ground for bombs. They didn't find any, and we carried on down to the belt of fields before the town. Poppy fields. Again the men waved at us cheerily as we rolled steadily past, with thousands of dollars of opium poppy on either side of us.

The poppy was a terrible scourge in the eyes of the American voting public, and a way of life to the farmers surrounding us. It was big business for the narcotics barons, a source of taxation for the Taliban, a powerful card in the hands of politicians and a rather exciting backdrop for our journey.

It also made the battle for hearts and minds an absolute nightmare, because it revealed that the whole system was based on a lie, and that lie was 'We're Here to Help'.

Were we here to help ordinary Afghans, or were we here to defeat terrorism? No one knew, not even our politicians.

Were we here to help farmers in the Helmand valley? Certainly not. Most of them did not love the Taliban, but they loved their families, and so they grew poppy to support them.

Alas, life in the West at the start of the 21st century was becoming far too uncomfortable, thanks to the terrorists and the heroin addicts. They needed to be stopped, but who should pay the price? Why, the simple folk of the Helmand Valley, of course. Chop down the poppy, cut off the Taliban's funds, stop the flow of drugs onto our streets. And then wave to the farmers whose lives you're destroying. Wave and smile. That's how you win hearts and minds. That's how you prove that you're the good guys!

Of course, we didn't *really* destroy the poppy at the same time as we fought to win over the people of Helmand. That would have been ridiculous. No, we fought to win over the people of Helmand while we paid someone else to destroy the poppy. *Voila*! Thank God for private military contractors.

By getting a private firm in, it was no longer the foreign invaders who were destroying the crops; it was contractors working for the Afghan government in Kabul. Much better. What right-thinking man could take issue with the policies of his own government? It is, after all, only there to serve him. But there was still a problem here. The private military contractors were generally ex-British and US Army and, although the Afghan government had paid for them, the Americans had paid for the

Afghan government. So the farmers of Helmand, in their naïve simplicity, might not see much of a difference between the contractors and the coalition armies.

The backwardness of the farmers was a difficulty, but luckily was not insurmountable. In fact, the answer was obvious. Just *do a bad job* of eradicating the poppy. Then the folks back home are satisfied, because they can see that the Afghan government is on our side and has the problem in hand, the farmers are satisfied because they get to keep their poppy, and the contractors are satisfied because they get rich on the taxes of the folks back home. Problem solved.

And this is exactly what happened. A firm of private military contractors was hired and given just enough resources to do a thoroughly bad job of eradicating the poppy. As we drove to Musa Qal'eh they were camped somewhere else in Helmand, probably getting mortared by the poorer farmers. The rich or well-connected farmers didn't need to use mortars, of course, because they just bribed the eradication force to leave them alone.

My squadron had given the eradication force a radio operator so that they could communicate with the British brigade headquarters, but this was a secret because we weren't supposed to have anything to do with them. Our radio operator was to stay with the contractors until the harvest was over, and most mornings he turned up at a farm with them, got attacked, retreated without destroying a single stalk, and moved on to the next place. It was a bit of a shit job.

Our convoy continued, and the farmers smiled and waved at us. We smiled and waved back again, and hoped they hadn't planted a bomb for us in the road ahead.

After a while the fields gave out. Our wheels plunged into fast-flowing water. We forded the murky Musa Qal'eh River and crossed a shingled flood plain, then the gates of the district centre opened in front of us and we entered the camp. Jumping down from the cabin I removed my helmet, feeling the wind in my sweat-soaked hair.

I was standing in a dusty, gravelled yard perhaps a hundred metres square. Clusters of shipping containers and parked-up vehicles lay scattered about the place, and a line of bushy trees grew through the bare stones at one side. In the distance, to the north, I could see the Musa Qal'eh Mountain: a sleeping monolith looming over the troubled town beneath it. In front of me stood the camp's headquarters building – two stark floors of grey concrete. Steel tensioners sprouted like flowers from the walls, reaching out for adjoining masonry which should have been added but never was. A balcony jutted out from the first floor with ornate and artistic sky-blue railings.

I turned to Sergeant Powell. It was time for another sally in the battle to win him over. Get in there with some conversation. Establish a beachhead.

'I think my luck was in, getting the truck,' I said. 'I didn't fancy your diesel tanker much.'

Sergeant Powell grunted in response.

The two of us looked into the state of comms in the headquarters. It was terrible. They only had one link to the outside world, and it was a satellite telephone that didn't really work. About one time in ten you could get it to produce a dial tone, and then you could hastily punch in the number for the manual operator in Whitehall, who had to route your call even if you only wanted to speak to brigade headquarters fifty kilometres away in Helmand. If you could make the operator understand you, over the deafening whizzes and crackles on the line, you could tell her what extension number you were after. Then, if you had the good fortune to get through to the person you wanted, you had about two minutes to talk to them before the line went dead and you had to repeat the whole process again.

Sergeant Powell set to work on the satellite phone with his soldering iron, and I sat down to write my report. We lasted for the whole afternoon before we'd both had enough, and then we gave up and went to waste some time with the infantry.

Musa Qal'eh was garrisoned by a company from the Argyll and Sutherland Highlanders, the original 'thin red line' of the Crimean War. Judging by the handful of men defending the camp, the line was still precariously thin. From the beating of the harsh Afghan sun on pale Scottish faces, it was also still a deep shade of red.

The hundred or so Scots in camp were charged with winning over the 20,000 hearts and minds in Musa Qal'eh, and they were starting by Scottish-ising the Afghan diet. They had taken the local flatbread, unchanged for centuries, and improved it. Now there was a new staple food in town – flatbread à la Yorkie bar. Simply open up the loaf, insert a slab of chocolate from the British 24-hour ration pack, leave in the sun for twenty minutes, then consume.

Night fell, and that evening I sat in the lounge by the gym to read my book. The gym was a single metal fencing picket with ammunition boxes strapped to each end and filled with gravel for weight. The lounge was three deck chairs next to the fencing picket.

The laundry area was next door. It comprised two metal bowls, a jerrycan full of water and a large grey puddle below a line of dripping clothes. You couldn't drink the water in the jerrycan because it came from the well, and the well was infested with bloodworm, but it was good enough for laundry.

From their filthy base, the Argyll and Sutherland Highlanders patrolled the town and tried to reach out to the people there. Thanks to myself and Sergeant Powell, they were now ever so slightly closer to reaching out to their higher headquarters in Lashkar Gah. Unbeknown to all of us, two men in the valley were trying to reach out to us that night. They almost did so, as I sat in the operations room with my book.

A shot rang out. Then another one. They sounded as though they had come from far down the valley – warning shots from a patrol base, perhaps, or a couple of locals in a dispute which had turned nasty. Then the sniper from the roof above us spilled into the room. He strode towards the operations officer, looking a bit like a child who was anxious to tell his parents about a trick he had performed. He had fired both shots.

Through his night vision he had seen two men setting up a mortar tube, preparing to bring it to bear on us. They were about 800 metres distant across the valley floor, and he killed them one after the other, both with single shots. The sound seemed far away because he was using a silencer on his weapon. All we'd heard was the shockwave as the bullets travelled through the air, not the crack of his rifle above our heads.

The sniper was still flushed with excitement. I wondered if these were the first men he had killed. When he saw them setting up their mortar he had got on his radio and asked advice from the operations room downstairs. The link had failed. Alone, and with no one to reassure or guide him, he decided to pull the trigger. How strange it must have been to kill them: two blobs in the hazy green sea of night vision optics. Seen, but not heard. Silently preparing to kill us and then silently dying themselves. Reached out and touched by the British Army. One through the heart and one through the mind.

In the morning Sergeant Powell and I headed back to FOB Edinburgh. My charm offensive was having no effect, and I was beginning to get demoralised. We sat in the back of an armoured Mastiff vehicle together, on the return convoy, and I did something that I knew would piss him off. I opened the top hatch to look at the view. It made us much more vulnerable to roadside bombs, and I'd thought about this, but then I came up with a counter-argument: fuck it. I was making no progress with Sergeant Powell, and I was tired of his silence. If he wanted the hatch shut he could tell me.

Our relationship with the locals was teetering between hearts-and-minds and open hostility. I was faring little better with Sergeant Powell and, when we got back to FOB Edinburgh, we discovered that our dealings with the Americans were going the same way. We needed a helicopter ride back to Bastion and we thought that the Americans were coming in that morning, but no one knew for sure. Perhaps they were trying to keep the element of surprise, having learned their lessons from Roosevelt. Confuse your enemies by all means, but don't forget to confuse your friends as well. That's the way you stay powerful.

Sergeant Powell and I walked out to the helicopter landing site in the desert. We *thought* the Americans were coming in. My friend the tactical air controller had told me, and he'd seemed confident. But where were they?

Three specks appeared on the horizon. It was them! Within seconds they were upon us, roaring down onto the landing site. Ten of us waited expectantly, steadying ourselves against the breathtaking downwash. Flying stones pinged against our helmets and goggles, and against the teeth of anyone unwise enough to leave his mouth open. The roar of the engines turned every man into a mute. The landing point commanders filed away from us, one to each helicopter. Two Chinooks and a Black Hawk. Now, in the distance, they held up fingers for the number of people that each fuselage could take. In ones and twos our little group was whittled away, as people peeled off towards their allotted helicopter and their ride home. Then, all of a sudden, I was standing alone in the sand, and no one was holding fingers up anymore.

This was not a good turn of events. I took matters into my own hands and ran to the nearest Chinook, where the door gunner shook his head at me. A landing point commander was on me now. He took me sprinting to the Black Hawk, with my Bergen swaying precariously on a single shoulder. Again we were turned away. Time was getting desperately short; pilots hate to linger vulnerably on the ground. We dashed to the final helicopter. At first glance there was no room but, with a supreme effort of pushing and shoving, I managed to free up a seat for myself. I strapped myself down and seconds later we lurched into the air.

We did not drop low into the wadi as we had done on the way in, but struck out instead over the green zone. We flew over what seemed like endless fields of poppy before finally setting down in an unfamiliar camp on the edge of the desert. I did not recognise it but I knew it wasn't Camp Bastion. The loadmaster ordered us to disembark. We obeyed, leaving our Bergens somewhere in the far recesses of the fuselage. Then we watched as Americans streamed out of the helicopters. After the soldiers came boxes and boxes of equipment.

After the boxes came black bin bags with something strange in them. It was wet and icy cold. The final item to emerge from our helicopter was a shiny red gravel compactor, half the size of a man.

It was satisfying to see the men and equipment pouring off our helicopter, because that way we knew we were going to get some leg room for our onward journey. We were disappointed when the loadmaster pointed to a second phalanx of American soldiers and they trudged towards the rear ramp, determined to fill our leg room up again for the next part of our trip.

Disappointment turned into alarm when we followed the Americans towards the Chinook and the loadmaster, raising his hand, shooed us away. We stood, agitated, on the flight line. I had a sudden vision of being stranded for days in an unknown American base, with my Bergen and all my kit flying off into the midday sun. I had SECRET classified documents in my bag. If the Chinook left us behind now, flying off to an unknown destination, this was going to be an interesting one to explain. I contemplated boarding the helicopter by force.

Three of us stood there, wondering what to do. Just as we became convinced that the loadmaster had filled his fuselage to the brim with Americans, he gestured with his hand and we ran gratefully towards him. He hadn't forgotten us! We tucked in among the neatly packed ranks.

We took off once more, whirling into the dry air, and the next time we landed it was in Camp Bastion.

5

They say that in combat the training takes over, but it gets inside you long before that. It changes you.

How many times could you practice killing a man before you wondered what it would be like for real? Ten times? Fifty? A hundred?

The number is immaterial. What matters is that it exists, and that it will always be surpassed, as it had been for me.

After the sniper killed the two men in Musa Qal'eh, we received intelligence on a planned Taliban attack that night. I was almost eager for it. At Sandhurst, and later in the mess, 'contact' with the enemy had been the elephant in every room in which we stepped. The great unknown that underpinned everything we did, and gave it purpose. The secret door, marked 'don't enter', and tempting because of it.

I walked up to the barricade and picked out a good firing point. I oiled my rifle. I sat my boots down next to my sleeping bag so I could reach them in an instant when the fighting started, and then I went to bed.

Boom! I jolted awake in the middle of the night. An attack?

No. The British mortar team on the hill, letting off an illumination flare.

I lay back down in my bed and slept peacefully until the morning, when Sergeant Powell and I began our return trip to Camp Bastion. I'd come close to the war but I'd not quite found it. We'd passed in the night and missed each other.

I fancied that I had one ally in my search for the war, or at least a fellow traveller – Jim. He was no stranger to the grind of the Rear Echelon, having already been to Iraq and had a very boring time there. Now, in Afghanistan, he could empathise with my position.

We had been taught about empathy at Sandhurst. We learned that it was good. We knew the importance of understanding what our subordinates were going through, but we also knew that empathy was not the same as sympathy, and that sometimes it was our men's jobs to suffer. Sympathy would only breed weakness.

Jim was not about to fall into this trap. Far from being a source of sympathy to me, he was quite the opposite, making me feel even more frustrated in my REMF-dom. I felt sure that he did it on purpose.

One morning I walked to the shipping container which served as my office in Camp Bastion, and gave Jim a call.

'Hi mate, any more reccies on the cards?' I asked.

'Oh no,' he said. 'You can't go off on too many jollies, mate. I've got a deployment in the pipeline now, so I need you to do my job for me from Bastion. I'm going to send you some files through.'

God he annoyed me sometimes.

'I've read your report from Musa Qal'eh though,' he added. 'Mmm … well done! Well done!'

He was lampooning an ancient general we both knew, a World War Two veteran. The general had attended so many events and parades in his career that, in his senior years, saying 'well done' had become a reflex action. Outside a country church he'd been introduced to a frail old lady with the line 'This is Margaret. Her sister was killed in the Blitz, you know.'

'Mmm … well done!' the general had roared maniacally back at her.

Now Jim was feeding the line back to me. Despite his faults, Jim was a very funny man. I couldn't help but like him.

'So what do you want me to do?' I asked.

'The brigade commander wants every unit to take it in turns giving interesting facts about Helmand for the evening briefs. He's tasked our squadron commander, and The Boss pushed it down onto me. So now I'm pushing it down on to you. Mmm … well done.'

'Are you *actually* joking? I thought you were running a fucking war? Don't you have more important things than Helmand facts to be worrying about?'

'Yes I do, mate. I'm worried about getting out of fucking HQ for a few days. That's why I'm tasking you with this. Look, the idea is they'll do the tactical update – all the killing and bombing and stuff – then everyone will throw their two cents in, then we finish up with a light-hearted but educational fact about the province. It's like the *Ten O'Clock News*.'

'Right.'

'Right.'

Silence.

Who was going to break the deadlock? I decided to throw a comment into the mix.

'For fuck's sake.'

More silence.

'So can I have twenty facts by the end of the day?'

'Yeah.'

I put my desert hat on. In a determined sulk I walked across camp to the internet terminals. They were mostly for soldiers to check their Facebook pages and send emails home, because there weren't many people who needed the internet in order to play their part in fighting the war. I, however, was an exception.

I spent an hour searching the web for interesting facts about Helmand, and didn't find a single one. All I did was confirm what I knew already. Helmand was a miserable province which, before the Taliban and the poppy, had existed entirely independently of world history. Even the British Empire hadn't bothered to conquer it.

I pulled up some figures on arable acreage, population statistics and river flow volumes, and noted them down. Then I invented a fact about Alexander the Great visiting Helmand during his campaigns. I made up three more facts about the adventures of a nineteenth-century gentleman explorer, whom I named Montague Stourbridge. Then I finished off with the 'fact' that, in the 1740s, tulip bulbs were more expensive in Helmand than gold. I cribbed it from a piece of half-remembered Dutch history.

I compiled all my facts, emailed them to Jim and went to lunch. Once I'd eaten I returned to the office, and saw Roachy sitting at the desk with a smile on his face and the telephone receiver in his hand.

'It's the OPSO for you, boss. He wants a word with you about the Helmand facts,' said Roachy. The OPSO was the operations officer. It was Jim. I was expecting a telling off. 'Not taking my job seriously enough', something like that. I picked up the receiver and readied myself to sound contrite.

'Hello?' I said.

'Mate, we need to talk about your Helmand facts.'

'Oh … how come?'

'They were *fucking* boring mate! The cubic flow rate of the River Helmand? Are you serious?'

'Well it's a pretty boring province.'

'And what's all this shit about tulips?'

This was getting personal. Now Jim was slagging off my ability to make stuff up. I grunted in reply.

'Anyway,' he went on, 'I suppose the ones about the Stourbridge guy just about scraped the interest level. Can you dig out some more stuff on him? No one else in HQ seems to have covered him yet.'

'Of course, mate, I'll see what I can do, no worries.'

And so Montague Stourbridge got a whole career invented for him. He had a scrape with a despotic emir, a fracas with three Russian agents and he discovered the source of the River Helmand.

CHAPTER 5

The Fact for the Day took on a life of its own in headquarters, and Sir Montague became a part of it. Some of the staff officers even talked about compiling them into a book at the end of our tour: *101 Things You Never Knew about Helmand*.

Luckily for me, it never saw the light of day.

The evening after the Helmand facts, Roachy, Brian, Sergeant Powell and I walked down to the Camp Bastion shop for a sugary drink. We had been in Helmand for six weeks now, and a languid submission to routine was settling across the camp, penetrating every recess as surely as did the fine dust which blew in from the desert. There was not a drop of booze, and all we had for company was each other. Gradually the quest for entertainment was drifting further and further from normality. I had not yet succeeded in finding the war but I was finding something, and that thing was strange.

As we walked we were flanked by Chucker and Paul – the Cunt from Blah – and their two corporals from the crypto cell. Then, as we neared the shop, they peeled off from us. Lost in the middle of the Afghan desert, in Camp Bastion, in a shipping container, there was a genuine, franchised Pizza Hut outlet, and this was their target. But they weren't going there to enjoy themselves. They were going to fight a battle, and it was the same battle they fought every Thursday night:

Chucker and the two corporals find a wooden table to sit at, like the ones you get in beer gardens. Paul walks over to the shipping container and places an order at the counter.

'Two Meat Feasts, two Hawaiian, a garlic bread, a pack of dough balls and four cans of blackcurrant Fanta.'

He hands over his ticket and sits down with the rest of the cryptography cell, waiting for their number to be called. Ten minutes pass. Fifteen.

Then, 'Number thirty-nine, please?'

Silence.

The pizza chef scans the tables through the night-time murk.

'Number thirty-nine?' he repeats.

The cryptography cell stays quiet and inscrutable.

Bemused, the chef puts their order to one side and goes back to his work.

Chucker, Paul and the two corporals stare at ticket number thirty-nine, which is sitting on the table in front of them. Who's going to be the first one to break?

Not Chucker, for in the hinterland of his cryptic mind lies a vast seam of stubborn determination.

An hour goes by.

Paul won't crack, because he's the Cunt from Blah, and if he gives in then all the other cunts from Blah might find out that he got beaten by the Parachute Signal Squadron.

Two hours elapse.

It won't be the two corporals either, because Chucker and Paul are senior NCOs, their superiors, and they're not going to lose face by showing weakness in front of them.

Three hours tick by.

Then – wait, I was wrong – someone cracks! It's Corporal Hume!

'For fuck's sake,' he grunts, as he snatches up the ticket and trudges to the counter.

The chef looks at him suspiciously and hands over his order, which is now stone cold. Corporal Hume brings it back to the table, and the crypto cell devours it with relief and with relish.

Pathetic really, we thought. It showed how geeky the crypto cell were. Roachy, Brian, Sergeant Powell and I weren't joining them for their silly pizza battle because we were real men, and we had bigger fish to fry. We had an entire *war* to fight, for tonight was Bingo Night at the coffee shop.

The four of us stepped inside the large room of wood and Formica, with a bar at one end and a man in one corner, who presided over a plastic dome of tumbling balls.

Soldiers walked solemnly to the bar to collect their cards and blotters, and took their seats in a sea of browned and camouflaged bodies, rifles stowed under vinyl-clad seats. We waited for the balls to start rolling.

Before they did so, one of our radio operators, Corporal McConnell, dropped by. He'd not come for the bingo, he was just picking up a can of Coke.

'All right,' he said chirpily.

'Evening, Corporal McConnell,' I replied.

The rest of the table ignored him.

Corporal McConnell was not well liked by the senior NCOs. He was an ally-Hat. That is to say, he thought he was ally – cool as ice and hard as nails – but, at the end of the day, he was a Hat. He was yet to pass parachute training. He was also skinny and talked too much, which didn't help his cause.

Roachy, Brian and Sergeant Powell disliked him because he was a soldier, like them, but he didn't measure up to their standards.

I was an officer, so I looked on him as one of my charges. Someone to be looked after. He worked on Helmand's casualty evacuation helicopter, and I worried about his well-being.

'Had a good day?' I asked him.

'Not bad, boss. We got called out this morning to extract one of the blokes in Sangin. He was firing the 51 mil mortar and one of the shells misfired and blew his hand off. We got him on the helicopter and then just as we were going to take off this sergeant came running over to us with a black bin bag. I figured it was all the personal kit for the guy we were taking.

'Anyway, we got the bloke to the field hospital, dropped him off and went back to the tents to chill out. We had a cup of tea, then I started going through the bin bag. I put my hand in and felt something cold and sticky, and pulled it out and it was the guy's hand!'

I laughed.

Roachy, Brian and Sergeant Powell gave Corporal McConnell a grunt of recognition, and their faces said *You smarmy little cock.*

Corporal McConnell left, and the conversation turned to the main-stay of soldiers everywhere. The constant drum-roll of complaint.

'Have you heard they're thinking of starting an Armed Services' Day back home? Be good to get a bit more recognition for this shit.' said Sergeant Powell, as we filled in our particulars on the bingo cards.

'Oh, fucking nice one,' said Brian. 'A load of civvies get an extra day off work, and we'll probably have to come in on a Sunday to do a fucking parade.'

A general murmur of agreement.

I left to take a piss. I hadn't noticed when I went but, when I came back, I realised that our table was enveloped in a rotten stench.

'It stinks round us,' I pointed out.

'That'll be the creatine,' said Roachy.

'Or the six eggs I scoffed for breakfast,' said Brian.

Roachy and Brian were massive already, but they were both on a weight-gain trip. The day before, I'd walked to the gym and found Brian using every single weight, so I'd had to go for a run instead. As well as the exercise, and the creatine, and the eggs, they were on Promax, Thermobol and Cyclone, and Roachy had just got some new pills off the internet.

'Check out these fuckers,' he said, pulling them out. 'I'm on six a day.'

I had a look at the bottle. Each pill was an inch long and on the label it said that they relied on nano-molecular hyperdispersal technology.

'Fast track to weight gain, these, boss,' he said.

'I reckon it's a fast track to kidney failure.'

'Nah, not these ones. These ones are all natural.'

The bingo master was a fat soldier from the Logistics Corps, and eventually he called for hush. The night's jackpot was seven hundred dollars. With stakes that high, no one on the other tables had bought fewer than ten number-sheets each. We had one between us. We were outnumbered and outgunned. But we were paratroopers, and that didn't faze us. It just made us angry.

'You're fucking rubbish with that blotter, mate, no wonder we're fucking losing,' said Roachy.

'This is fucking dog shit. What a fucking waste of a dollar this was.'

A cheer of 'Bingo!' went up from the next table.

'We're getting beaten by a bunch of fucking Hats here.'

'I'm going to start throwing chairs in a minute. Those fucking Hat cunts.'

And so it went on, as Roachy, Brian and Sergeant Powell vented their wrath.

I only chipped in with the occasional comment, because I was not one of them. I was a young officer and they were senior NCOs: sergeants and staff sergeants. The army ran on class, and there was an unbridgeable divide between us. None of us would have it any other way. It was how the system worked. Why else would you take orders from a man fifteen years your junior, whom you could kick the crap out of if the inclination took you?

Still, I was tolerated. Sometimes even appreciated. Roachy and Brian got on well with me. Sergeant Powell was coming round to me. And at the end of the day I wasn't a Hat. That is to say, I had undergone parachute training.

It was what bound the squadron together. Fewer than half had passed it, but every man aspired to it.

It was a privilege to be allowed to exit an aeroplane as it flew at six hundred feet above the ground and, before the honour was bestowed, the prospective parachutist had to prove himself worthy in six and a half weeks of physical trials. Loaded marches were the mainstay; toiling for hours under a heavy Bergen until your shin muscles ran with fire, or sprinting full tilt, with the hard shock of tarmacked roads pounding into your knees.

P Company, as it was called, and the preceding beat-up training, was more to do with displays of bloody-minded determination than it was with physical fitness. Every so often an athletic-looking celebrity would attempt the course for a television programme. To everyone's amusement they always failed miserably.

We all got injured. Our muscles tore, our tendons stretched, our cartilage cried out in agony. We ate painkillers, in exotic varieties and combinations, as if they were sweets.

The worst injury that could befall a candidate was shin splints. It was the gradual detachment of the lower leg muscles from the bone. Each fibre, when it departed, ripped a little bit of bone with it, and once the shin was stripped of its strong outer core it would crumble away. We started with a hundred and twenty men on my course, and thirty finished. A good-sized handful spanked in with shin splints. Every time someone packed his bags and sloped off home I worried more about the deep, spasming pain in my own shins.

We had a young soldier on our course, skinny as a rake, whose shins started giving way around about half way through – three weeks in. He took a lot of pills, but they couldn't put the bone back where it was supposed to be. Any doctor could tell you that. Even the army doctor who'd failed the course six months beforehand, who'd started taking opiates from work and injecting them into his thighs so he could carry on.

Despite the drugs, this young soldier was in a lot of pain. He couldn't even walk to the cookhouse properly. He took three-inch steps with his left leg, then brought his right leg up to meet it, and it took him ten minutes to walk three hundred yards. But, somehow, when we got onto the exercise area and our instructors called 'Prepare to double ... double time!' he *ran*. He stuck it out. He beat his pain, day on day. Minute by agonising minute.

It wasn't enough though. His mind was strong but his body shat on him, three days from the end, on the log race. We were sprinting across open country, determined to carry a telegraph pole over a two-mile course, with speed and guts and bloody-minded determination, back to where it had started from.

We were charging down a slope when he collapsed. He stayed on the log because it had a rope tied to it, and the other end was hooked around his wrist. It dragged him for twenty yards across the gravel.

'Don't help him, let him stand up on his own!' shouted the instructor. 'He'll take himself off the log if he wants to.'

This turned out to be a tall order. His shin had given way, and the bone had turned to mush. We ignored him, lying screaming by the side of the track, and finished the race. Then, later on, the medic who had treated him arrived at the finishing posts and we crowded around him to hear his diagnosis.

'Feeling his shin,' the medic said, 'was a bit like putting your hands on a bag of warm porridge.'

This was the challenge laid down in front of the prospective para-chutist. Only if he succeeded would he earn the right to attend the Basic Parachute Course, and experience what recruitment literature de-scribed as 'an adrenaline-fuelled thrill ride; racing through the air while the fields are a patchwork beneath you!'

Army recruiters have never been the world's most objective com-mentators, but this still represented a low point. First of all, the fields are far from a 'patchwork'. From the door of a Hercules at 600ft you can make out the features of people on the grass, and the drop below your feet seems very real indeed. Secondly, while military parachuting is indeed adrenaline-fuelled, it is more of a series of fears and discomforts than a thrill ride.

You're flying to the Drop Zone. Loads of blokes in parachute smocks and camouflage paint are sitting next to you. Everything is as ally as fuck.

This feeling lasts for about ten minutes, but the flight to the Drop Zone takes two hours. The Herc is hugging the contours of the land amid a whirling sea of turbulence. Half an hour in, someone will succumb to air sickness and throw up. The blast of the air ducts pushes the smell into every nook and cranny of the cabin. Someone else follows suit. A chain reaction has been started. By the time the call comes to 'Stand up, fit equipment,' the thought of jumping from the vomit-soaked plane into the breathtaking tumult of the slipstream seems heaven sent.

The dispatcher heaves open the parachute door and stares grimly into the space beyond. Wind batters his face at a hundred and thirty miles an hour. Your legs tremble. You genuinely have no idea whether it is from fear or because of the thirty kilos of equipment that hangs suspended between them. The dispatch light is still unlit. You're safe for now.

Unless – that is – someone's reserve parachute is accidentally pulled amid the press of bodies. Then, as happened to a friend of mine, you find the rogue parachute bouncing out of the dispatch door and opening itself. Its hapless owner – and on this occasion the eight people in front of him – are then dragged out of the plane and into the unfriendly night: surviving, but with their enthusiasm for parachuting well and truly dented.

If this does not happen then the plane will fly on to the Drop Zone. 'Action … stations!' cries the dispatcher, and a neat line of you shuffle forward towards the gaping doorway. At this point a pungent fear starts to fill you up. You cannot yet see out of the door. 'What if,' you ask yourself, 'I turn into the doorway and, confronted with the howling emptiness, my legs set solid?' There's a man pressed in front of you and a man pressed behind you. You only have a split second to exit the plane. No matter what you see beyond the doorway, you cannot allow yourself to hesitate for an instant. It is a fear which strikes deeper into you than fear of physical injury can ever do. 'What if …' you ask yourself, 'what if my body refuses to jump?'

CHAPTER 5

Of course, the prospect of physical injury is not to be disregarded; hesitate, trip, lose the cadence or otherwise bungle your exit and the consequences can be unpleasant. A lapse of concentration in the plane might leave you dangling feet-first out of the doorway, with your parachute line around your neck and the rear lip of your helmet jammed up against the exit step. Then you're left, flailing and choking, suspended in mid air by your chin-strap, until the dispatcher gives you a firm kick in the back of the head and you're sent spinning away into space.

Even outside the plane, descending under a billowing green parachute, the prospects for injury remain as tantalising as they are diverse and bizarre. Men collide in mid-air and spiral downwards together as a tangle of limbs and rigging lines, descending towards the bone-snapping earth beneath them. Parachute drops go awry and deposit their charges into tall pine trees. The branches hold for a while and then give way, letting men slip down into space trailing their shattered canopies above them, as the field ambulances wait below.

This was what it meant to be parachute trained, to be airborne. It was a common bond between men, a shared knowledge that those around you had the mental strength to drag themselves through P Company, and then to plunge outwards into the slipstream, unhesitatingly, on a single word of command. We were special, and we even had a different coloured beret to prove it. Maroon was our colour, and we were loyal to it.

In recent years it had been hijacked, so that anyone in the Air Assault Brigade could wear it, parachute trained or not. But we knew whose it was really. They were just borrowing it and, deep down, they were really blue beret wearers. Crap Hats. Hats. Harry Hats, Harrys, Haraldos, Harry Screamers and Scream-bags. Fucking Screaming Bastards. The airborne forces have as many words for their non-airborne comrades as Eskimos do for snow.

Though, of course, being 'a Hat' was a relative term.

As far as the Parachute Regiment infantry was concerned, all of their supporting arms were Hats, whether they were airborne or not. The infantry were the only real paratroopers in the army, they'd say. We disagreed. As far as the engineers, the artillery, the logistics, the signals and all the others were concerned, it was the rest of their pallid and slovenly corps who were the Hats. Airborne signals was a tiny kernel within a vast organisation which looked on us as arrogant and aloof. We in turn looked on them as tedious and embarrassing. We imagined that we were a class apart.

We'd taken our places in the front rank of the British Army, facing off against enemies from the east. Ready to fly across France and Belgium, leap down screaming onto the north German plain and smash the crap out of the Russians.

But now we were in Afghanistan, and we were faced with a different kind of foe. A foe you couldn't beat with a gun and a parachute. All of our training seemed to be for naught.

We'd got caught in a bingo war, and the Hats were beating us. We were surrounded and out-blotted and the taste of defeat was in our mouths. Those fucking Hat cunts.

The bingo ground on to its bitter end, when a pasty-looking team from the dog-handling section made off with the jackpot. Roachy, Brian, Sergeant Powell and I sloped off into the night, wallowing in our ignominy.

Then we had an idea. There was a way to exact our revenge. We'd bully the crypto team! Chucker and the two corporals were Hats, and Paul didn't count as proper airborne because he was from Blah. Everyone knew that Blah's selection course was easier than ours – hillwalking at three kilometres an hour in Wales? We could do that in our sleep.

A week ago, Roachy had taken a Land Rover from the Royal Military Police. He'd recognised the number plate. It was one that had been in his troop back in the UK – three years ago, on a different continent. He flagged it down, kicked out the two corporals inside and told them it was ours. Then he drove off with it, and left them standing in the sand. The Rover was battered to hell, and the windscreen squirter was broken. It fired its fluid out in a ten-foot arc straight forward.

We spotted the crypto team walking back from their pizza battle and lay in wait for them in an alley with the headlights off.

Then, when they passed us, we opened up with a vicious squirt of washer fluid. They flailed around in surprise and we bowled off into the night. Four grown men, airborne soldiers, howling like schoolgirls. Victory.

Away from the bingo and the pizzas, somewhere else in Helmand, there was another war going on.

Jim was still stuck in Lashkar Gah, and he was fighting to get out on the ground, but his campaign was going badly. It was bad news for him but good news for me, because it meant that I didn't have to do his job for him from Camp Bastion. So, maybe, I could get out on the ground instead.

In other recesses of the province there was yet another war going on, and this one was against the Taliban. This was the war I was looking for, and if I got out of Bastion again then maybe I could find it. I rang Jim up one morning.

'What's next for the comms reccies?' I asked.

'You want to go to Sangin?'

Did I ever. Sangin was a town mid-way between Musa Qal'eh and Gereshk, on the Helmand River, and it was the very epicentre of the insurgency. We were pouring more and more troops into the town, and pushing the Taliban further and further back into the countryside. The district centre in Sangin had been besieged two summers ago – a tiny dot of British soldiers adrift in a town ruled by the Taliban. Now we were muscling our way in on every block and street.

Sergeant Powell and I packed our bags and hopped on the next Chinook out of Bastion. The war was in Sangin, and I was determined to find it. But first we had to find the town itself. We spent thirty minutes in the back of the helicopter, as the pilot sat with the map on his knees and talked to the door gunner with a concerned look on his face. Then Sangin appeared from the desert, and we smacked down on the hard earth of the district centre.

It was closer to the river than its counterpart in Musa Qal'eh, and greener. All life in Helmand depended on proximity to running water; without the criss-crossed maze of irrigation ditches and canals nothing could survive the heat of the desert. Starting in the mountains in the heart of Afghanistan, the River Helmand descended steadily southwards, sustaining a fragile wisp of life along its path. About half way down its length it met and watered the town of Sangin. Eventually, in Iran, it flowed into a huge lake and went no further, abandoning its quest for the sea.

Water was life. If an air conditioner trickled condensation into the sand, then plants would burst out of it. Here, in Sangin, greenery suppurated from the land for a kilometre or two either side of the river, and the weeds on the helipad were the first green things I had seen in the month since Musa Qal'eh.

We were led from the helipad, past the mortar team in a mud hut and a gang of engineers sawing timber, to a large concrete building. It was of a striking 1960s design which I'd seen many years before near the western border of Serbia. The two buildings were thousands of miles apart but the similarities were unmistakable – the strange modernist lines, the inward sloping skirt around the first floor, the tiny second floor dumped on top – the centre-pieces of two small towns in the backwaters of the world, where the long fingers of Soviet influence had extended just beyond the borders of the USSR. It was the British battle-group headquarters, and it was where the work lay for Sergeant Powell and me.

It took us all of half an hour to figure out that we were superfluous. Sangin didn't need our expertise. Their comms worked OK, and where they were going wrong we didn't have the power to fix them. Nor were we going to find any war, because the Royal Irish were on top of it and didn't need a couple of radio-twiddlers to help them out. We were cocooned inside the compound wire, but the next helicopter out of Sangin didn't leave for three days, and so we were marooned.

Killing time in Sangin became easy, because life there had an epic quality about it. It was normal life without the boring bits. No one in Sangin had to fill out a form, or get caught in a traffic jam, or have grown-up conversations with women about their feelings. There wasn't even any bingo to worry about, because there was no need for it. Men didn't need to turn on each other. It was a place to unravel, and let the simple things in life take over: three square meals a day, the heat of the sun and the cool of the river, and the constant struggle of life and death.

Even that had gone back to basics. The Royal Marines had occupied Sangin over the winter, and found the terrain too rough even for quad bikes, so they'd bought themselves a patrol donkey from the market. They loaded it up with spare ammo and grenades and then, when a firefight kicked off, they all ran to it to gear up. It patrolled with them for the entire winter. When it had some downtime it lazed around camp eating the grass.

In the Crimean War the Russians had called their British adversaries 'lions led by donkeys'. Well, it had taken a hundred and fifty years, but finally we were shaking the stigma off. At long last, *the donkey was being led by the lions.*

For a while, at least. The marines tied an empty jerrycan to its foot so it wouldn't wander off but then, one day in the spring, it walked straight out the front gate. The sentries didn't even bother to challenge it. Whether it returned to a pastoral life in the valley, or whether it turned traitor and became a patrol donkey for the Taliban, we never found out.

The Sangin District Centre was split into two. Between the halves was an offshoot of the Helmand River, and it was a godsend. Its source was the meltwater in the high mountains. It was cool and deep, and the daytime temperature was becoming unbearable.

The locals didn't go out in the day any more. When they saw British soldiers march under heavy loads in the sun, they built up a myth that we took a pill each morning which stopped us from feeling the heat. As it was, the heat and the discomfort were simply endured until a plunge in the river gave a torrent of relief; entire patrols staggered wearily through the gate, peeled off their sodden body armour and plunged gasping into the swirling green water. Its touch electrified the skin.

It flowed quickly, too – so quickly that it was impossible to stand against its full force without being swept downstream. A safety line was suspended over the water near its exit from camp which – if grabbed – offered escape onto dry land. Over the winter two marines had come back from patrol, jumped in the water, missed the line and been swept by the river into downtown Sangin, where they found themselves on patrol all over again, but this time unarmed and wearing nothing but boxer shorts. They sprinted through the bazaar back to camp with smiles on their faces.

Every day after lunch I bathed in the river, and watched Afghan and British soldiers dive and splash each other as if they were children. All was quiet in Sangin. The poppy harvest was in full swing and every local man of fighting age, plus half a million migrant workers, were busy with it. There was a time to reap and a time to fight, and this simple wisdom was not lost on the Taliban. We knew they were out there. Some of the Afghan soldiers even knew their mobile phone numbers. The Taliban existed, somewhere nearby, but they were keeping quiet.

It was the calm before a terrible storm.

6

Three days later a burst of machine gun fire rang out in the night.

I was in Lashkar Gah, the British headquarters which ran the war for the whole of Helmand, and someone was getting a magazine-full at the front gate. It was an anxious Afghan father and his sick little girl.

The father was speeding towards the camp, driving his daughter to the field hospital before it closed for the night. The sentries saw the car pelting towards them and gave a warning shot. It could have been a suicide bomber. The father didn't notice, and kept his foot on the gas. The sentries let him have it. Bullets all over the place – into the engine, through the seats – but, by some miracle, both father and daughter walked away without a scratch.

I turned my back on the gate and the shooting, and walked towards headquarters.

Over the next few weeks, I was to learn the truth about war. I was to have it rammed home that war was vicious, brutal, bloody and horrific. I was to find out, because my computer was going to tell me so.

When I was a teenager, and NATO was bombing Serbia, we had been told that war was no longer a slugging match, *mano-a-mano*, in which men tear and gouge and piss and shit. No, it had become a high-tech pursuit, where enemies could be dispatched at the press of a button, in the flash of a laser-guided rocket, and where NATO always, always knew where you lived.

Actually, NATO didn't know where I lived at the time. But it did know how to influence me, and the people around me.

It is much easier to sell a war to an unwilling public when you can convince them that the spectre of British sons and daughters fighting vile, dirty wars is a thing of the past. The public seemed insulated from war with a simple reassurance: 'Don't worry, we can fight without risking your little ones' lives. It's only the other side who are going to get killed. And you don't even have to feel bad, because these days we need only kill the *bad* ones.'

Iraq had eroded this pretence, and Afghanistan had shattered it. The public was no longer insulated from war by a double-glazing of high-tech. Instead, that privilege was reserved for me, and a handful of others. I'd sprung back from Sangin, bounced through Bastion and ended up as a watch-keeper in brigade headquarters in Lashkar Gah, to sit behind a computer. My jobs were going from bad to worse.

I'd arrived in Lash to see Jim and debrief him on my trip to Sangin. He'd heard what I had to say, thanked me for my good work and reported up to our squadron commander, The Boss. The Boss had 'listened to my findings with interest', then told Jim to tell me that I wasn't going to be doing comms reccies any more. He was going to put one of his other troop commanders on to it. Brigade headquarters were short of a watch-keeper and, having two arms, two legs and two pips on my shirt, I fitted the bill for the job perfectly.

Watch-keeping was a task which came to every young officer sooner or later. I was to do it for three weeks, and during that time Roachy was posted out of Afghanistan. He exchanged the desert, his weight gain and his bingo for a reunion with his wife and child, and a job teaching comms to university students at an Officer Training Corps. Quite an improvement as far as he was concerned. I never got to say goodbye to him.

I walked to the headquarters building as the gun reports from the front gate faded in my ears. We were still hidden by the high walls of a British camp, but now we were also nestled in the heart of a crowded town, so spats at the gate were a frequent occurrence.

Our location was a necessary difficulty, because the brigade staff needed to work with the Afghan provincial governor who lived in the town. His name was Gulab Mangal, and he was known as 'Joe' after the famous *Neighbours* character. Joe was new in the job, and he was not a native of Helmand; he'd been drafted in from outside on the back of his strong anti-corruption record. Great things were expected of him.

I walked into headquarters. It was a sheet-steel building, open plan inside, with a hundred cheap chairs and tables, like you'd find in any drab office block in Slough. Only less charming. At the back was the operations room – the ops room – where the day-to-day running of the war took place, and this was where I worked.

'All right,' I said to the battle captain, who was a short, podgy ex-ranker with personal odour issues that he covered up with sickly-smelling deodorant. I took my seat next to him. It was his job to know everything that was happening in Helmand, and to issue direction where it was needed.

'All right,' he replied to me. I was his watch-keeper. It was my job to handle the information which flowed into the room, and pass it on to whoever needed it.

'What's happening?' I asked.

'Fuck all.'

Not surprising, really. We ran the night shift, and even the Taliban appreciated the value of a good night's sleep. I settled down in front of my three computer screens, which in a different life might have made me look like a slick young operative in a twenty-first century command node.

I belched loudly. I'd slept all day then come via the cookhouse, where they were dishing up the evening meal. Roast beef for breakfast didn't agree with me.

On the wall in front of us were six large plasma screens, with data and streaming video for the whole room to digest. Through a military version of Instant Messenger we were connected to Musa Qal'eh, to Sangin, to Gereshk, to the Joint Helicopter Force, to the Explosive

Ordnance Disposal team, to the RAF and to countless others. We were in the nerve centre of the battle for Helmand. Right at the crux of the conflict that was defining our generation, and we were watching its progress – one line at a time.

This was war, and its font was Arial.

For hours, nothing happened. Absolutely nothing. I made some coffee, did the crossword and tried to keep upwind of the battle captain. Then, at about 5 a.m., a line popped up on my screen:

EF Eng SAF. FF Rtn SAF, 81mm, Arty, CAS. 1x EF KIA.

It was from the American 24th Marine Expeditionary Unit, 24 MEU. They were in Garmsir, in the far south of Helmand, pushing ever further into Taliban territory. In the weeks to come they hoped to break out into the southernmost deserts, cutting off the Taliban's supply routes from Pakistan. This was pissing the Taliban right off. They were fighting tooth and nail, but the Americans were giving back much worse than they got. The line on my screen meant 'Enemy Forces engaged us with small-arms fire. We returned small-arms fire, 81 millimetre mortar fire, an artillery barrage and bombs dropped from a fast jet. One enemy fighter was killed in action.'

The Americans could always be relied on for a subtle approach to counter-insurgency.

I reported the engagement to the battle captain. He nodded, making a mental note of the situation. One to keep an eye on.

That was what we did, mostly. We kept an eye on things. People told us what they were doing, and asked us when they wanted to know what other people were doing, and we kept the war ticking over. The only time we really earned our pay was when a line popped up like:

1x UK mil T1 GSW t of ace.

CHAPTER 6

A British casualty, medical priority 1 (most urgent). Gunshot wound to the face.

We couldn't see the injured soldier, the spurting blood and the bullet-shattered features. We couldn't hear his cries of agony or read the panic on his friends' faces as they waited for the helicopter we had dispatched to them. But the tragedy wasn't lost on us. When a line like that appeared the room was transformed. The entrance to the ops room was barred. The red light went on. The outside world was shut away, and a deathly silence slipped down over us. Even the walls seemed to move closer together. We waited on tenterhooks as the tragedy progressed towards its closing line.

IRT w/d BSN

The Incident Response Team has landed, 'wheels down', at the Camp Bastion field hospital.

Whatever happened afterwards was out of our hands. The steady roll of reports and requests could flood back across the ops room. We moved on to the next thing.

Everything that happened in Helmand had an echo in the ops room. We weren't numb to it, we were just detached, like doctors with their patients.

Sometimes we could even listen to the Taliban when their radio transmissions were intercepted and passed back to us. Then they seemed like ghosts in the night, out there somewhere, un-get-at-able, but with their conversations popping up on my screen as regular as clockwork. When it was horrific, I felt a tiny echo of the horror:

ICOM intercept:
Taliban 1: I have the spy we captured, what should I do?
Taliban 2: Keep him with you until I arrive.

It appeared one night, and I felt sick contemplating the man's fate.

Then, on other nights, it was downright eerie. Like when the Danes were out on a dawn patrol, in their area of operations around Gereshk, in the east of Helmand. They intercepted Taliban radio transmissions, from a team that was about to attack them:

ICOM intercept:

Taliban 1: They are approaching the tree line now. Do not open fire until they reach it.

How strange it must have been, walking across the fields, listening to an unseen enemy describe your own movements.

It was too much for the Danish patrol. They radioed for an unmanned reconnaissance plane to find their attackers. They didn't get one. Instead, they got an American Reaper drone, armed with a Hellfire missile.

They couldn't see its video feed, but we could. A buzz filled the ops room. We crowded around the screen, waiting for the Taliban to appear in the thermal scope. They were going to get fucked. It was a car-crash moment, disturbing but utterly compelling.

The drone circled for half an hour and then gave up in frustration. The enemy wouldn't show themselves. When I left the Ops Room at seven that morning the Danish patrol hadn't even been shot at. A few people still lent half an eye to the video feed, just in case, but it seemed the Taliban had lost heart and decided to fight another day. They didn't know it, but they'd just saved their own lives.

It wasn't just us who could play the listening game. The Taliban knew it as well, and liked it.

One night I took a call from the Ministry of Defence in Whitehall, asking if we had any unreported soldiers missing in action. They had been contacted by a frantic mother who had just taken a call on her mobile phone while she was at a party. An unfamiliar female voice had told her that her son had been captured by the enemy, and that his whereabouts were unknown.

The MoD smelled a rat, because no one official would break that news to a mother over the phone. Still, to make sure, I set about waking up a string of people at Kandahar airfield. Eventually someone there was sent to check on the soldier in question. He was sleeping safely in his bed, and woke up to see his mate standing over him.

'Just checking you hadn't been kidnapped by the Taliban, mate,' was the only explanation he received.

Perhaps he'd used a mobile phone and a Taliban sympathiser in the telecoms company had passed on the number he'd called. Or perhaps he'd given his mother's home number away on the internet. Who knows? It went to show that, just as we were prepared to slide down the technological scale when it suited us, the Taliban were equally as pre-pared to slide up it.

Cavemen with AK-47s they were not. Neither were they faceless goons who thought only of expelling the infidels. Each time a line appeared on my screen, a tiny bit of light was shed on the Taliban.

It was like when we were at Sandhurst and an illumination flare went up, showing the outline of the base we were about to attack. The buildings were brought out in hazy orange relief. A little bit more knowledge given on the nature of the enemy.

Sometimes, when a flare went up and we glimpsed the Taliban, they looked surprisingly human. Noble, even:

ICOM intercept:
Taliban 1: The man still refuses to leave his house, what should I do?
Taliban 2: Tell him it's for his own good. We will fight the British nearby tomorrow,
and we don't want him and his family to get hurt. We are responsible for his safety.

Then sometimes they were ludicrous:

Taliban 1: Go and bring me the two-headed thing that uses a lot of ammunition, not a pickaxe!

(He was talking about a rocket-propelled grenade)

Taliban 2: OK
Taliban 1: One time, when I asked this, someone brought me an actual pickaxe!

And sometimes they bickered like children:

Taliban 1: There are some helicopters flying tonight, I think they are heading your way.
Taliban 2: Don't discourage anyone, motherfucker.
Taliban 1: I'm not discouraging anyone, I will not say anything ever again.
Taliban 2: Good, thanks a lot, just make sure you don't say anything.

And sometimes they were just beyond my understanding:

Taliban 1: Hello, how are you?
Taliban 2: I'm fine, thank you.
Taliban 1: OK, here there are a few devotees, they all say hello to you. One of them says he wants to blow himself up first, but the others argue and say they all want to blow up themselves first!
Taliban 2: OK say hello to them from me.

No matter how human they were – how inscrutable, how exotic, how vicious or how noble – they occupied a special place in our war for the population of Helmand. Theirs were the hearts and minds which we had decided to snuff out, and we applauded their misfortunes.

A week into my stint of watch-keeping, in the Musa Qal'eh valley, soldiers at the hilltop Roshan Tower observation post saw four men herding a group of local farmers into the back of a truck at gunpoint. Then they climbed into a car and drove off in convoy, with the truck in the lead. The soldiers at the Roshan Tower couldn't touch them. They weren't putting anyone's life in immediate danger so, even though they were clearly kidnappers, the rules of engagement said they couldn't be touched. But then the Taliban screwed up. The car drove close by the tower, and one of the men made a fatal mistake. Inexplicably, he leaned out of his window and sprayed inaccurate AK-47 fire at the observation post. This was all the provocation the soldiers needed, and they replied with a £40,000 computer-guided Javelin missile.

A Javelin missile (the MoD assured us) could destroy any tank in service in the world today, and turn its entire contents, human or otherwise, into a finely ground pâté. So it came as a surprise when four living men emerged from the annihilated vehicle. It was probably something to do with pressure differentials, because cars fell to pieces under the hammer-blow of a Javelin missile instead of containing the explosion inside them like a tank would.

One of the men was missing a leg. He couldn't run away, so he was picked up by the patrol dispatched from Roshan Tower to investigate the wreckage. The other three, despite being seriously injured, managed to escape down a dried-up river bed into the town.

An hour later they presented themselves at the front gate of the Musa Qal'eh District Centre with burns, deep gashes, internal bleeding and broken bones, pleading for medical treatment. They explained they were local men who had all been involved in a freak farming accident while tending their fields.

We had the whole war laid on for us there in the ops room. It just came to us in text speak. When it was darkly humorous we laughed, like when the Parachute Regiment shot dead a suspected suicide donkey. Maybe it was the same one the marines had kept in Sangin over the winter, gone rogue. The Para Reg squad were on rural patrol when the donkey came charging towards them, with its saddle bags rammed full of something or other. Not worth taking any chances on. One of the privates took aim and let rip, and the donkey fell down dead. A few seconds later he saw its owner, looking pissed off and wondering how he was going to get his food to market now he'd lost his transport. The patrol commander took $10 of his own money out of his wallet, gave it to the man, and continued on his way.

It was a stingy amount for a dead donkey, and a misfortune for the man in question, but it gave the lads on patrol a laugh. And the laugh rippled and washed up in the ops room, and we laughed too. Then, when the story was poisoned by tragedy, the ripples spread out and we in the ops room felt the bitter taste in our mouths. Two days later the donkey owner was beheaded by the Taliban, for accepting money from the infidels.

There was no shortage of other tragedies in the ops room. It was the place to go to realise that life was cheap. Not a precious pearl, to be closely guarded, as it was thought of back home, but a silly thing, which has come into our possession lightly, and which can be discarded equally as lightly. But not only that. It was a thing that could be taken from others with just as much lightness and carefree panache.

One night the computers told us that two Afghan National Police were seriously wounded at a checkpoint. Bleeding and broken, they made their way across the desert to the nearest coalition base, Camp Jupiter, desperate for help.

Ten minutes later a few more lines of text popped up on the screen. It wasn't just two wounded policemen. There were three more, too injured to move, still bleeding away at the checkpoint. Five of their colleagues were lying beside them as corpses. The entire checkpoint had been wiped out.

How had the Taliban done it, we wondered?

First we heard that they had pulled a trick. One man had entered the checkpoint shouting and raving, in order to distract its occupants. Seconds later, another man had stepped through the doorway and

The firing ranges at Camp Bastion and the General Purpose Machine Gun.

Tea with the US Marines in Strongpoint Bravo (Chapter 13).

The view across the Helmand River from Musa Qal'eh.

The Mobile TOC (Chapter 9). Second from left is Captain Asif. In the centre is General Muhayadin. Third from right is the Commanding Officer of 1 Royal Irish and I am on the far right.

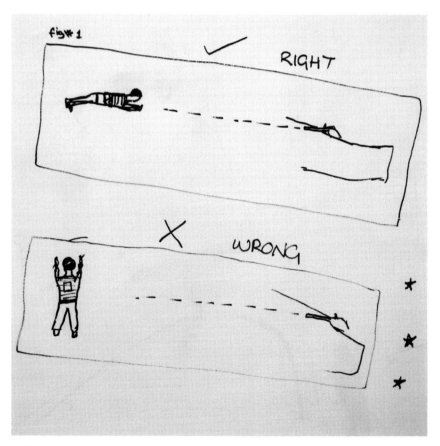

Instructions for interpreters during a fire-fight, drawn on a wall in Sangin.

Desert convoy from FOB Dwyer to FOB Delhi (Chapter 11).

Gaffer-taping the armoured panels back onto the Pinz (Chapter 11).

An Afghan National Policeman outside his sentry box.

A view of Sangin from the British base.

Our accommodation in FOB Delhi, before the stealing started (Chapter 12).

The WMIK on the way to Strongpoint Bravo, near to where it would be hit by an IED a few days later (Chapter 14).

Strongpoint Bravo. Walking to the burn pits with a bag of one's own waste (Chapter 13).

Patrolling in Garmsir.
ANA soldiers killing time
with the local children.

Recruit training.

sprayed the entire room with machine gun fire, cutting down everyone inside.

Then, a few hours later, a different story came to light. The survivors revealed that they'd been attacked by one of their own. The eleventh man who worked with them at the checkpoint, day in, day out. We never found out why. For some reason he'd got pissed off, so he'd picked up his rifle, switched to automatic and squeezed the trigger.

But this was not the worst thing that happened while I was watch-keeping. The worst thing was this.

One morning Helmand's governor, Joe Mangal, was whisked to a meeting in Musa Qal'eh by a British Chinook. Somehow, news of his journey had leaked out to the Taliban and, as his helicopter slowed over its landing zone, a slew of RPGs whooshed up to meet it. One scored a direct hit, smashing into the rear pylon of the aircraft just below the rotor blade. Had it exploded, Joe would have died, along with everyone else who hung in the air with him. Miraculously, it was a dud. The warhead passed straight through the metal housing and out of the other side, where it struck the underside of a rotor blade. Again it failed to detonate, and it careered off harmlessly into the open sky.

Were it not for that unreliable trigger mechanism, the Taliban would have killed Mangal and scored a resounding victory against us. In the blink of an eye, the whole balance of power in Helmand would have been altered. They failed, and that gave them a score to settle.

Two days later, they attempted to get their revenge. They needed to force us into sending a second helicopter into Musa Qal'eh for them to shoot down, and they devised a sure-fire method of doing so – a suicide bomber was dispatched to a police checkpoint and he blew himself to pieces. He killed several civilians and injured many more, in the certain knowledge that we would despatch the casualty evacuation helicopter to pick up the survivors. When the helicopter appeared above the town the Taliban opened fire on it with heavy machine guns. The helicopter had to retreat and abandon the casualties. The Taliban failed to bring it down, but they escaped unscathed. Once the brief battle was over it was only the innocent civilians who lay twisted and broken in the blinding sunshine.

So much for the cleanliness of high-tech war.

The computers in the ops room, or wherever, didn't change the way we did business. They were a tool, to be picked up and discarded at will. A way to empower Man to reach his true potential.

On those nights of watch-keeping, it just seemed too bad that Man was such a shit.

This was the dawn of the twenty-first century and yet here we were, in the desert, and all our skill, all our endeavour over the millennia, was leading right back to the simple act of being brutal to one another.

So where were we going wrong? Man was never knowingly a shit. Everyone in the world had good intentions. Everyone was proud of their achievements, felt they'd done the right thing, stuck to their principles and only did wrong because, by doing so, things would be better in the end. Even the Taliban thought that way, I'd imagine.

So if none of us felt that we were shits ourselves, why were we being so shitty to each other?

Well, although I don't consider myself a shit, I *did* use to enjoy watching fights at school. When I was a child, if I picked up a stick in a forest then it became a gun in my hand. If I picked up a sea shell on the beach then it became a grenade.

It's a thread that's woven in deeper than missiles and computers and radio intercepts, deeper than swords or clubs or even clothes. Stanley Kubrick was bang on when he made an ape pick up a rock and kill another ape, and he called it the dawn of Man. And I wasn't alone in thinking so. Jim agreed with me.

When I was in Bastion and he was in Lash he shared the pain of the rear echelon with me. But now that I was in Lash as well that wasn't all that we shared. I'd moved into his room. It was a drab concrete cell in a crumbling 1960s building, and we lay in it on metal bunks and dreamed of action together.

It was not a happy time for me, because my prospects were waning and Jim's were on the up and up, and he spared no effort in ramming this message home.

'Fuck me, mate, two months already in HQ, I'm about ready to crack. I'm getting out though, thank fuck,' he said, as we stared at the cracks in the plasterwork above our heads. 'It'll be good for you as well, 'cos you'll be able to share in the action second hand. You know, I'll be out there doing the business and I'll get on the radio to you and be like, "Graham, we need ammo resup – heli drop. Make it happen," and you'll be able to go from your desk in the ops room to the battle captain's and tell him we need more ammo, and he'll sort it out for us, so you'll kind of get a slice of the action as well.'

'So do you reckon The Boss is going to let you out, then?' I asked, trying not to rise to his baiting.

'Yeah, he's well on-side. Once the Americans finish off the push down south, and clear out, there's going to be three new British bases built down there. The Boss wants to send me out with the location recce team from the Engineers, to advise them on comms. But after we've done the base reccies, the Engineers are going on a long-range desert recce, out beyond the Hook of Helmand, towards the Pakistan border. The guy leading the team's a mate of mine from Sandhurst, so he's going to get me on it. No one's been that far south yet. We don't know what's out there. Anything could happen. We could get *besieged.'*

Jim drew his Browning from its holster. 'Bang, bang,' he said. 'That'll be me in a week, mate,' he said. Then he put it back. Then he drew it again. 'Bang, bang.' Then back in the holster for a third time. He pulled it out *again*. Thus time the pistol's elastic lanyard came off his belt, and slapped him square in the face.

'Ah – *fuck*,' he said, clutching his lip, and he walked off down the corridor to look in the mirror.

Getting besieged. Nothing in the world felt more desirable to me right then. Not drinking a beer in a sunny garden. Not making love to my girlfriend. Nothing.

Jim returned from looking in the mirror, and I could tell that he sensed he'd gone too far in needling me. I'd been watch-keeping for three weeks now and, that morning, I'd been told that I was soon to move all of ten yards to take up my next job, as commander of the brigade comms troop, in the back room of the headquarters building. I would be there for a month and a half. It was the very epicentre of the rear echelon and I was becoming deeply despondent.

'You'll get out soon, mate,' Jim said, in a sad tone which he used only occasionally. He brought it to the surface to remind me that, beneath all the piss-taking, there was a foundation of genuine solidarity between us. He had to, really. I was the only ally he had.

Two days went by, then Jim flew south to Garmsir for his reccies. I moved from watch-keeping to running comms troop, which comprised a dozen or so soldiers, who worked the radios for headquarters and who were all as bored and frustrated as I was. We worked together in the back of the headquarters building, them operating and maintaining the radios, me as their leader. Except turning dials and pressing buttons requires almost no leadership, and so I became a manager of shift rotas and a drafter of documents for The Boss. I moved off the night shift and settled into a daytime routine: meet the lads in the morning for an update, talk over new projects with Jim, have a game of Tanks on the computer with the troop sergeant, draft a proposal or two, go to the daily squadron conference, and so on and so on.

What was it that made me long to be holed up and besieged, somewhere south of the Hook of Helmand?

CHAPTER 6

It was something to do with what I had glimpsed in Sangin. Simplicity. The Game of Life, with the background noise turned down to zero, and all the petty side games done away with – but with the stakes turned up to maximum. No shopping runs, no credit agreements, no congestion charge. Just a gun and the desert and life and death.

That was the big war. The bare bones of existence. And if the big war wasn't there to fill up the hours of the day, all the small wars rushed in to take up the slack.

In brigade HQ the big war was all around us. It had to be, we were running it. But it didn't fill up the day. The small wars washed over it, and they were different for everyone.

The ones that plagued me the most were the squadron commander's wars. The Boss's wars. He was responsible for all the radio comms in Helmand, and he was bloody good at his job. A truly impressive force. But he knew that excellence in comms just wasn't sufficient to get him his promotion to lieutenant colonel, and so he fought his small wars of memory, and he tried to enlist everyone to fight alongside him. His battleground was the squadron's daily meetings, in a small concrete courtyard under a wicker canopy, lit by a single sodium bulb.

'Graham,' he would say, as he fixed me with a stare across a table filled with the officers and senior NCOs who served under him.

'Graham, what is the name of Officer Commanding, Cryptography, Southern Afghanistan?'

Silence hangs in the air.

What the *fuck* is he talking about?

I suppose there must be *someone* in charge of cryptography for southern Afghanistan, but what's it got to do with me? The new crypto keeps arriving on time each month, whether I've learned its master's name or not.

'I don't know, sir,' I reply, as humbly as possible.

The Boss gives me a dirty look, and trots off the name of Officer Commanding, Cryptography, Southern Afghanistan as if he has learned it by rote. Which, to be honest, he probably has. Of course he has, because playing your part in defeating the enemy isn't enough to earn you a promotion to lieutenant colonel. You have to drill your mind until it resembles a Filofax, where each page corresponds to one of your peers, competitors or superiors, and the headings on it are Name, Rank, Position, Personal Gripes when Conducting Inspections and Best Ways in which to Schmooze. This was his small war, and he was brilliant at it.

I was shit at it, and he never let me forget it, but that was the least of my worries. His second in command, David, was an expert at small wars, and I was shit at all of them.

David had joined one of the biggest small wars in the army. He had taken up his place in the Defence Writing militia, and he had vowed to uphold its principles, even unto death: 11-point black Arial typescript, capital letters for titles, bold and underlines for subtitles. No 'th' after dates. And, when referring to other documents in the header block, no full stops after document names. This was crucial. The army relies on discipline and iron rigidity. Holding the line. How on *earth* could we hope to defeat the Taliban if rogue lieutenants went around putting full stops after document titles? Non-conformist writing had to be stamped out, and David had taken it upon himself to do so. Sometimes it meant that paperwork got stuck in the squadron for a month or so, while all the errant full stops were tracked down, but this was a war, and in wars there is always collateral damage, so we had to harden our hearts to these unfortunate events.

Then there was Sidney the stock-taker's war. He pushed paper for the squadron, and during the day his wars were smaller than anyone's. But then at night, when he phoned home to his wife in England, his war was the biggest of them all.

'So what have you been up to?' she asked.

'The squadron's dead short of manpower,' he replied, 'so I've been getting out on the ground with The Boss. You know, he's been leading the lads, and I've been backing him up, getting my hands dirty. I can't really say any more over the phone.'

It was a good little fantasy for a frustrated REMF but, unfortunately for him, it backfired. His wife was a formidable woman, and wasn't going to take that sort of thing lying down. She rang the squadron rear party, back at our base in Colchester, and said 'What the hell is my husband doing on patrol with the squadron commander, when he should be taking care of the paperwork in HQ? What sort of tin-pot squadron are you running here?'

The head of the rear party said he didn't know, but he would find out. He rang Lashkar Gah and asked why The Boss was taking Sidney the stock-taker out on patrol. The sergeant who answered the phone said that he wasn't, and then walked to the cookhouse to tell everyone he could find about the tales that Sidney had been spinning to his wife.

But even in the cookhouse, where he ruined Sidney the clerk's life that afternoon, a small war was being fought. The master chef had just issued a decree that under-armour shirts were not to be worn at meal times. Some of the infantry had started eating while wearing them, when they'd just returned from patrol and didn't have time to change before the cookhouse shut. But, because they had been on patrol, they were sweaty and unpleasant to eat next to. So it had been proposed that the infantry should go without their meals, rather than disturbing the pleasure of other people's, and the master chef had agreed.

I was suffocating under everyone else's small wars, and so I fought my own small war with even more determination than before. It was the war to get out of HQ, and I was desperate for victory.

During my nights as watch-keeper, I had been developing a new strategy. The day after Jim left for Garmsir, I put it in to action. I got the nod from The Boss, and then walked down to the psychological operations cell at the far side of camp. I wanted to see if I could offer my services to them, because I knew they were undermanned, and that they patrolled out of Lashkar Gah. I could work for them, making up the numbers on PsyOps patrols, chatting with the locals, assessing their mood and trying to gather intelligence from them, and still keep The Boss happy by putting in the hours running HQ comms troop. Perfect.

I pushed back the door to their shabby little office. It was another small concrete cell, like the room that Jim and I shared. Grey and messy. But behind a desk, a few feet in front of me, sat a pretty blonde corporal. Her face broke into a luxurious smile.

'Hi,' I said, 'I'm in Lash for a couple of months with some free time on my hands.'

I explained my situation to her.

'I'm sure we could use you,' she said, splaying her fingers over the wood of her desk and still smiling.

Her name was Sarah, and over the next few weeks I would come to think of her as a ray of sunshine in the dirt-dim greyness of Lashkar Gah. She was young, newly married and with everything possible going for her.

'How about popping over to see the captain?' she asked.

I did, and the PsyOps captain jumped at the offer of extra help. First, though, I'd need training. His sergeant major could train me, but he was away and wouldn't be back in camp for a week or two. I would have to wait.

In the meantime, I had HQ comms troop to get settled in to. I spent a day going over equipment inventories and emergency procedures. Then a morning doing the crypto accounts. By lunchtime everything was put in order, and I went back to my bunk for a nap.

I walked into the room and saw Jim lying on his bunk. I wondered what he was doing there. He'd only been gone three days. Why did he look so miserable?

'Hello, mate,' I said. 'What happened? Did the recce around the Hook of Helmand not go ahead? What happened to getting besieged?'

'No, it went ahead,' he said in a sulk. 'We all did the base reccies together, but then when it got to the long-range recce the Engineers said there was no spare space on the vehicles, so they told me I couldn't come.'

This was music to my ears.

'I'm really sorry to hear that, mate,' I said. 'That was your one big chance to get away, wasn't it? I guess you'll be stuck in Lash for the rest of the tour now.'

'Yeah,' he said, looking broken-hearted.

'Well, at least I'm probably getting out with PsyOps soon, huh?'

'Yeah.'

'Don't worry, though, I'll make it really live for you when I tell you about it. It'll be almost as if you were out there yourself!'

Jim sighed. He didn't have the energy to do anything else. I left him, and returned to HQ comms troop with a spring in my step.

But, despite my boasting, my plans to get out with PsyOps didn't go smoothly. Over the next few weeks I was a regular feature at their office, calling in every few days to ask Sarah when their sergeant major was going to arrange some training for me. Every time, she replied with the same smile and good-natured shrug of the shoulders. It was a project which seemed destined to hover on the horizon, permanently out of reach. I decided I needed a back-up plan. I started lobbying The Boss for a trip to the Danish area of operations, where O'Hagan had been blown up, to visit my soldiers who were still working there. And, in the meantime, I killed time in Lashkar Gah.

Running was the best way to make a couple of hours disappear. You could slip down an alleyway of blast walls and then sprint across the front of the headquarters building, crunching on the gravel, before heading across the vehicle park and around the helipads, and back to the start past the accommodation tents, ending at the foetid and stinking pool of the camp's open cesspit, which we called the Boating Lake. It took about ten minutes.

It was June now, and the temperature was nudging fifty degrees. I could manage three or four laps of camp before I began to feel faint and dizzy. Then I would run one more lap, to push back my limits of endurance, and retire. After that I took a cold shower, then ate an ice cream from the camp shop, then stood under the A/C for half an hour to try to stop sweating. Hey presto, two hours disposed of. After that you could always read, but if you didn't want to be disturbed you had to find a quiet corner outside. Away from the A/C it was so hot that the glue in books' spines melted, so after about ten minutes of reading all the pages fell out. It made for a tedious pastime.

I did this routine for six weeks, and in that time we suffered a plague. We were beset by Diarrhoea and Vomiting.

In civilian life diarrhoea and vomiting are two separate words, and they are symptoms of an underlying illness. But in the army they are inextricably linked, and they are not merely symptoms, but a disease in their own right. In fact they, or it, is the only disease the army feels truly comfortable with.

D and V.

If you just *say* you're ill, or in pain, then you are a malingerer. You are showing that you lack moral fibre. But as soon as you can produce some evidence to back it up – puke, pebbledash shit, whatever – the situation turns itself inside out. Suddenly, you are one of the Infected. You're kept in isolation. Someone brings you your meals to eat in your room, and then washes their hands afterwards. You get a sink and toilet cordoned off just for you. You can stand up, tall and proud, and proclaim 'I have D and V'.

You don't even have to produce evidence from both ends. If you puke, then you are suffering from Diarrhoea and Vomiting. It doesn't matter if you're shitting or not. You have diarrhoea by association.

Likewise, if you're shitting, it is a mathematical certainty that you are vomiting, regardless of what is coming out of your mouth.

If an entire disease can be contracted purely by linguistic association, then no wonder it was so contagious. It was spreading through Lashkar

CHAPTER 6

Gah like wildfire. By my fourth week in comms troop, nearly a third of the camp's manpower was bedridden. People were starting to talk about the whole place getting quarantined. No helicopters in or out.

Then, thank fuck, the D and V plague subsided a little. The threat to the heli flights lifted. The Boss got less twitchy about his manpower and one day – to my surprise – he agreed to let me get out for a week and visit my soldiers in the Danish area of operations. I was free!

I put some plans together, booked my flights, let the lads know I was coming, packed my bags and waited. Another few days rolled by, and then the day of the flight arrived. I walked down to comms troop to make sure everything was in order for my departure.

Sergeant Powell was there. He'd come over from Camp Bastion to work in the headquarters' technical workshop. As I walked into our steel-box office, there was a crowd of young soldiers gathered around him, and he was holding court.

'I'm stacked enough now,' he said. 'so I've switched from the weight-gain pill to the weight-loss pills. You know they're doing the business, 'cos they make your sweat all thick and treacly. It lets you see all the unhealthy shit that's leaving your body.'

Barnsey joined the fray. He was my troop sergeant from HQ comms troop – thick-set, bright and easy-going. Built like a brick shit house. He started telling the crowd about his weight-gain regime in Kabul, when he was posted there way back in 2002. Then, for no particular reason, he moved on to the football match they'd organised there.

The Taliban had just been deposed, and the victorious coalition had organised a game in the newly liberated Ghazi Stadium between two local teams. Under Taliban rule, the stadium had been used for public executions, and for the punitive amputation of limbs.

'We got tasked to clear the place up before the match,' said Barnsey. 'We spent a day going round the grass picking up bits and pieces of people. We weren't sure if it was mined or not, but we didn't have any detection stuff. Anyway, they had the match, but the stadium was only designed for 30,000 fans, and 80,000 pitched up. The Taliban hardly ever let them have football games, and when they did they banned cheering, so the locals were going nuts for a proper match.

'There was a handful of Brits, and we were supposed to control this crowd of fucking 80,000. If anything had have kicked off then we would have been right in the shit.

'Then, after a while, the Afghan police turned up. Whenever the crowd started acting up they took live RPG warheads and started beating them with them. It was fucking mental.'

I didn't doubt it.

I said goodbye to Barnsey, Sergeant Powell and the lads, and went to find Jim to tie up some loose ends. They took about ten minutes, and then I found myself sitting with him at his desk with another hour to go before my flight.

'Game of Tanks?' I asked, pointing at his computer.

'Yeah, best of three,' he nodded.

'And if I win this time, then get killed in Gereshk, that means I'm champion forever, right?' I asked.

'Right.'

I beat him 2-1, and made my way to the helipads for my Chinook ride to Camp Bastion, brimming with enthusiasm.

On the way I passed through the medical centre, which was still in the grip of the brutal outbreak of D and V. So many people had succumbed that the isolation wards weren't able to cope, so men spilled out into the corridors, lying in camp beds, in a tumultuous scene reminiscent of a World War I dressing station. A pungent smell hung in the air, and medics stepped gingerly between the serried ranks of sweating, shaking and shitting soldiers. Perhaps it really was the plague.

When I arrived at the flight line I heard some news which made my heart sink low and my blood run cold and sickly.

CHAPTER 6

Four British soldiers had been killed the night before when an IED had detonated beneath their vehicle, just on the outskirts of town.

Three of the dead were men.

The fourth was Sarah, the pretty blonde PsyOps corporal whose smile had lit up Lashkar Gah.

7

It was a big bomb that killed Sarah. It scattered bits of their vehicle over a kilometre from the blast site.

It was the final act in a rash of tragedies. In the week and a half before the bomb that killed Sarah, five Parachute Regiment soldiers had also lost their lives.

Three of them were blown up by a suicide bomber in Sangin. As they patrolled through the maze of compounds a man appeared from a side alley. In the blink of an eye he was on top of them, detonating himself and carrying three young men along with him.

That evening, in Lashkar Gah, the brigade commander remarked on the Taliban's growing use of suicide bombers. 'It is noteworthy,' he said, 'that there has not been a single British death in Helmand from gunfire for over a year.'

Four days later, another Parachute Regiment patrol near Sangin was ambushed, and two soldiers were brought down in a hail of Taliban bullets.

Of the soldiers who died in the suicide bombing, two were nineteen years old. They had both been born in 1989, the year of Tiananmen Square and the fall of the Berlin Wall, which might as well have been yesterday. They had missed out on seeing history unfold because they had been born too late, and now they would miss out on everything which lay ahead, because they had died too early. They had had a brief interlude from their normal state of oblivion, book-ended by world-changing events on one side and a burst of machine gun fire at the other, which had now marked the resumption of normal service.

CHAPTER 7

The Taliban's summer offensive was in full swing. The storm had well and truly broken.

It was generally the infantry who got the worst of it, out on foot patrol. But that's not to say that some of my soldiers weren't equally as deep in the shit. None of them had been killed or injured since O'Hagan got blown up during our first week in Afghanistan, but that was more through luck than anything else. My lads, attached to the infantry, had had a series of near misses.

One detonated a roadside bomb when out on foot, but the Taliban had dug it into the ground the wrong way round, so it shot out harmlessly over the river.

Another one had been in an armoured personnel carrier when it rolled over an IED. It failed to detonate, but then it exploded under the vehicle behind him, killing one of the crew.

Then there was the lad whose patrol got ambushed. He was on the heavy machine gun and, as soon as the bullets started flying, he puked all over it in terror. Then he returned fire, and luckily the lumpy bits of vomit in the mechanism didn't stop the bullets from coming out of the end of it.

They were all my soldiers, attached to the infantry to assist them with comms, but they didn't feel like mine any more. My troop, our team, had been broken up and cast adrift – an archipelago of voices on the radio net, and a cast of characters in stories told in the cookhouse. For a troop commander, the situation was very bad. I wanted to *see* some of my lads, to find out what they were up to. And, after too long spent in HQ, it looked like I was finally going to make it happen. I'd blagged myself a week to visit my soldiers in the Danish area of operations, and now I was at large in Helmand. Just me and my Bergen, and no real plans. It was like going backpacking around Asia, except with the ever-present threat of violent death. Ally as fuck.

On paper our signallers, my soldiers, were with the Danes to run the British Army radios we'd given to them, so they could talk to our HQ in

Lashkar Gah, among others. It wouldn't have taken too long to train Danish signallers to operate our radios, but our lads also provided a secondary, completely indispensable service. Almost all the Danes spoke fluent English, but none of them understood Geordie, Scouse, Brummie or Jock. Face-to-face maybe, but not on the radio net, no chance. So our lads were part radio operators and part interpreters.

The Danes had half a dozen of them, spread over a handful of patrol bases, and I was going to try and visit as many as I could. I had to work fast because my mid-tour leave was coming around, and it was down to me to get to Bastion in time for the flight home. I also had to keep The Boss on-side because, after my leave, there was a chance that he was going to transfer me to mentoring the Afghan National Army. If I cocked things up, spending too long with the Danes, then that was going to go right out of the window.

Today I was going to fly from Lash to Bastion, where a Danish road convoy was due to drive up to their area HQ, FOB Price near Gereshk, which I visited after O'Hagan got blown up. From there, I'd just see what happened.

I walked to the helipad at Lashkar Gah. We waited. A dot appeared in the sky. A few seconds later, bang! It was a fully-formed Chinook on the concrete in front of us. The rotors boomed. The wind howled. We received our signal to board. As I approached the aircraft, a strange pair emerged from the fuselage in front of me: a prisoner and his guard. The prisoner was an unusually muscular, middle-aged Afghan man, with a wiry beard stained bright orange by henna dye. His wrists were bound in front of him with a plastic cable-tie and his eyes had been blindfolded so that he couldn't see the camp. He clutched a plastic bottle of water awkwardly in his bound hands, and shuffled down the ramp with a measured calmness. The blindfold made him sightless, and with the roar of the rotor blades overhead he was almost completely senseless.

Taliban, presumably. Here for interrogation, then handover to the Afghan Police. 'To be handled through the local system,' as we liked to say. This might entail incarceration and torture, or alternatively bribery and release, or perhaps something in between. We didn't know which, but we knew that there was a system in place, and from this we drew comfort.

I wondered what the man was thinking.

Ten minutes later I was running from the same Chinook onto the gravel of the Camp Bastion flight line.

I spent twenty-four hours in the camp, and the following morning I made my way to the Danish compound for the 0800 hrs convoy to FOB Price. When I arrived the Danes were formed up in a hollow square, half way through a brief by their squadron commander. I stood a little distance away, waiting for the end of the briefing. As I listened to the unfamiliar language, I watched the ranks of Danes in front of me.

The women were invariably beautiful, blonde and clear-skinned, with pistol holsters strapped around athletic thighs. By contrast, the average female British soldier had lank hair, huge, blotchy upper arms and a bottom that spread to swallow up the extremities of her back and thighs.

The men compared equally poorly. The Danes had sculpted torsos and golden tans. British soldiers usually came with pock-marked faces and bad teeth, ruined by a diet of sausage rolls and Irn-Bru. But I have always been strangely proud of the unsightliness of the British Army, and the ethos which created it.

Sculpted muscles – gym muscles – were vanity muscles, not muscles designed to serve a purpose. In fact, when it came to fighting wars, the whole upper body was pretty much bullshit. Runs and loaded marches were what mattered: the ability to move fast with weight on your back – for hours if necessary.

Last time my squadron was in Afghanistan, a few of the lads had been stationed with some US special forces soldiers. One day, they all decided to run around the perimeter together. The run lasted for about twenty minutes, and by the end the fastest American was so far behind the slowest Brit that he could barely be seen. Eventually, once they'd stopped, he caught up with them, panting and exhausted.

'Oh, man, you guys are fast,' he said. 'I tried to keep up with you, but you were so fast I couldn't even *sing*.'

I thought of that story now. I'd always liked it. It gave me a warm glow inside.

The Danish squadron commander called his soldiers to attention and dismissed them, and I homed in on a sufficiently junior-looking officer and asked where I should go for the convoy to FOB Price.

'I'm afraid it has left already,' he told me apologetically.

'But they told me last night that it was going at 0800 hrs this morning, and it's still only seven-thirty,' I said.

'Yes, but at 0100 hrs this morning they changed the convoy time to 0600 hrs. I do not know why.'

'Right,' I replied. 'Do you know of anyone else who's going up to Price today?'

'Try the Piranha platoon,' he gestured. 'They could have a spare space.'

The Piranha is a Danish armoured personnel carrier. Three of them sat on the other side of the courtyard with twenty soldiers milling around them. I walked over, and their platoon commander introduced himself.

'We have a space, yah,' he said. 'You can come with us.'

It took us a few hours to get to FOB Price, travelling down Highway 1, Helmand's main artery. About half way there, with a bump and a slide, we came off the road. The vehicle scrabbled for traction against the sand as we plunged steadily down an embankment. We didn't turn over. We just came to rest, flopping down onto the soft ground. The driver had fallen clean asleep at the controls and a volley of Danish swear words were hurled up to him from the rear cabin. Smiling and shrugging, he turned the vehicle back up the slope and we climbed onto the road. At the top we saw the other two vehicles waiting patiently for us, as if this was not a rare occurrence at all.

When we pulled in to FOB Price, one of my squadron's senior NCOs was waiting to greet me. It was Sergeant Wilkinson.

'All right, boss,' he said, as I jumped down from the Piranha.

'How's it going?' I asked.

'Not bad,' he replied, pushing his shock of black hair away from his forehead. 'We had a bit of drama yesterday, I tell you.'

'Yeah?'

'Yeah. You remember that suicide attack that took out O'Hagan? They did it again, in Gereshk, to the US Marines. This fella asked the patrol where they were from, they said 'America,' and he walked away. Then this other guy came up to them and blew himself up, right in the middle of the street. Killed one of the marines, two local men, three women, seriously injured about two dozen. They brought the casualties here, and I spent the whole day carrying round bodies and bits and pieces. Some of them were just coming apart in my hands. Anyway, that was my day.'

Of course it was, because Sergeant Wilkinson was submerged down to forward operating base depth. He didn't notice how deep he was, because he had grown accustomed to it. What happened outside his head was balanced by what happened inside. I was coming from nearer the surface, from headquarters depth, and I was passing him on my way down, for I was descending to patrol base depth.

I fancied that I was doing it to reach my soldiers, and to see how they operated so deep down. Roachy, who was less prone to metaphor, would have probably said, 'Stop talking shit, sir, you're going on a fucking jolly,' but that's another story.

'Who's at PB Armadillo?' I asked Sergeant Wilkinson.

'Rabuka, Lowry and O'Malley.'

'Is there a convoy going there any time soon?'

'As luck would have it,' he said with a sardonic flourish, 'there's one in half an hour. I'll get you a place on it.'

We found the new convoy and I climbed into the back of another Piranha, squashed in with some Danish soldiers. The hatch swung shut, the handle turned, we sealed ourselves from the outside world, and we descended one level deeper.

The next time the hatch swung open, it let in the blinding sunshine at Patrol Base Armadillo.

The camp was an erratic mixture of local mud-brick buildings and modern blast wall bunkers, sitting a few kilometres from the rural green zone, which hung mistily on the horizon. Unlike Sangin or Musa Qal'eh, the camp was far from the life-giving River Helmand, and two of its three wells had dried up as soon as the summer came. The third well was infested with bloodworm, so bottled water was all the lads had. They had transformed themselves from smartly-dressed soldiers into bearded men of the desert, and were relishing the officially sanctioned disorder.

Shaving was banned and laundry was frowned upon, which was like an early Christmas present for the three British radio operators on camp. I couldn't help feeling proud of them.

The four of us climbed onto the roof of the mud hut where they slept and sat down together.

'How's things then?' I asked.

'All right.'

'Danes treating you OK?'

'Yeah.'

'You eating their rations?'

'Yes, it's all fucking fish.'

'How are the patrols?'

'Not bad.'

My eyes fell on Rabuka, the Fijian, and he opened up a bit.

'We got ambushed yesterday,' he said. 'We were patrolling in the Leopard tanks and Piranhas up to PB Attal and got a load of RPGs fired at us. One of them landed two feet from our vehicle,' he explained, as calmly as you like.

CHAPTER 7

Rabuka had joined the British Army a few years ago, when there was a recruiting drive on for Fijians. His eyes lit up when he talked. He radiated morale.

'We're doing the same patrol again tonight,' he said. 'Up to Attal, where the Afghan Army are doing a foot patrol into the green zone. We'll sit on the ridgeline above with the tanks and scare off the Taliban from attacking. Well, if they don't ambush us again. You want to come along, boss?' he asked.

'Yeah.'

'We're going at 0200 hrs tomorrow morning.'

'Happy days.'

'Shall we go inside the hut for a bit?'

'Yeah, is it cooler down there?' I asked.

I assumed that it would be, that the mud-and-straw huts followed a pattern which had been handed down from father to son over centuries to provide simple, effective relief from the heat.

'Nah,' Lowry chipped in. 'You're out of the sun, so you don't get burned, but the air's stuffier, so you feel sick. Inside and out are both shit in different ways, so at least if you change around now and again you get some variety.'

The four of us whiled away the afternoon together, chatting, drinking our water and sweating. Then the evening rolled around, and we slept in camp beds under the stars. Eventually two a.m. arrived, and Rabuka and I got up for patrol.

We stepped silently into the armoured carrier, unwilling to break the silence of the pitch-black night. Rabuka tinkered with his radio set, and I made myself comfortable. Then, once all the Danes had arrived and everything was in place, the patrol rolled out of camp: three personnel carriers and two battle tanks.

We drove through the night, and through the desert, for an hour, before pausing in the desert.

'We stop here for twenty minutes,' said the driver in the front compartment, and he slung a pack of water bottles back to us. Rabuka and I got off to stretch our legs.

The night was utterly still, and the sky was as black as coal. Only the faint glow of starlight illuminated the silent and sleepy scene around me. We stood motionless, wrapped up in our own thoughts. I looked down at the dust around my feet. It was fifteen inches deep, as fine as flour, and as you moved your feet great stacks of it exploded around you. I imagined the tiny crystals laid down with the infinite care of a soft wind, untouched by human foot or animal hoof in many years – only to be burst by our desert boots.

Rabuka joined me in the dust. 'It was a near miss we had yesterday, boss,' he said. 'Chances are they'll be waiting for us again this morning.'

'We'll see,' I replied.

Ten minutes later we loaded up and drove for another hour, coming to a stop overlooking Patrol Base Attal.

I had a look out of the observation hatch. It was just beginning to get light, and a hundred yards away a single file of British and Afghan soldiers was leaving the camp, which was an old mud-brick compound. It used to be someone's house.

The Brits looked grumpy and dutiful, carrying on the daily grind. The Afghans looked bored. They shuffled off together through the night towards the green zone.

They were submerged at the very bottom level, where life was cheap and death came easily, and I was looking at them through my porthole. Strange things happened at their depth.

Two days ago, the company at Attal had been scheduled for a joint patrol with the Afghan company at FOB Sandford, which lay across the river. The two companies despised each other because a soldier from one company had nearly shot the commander of the other company, probably by accident. So when the Sandford soldiers rolled through the gates of Attal, and the Attal soldiers realised who their visitors were, war nearly broke out. The company commanders fired shots at each other, men in the sentry towers started fitting warheads into the muzzles of their RPGs and the British mentors radioed Armadillo for emergency extraction. In the end, like a brawl in the street, the situation petered out, but the Sandford company returned to their own base across the river, never to patrol with the Attal Company again.

That was honour in Afghanistan: sticking up for your own kind. Being ready to die with your own, no matter how senseless the cause.

Attal was two months old, and the defences had been built by hand. Officially built by the Afghan Army, but not in reality, because filling sandbags was not honourable. It was peasant work, not warrior work, and so the Afghan soldiers at Attal did not do it, but someone had to. In the end the Afghans sat back in the sunshine and watched the British mentors do it for them. After all, the Brits weren't going to live in an undefended base, and the Afghans knew that only too well. What's the point in filling sandbags, when all you have to do is refuse and someone else will do it for you? The Afghans had us over a barrel.

At the surface, of course, the picture was different. There were several layers of murk separating it from the dark depths, and it offered a pleasant view.

On the surface, it was observed that Afghan soldiers were building their own base in the heart of former Taliban territory, and patrolling from it bravely.

Occasionally a bubble would rise up from the deep, indicating that all was not well, like when twenty Afghan soldiers sneaked into a supply truck and escaped Attal, then were discovered at brigade HQ, beaten, and sent back again. But this caused little concern at the surface. Up there, unpleasant bubbles had a habit of turning into comforting phrases like 'a need for further capacity building in the Afghan National Army'.

The patrol walked into the green zone, and we waited. Nothing happened. There wasn't even a peep out of the ICOM scanner – no Taliban radio traffic. Even if they weren't going to attack us, they should have at least got on the net to report our presence, but there was nothing. They'd just gone away.

We started to feel relaxed. We opened up the top hatches, and I sat on the uncomfortable inches of armour plating and watched a grimy sun rise over the valley. Rabuka went to chat to the driver with whom he'd become friends. The two of them had bonded in the desert, a Dane and a Fijian, passing the time of day as the sun rose over Helmand.

After an hour the foot patrol came back up the hill. The Brits looked grumpier, and the Afghans looked more bored. They were swinging their rifles around, one-handed, to amuse themselves. No fighting today.

This had been my last, sad lunge at seeing some action before mid-tour leave, and it had failed.

'Let's go,' shouted the Danish patrol commander, and our vehicles roared into life. We swung the hatches closed.

I had briefly reached maximum depth, and now I was starting my journey home. Going up.

The first leg of the journey was sleepy but dangerous.

There was a chance the Taliban had laid an IED on our route back. A good chance, actually. The Danes had done the same patrol the night before, so the Taliban knew our pattern, and we'd given them enough time to dig something in, while we sat on the ridgeline overlooking Attal.

We could die at any second, I told myself, as we rolled through the desert. *We could die at any second.*

But even the most shocking thoughts can only roll around your head a handful of times before they become banal. After a few minutes, a new one arrived, 'That antenna coupling's really digging into my back … I wonder … if I move to the right just a little and dip my helmet sideways … Ah, that's much better.'

CHAPTER 7

A growing comfort and tiredness spread over me, and I drifted off to sleep.

I was jolted awake back in PB Armadillo, where an exodus was in progress. Fenris company, who I had accompanied to Attal, was leaving, to be replaced by Odin company. Fenris were adamant that Odin's stay should be no more comfortable than absolutely necessary, so they were stripping the camp of everything they could lift. I made arrangements with Fenris for a ride down to Gereshk that morning, and the Danish operations officer assured me that someone would fetch me as soon as the company were ready to leave.

He gave the impression of a man who had every confidence that the event would come to pass, without feeling the slightest need to issue instructions to make it happen. Still, his confidence reassured me. I settled down to sleep in a deck chair, as a chest freezer was guided past me to a waiting truck. Three hours later, I was nudged awake. I looked up. Good old Rabuka was standing over me.

'Sir, aren't you leaving with Fenris Company?'

'Yeah,' I reassured him, 'they're sending someone round for me when they're ready to go.'

'They're driving out of the front gate now,' he replied.

'Fucking Danes,' I said, pulling my shirt on over the crisp white silhouette of my dog tags, burned into my torso. Perhaps I'd slept too long in the sun.

Within seconds I had my body armour on and my Bergen on my back, and was sprinting full-tilt towards the main gate. I got there just in time to see the rear wheels of the last vehicle slip past the exterior blast wall. I cursed the Danes again. That was the last convoy out of Armadillo for a week.

Or was it?

I saw three armoured carriers parked up against the perimeter wall. Fuck knows what they were doing there. I ran over.

'Are you going to FOB Price?'

'Yes, in twenty minutes,' the patrol commander replied.

'Do you have any spare space?'

'Yes, we can do that for you.'

Who needs organisation, when you've got luck?

I squeezed myself into a Danish troop carrier again, and we drove to Price. I booked myself a space on the midnight chopper to Bastion, and settled down to kill some time, again. It was a pause in the upward surge out of Helmand.

My first port of call was the British comms detachment, a back room in a shabby headquarters building, where I found Lance Corporal Pickford.

'All right, Pickers?' I asked.

'Not bad, boss,' he replied. He was a small lad. Mousey hair, angular features. He sat behind his desk, dwarfed by the banks of radios on either side of him, looking like his daddy had left him in charge of comms for the day. Which, if you switched 'daddy' for 'Sergeant Wilkinson', was basically true.

'Comms working OK?' I asked.

'No.'

'What's wrong?'

'I can't talk to anyone on the radios.'

'That's not good.'

'No. I reckon we're getting interference from somewhere.'

'Let's go and have a poke about,' I said.

We did a circuit of the large desert base, looking for convoys which had just arrived. We found a couple, and both times the conversations were the same:

'Have you guys got your emitters on still?' we asked.

'No,' shrugs the guy in the cab, without even glancing down at the power switches. It's too much like hard work for them, getting pestered by the fucking Signals.

CHAPTER 7

So, after twenty minutes, Pickers and I lost heart.

'Let's go and have a look around the jingly market,' I said.

We gave the quest for comms a rest, and walked over to the small collection of stalls in the corner of camp.

Jingly markets were a feature of every largish base in Afghanistan, so-called because of the bizarrely decorated trucks in which the locals arrived to sell their tat. Where the traders came from, nobody knew. Nobody even particularly cared. They simply appeared on the sandy horizon at the appointed hour.

We wandered in and out among the stalls. I thumbed through the DVDs.

'What have you got there?' Pickers asked.

'*The Office. The Total of Secondly Series.*'

'Fucking cheap Chinese forgeries. We bought a Cameron Diaz special the other day, twenty films on one DVD. Then we got it back to the tent, and none of them had Cameron Diaz in. So we took it back and swapped it for an action film special. Same deal, twenty films on one DVD, except thirteen of them were *The Bourne Ultimatum*.

'This market's boring though. We had a jingly market in Iraq which sold battery-powered torches, except they doubled up as Taser guns.'

'Nice,' I replied.

We walked back to the comms detachment, and we never did find out the root of the problem with the radios.

'Probably the Americans,' Pickers speculated. 'Electronic warfare burn. High altitude flyover. Too secret to tell us about.'

This was the usual explanation when comms didn't work. I suspected it was the Helmand equivalent of an urban myth. But, either way, after a couple of hours comms simply improved of their own accord, as they often do.

I left Pickers to his comms and tracked down Sergeant Wilkinson, with his haystack of black hair and his permanently sardonic tone. Evening was settling onto us, and we walked to the cookhouse together for dinner. We ate a mediocre meal, and then we walked through half a kilometre of open desert to a sandy extremity of the camp where a crowd of people were gathering to mark Danish midsummer. A faint orange glow resolved itself into a burning pyre, with a poor effigy of a Scandinavian witch smouldering on top of it. Closer still, and we saw two trestle tables laid out with cans of soft drink, in a sort of pyramid formation.

'Help yourselves,' said one of the Danes, and we fell upon the fruits of their hospitality.

There was something deeply unsatisfying about standing around a bonfire with a can of lemonade, when your mind expects beer. Still, as soon as one can was finished, your idle right hand craved another one. The conversation, unlubricated by alcohol, was stiff and half-hearted. A tinny CD player rattled music out into the night air, competing with the roar of the heavy machine guns which were being test fired on the perimeter wall.

These were 50-calibre guns, with bullets half an inch wide. When you put a cartridge in your palm it took up nearly your whole hand span. They were so large that they were obscene, and if a 50-cal bullet passed close enough to you its shockwave would take your arm off.

As the guns blasted into the darkness, a song struck up around our small circle of firelight. It was stirring and, when it had finished, I asked a Dane what it had been about.

'We are singing about how happy we are, as it is harvest time, and about how fertile the world is,' he replied.

The barren, rocky ground stretched endlessly away from us. The guns went on firing. We were both very far from home.

Within a few minutes the Danish national anthem struck up, and we rose from our seats. I sang along in the same way that I would with a hymn I did not know, by making grunting sounds which I hoped would augment the overall performance.

Once it had finished, our gathering broke apart and we went our separate ways into the darkness.

CHAPTER 7

I walked towards the helipad for my flight back to Bastion and, as I did so, a firefight lit up Gereshk. It was three kilometres away, and long plumes of orange tracer peeled up into the sky.

Not too far away from me, people were fighting for their lives. But not me. I was safe, and it was time for me to go up yet another level, to Camp Bastion.

My ascent was gaining speed and, what's more, I was gathering fellow travellers. In Bastion I met up with six young soldiers from the squadron, whom I was to shepherd back to England. Like mine, their mid-tour leave was due. Some of them were pressurised to headquarters depth like me, and some had been pulled up from the deepest fathoms of the infantry patrol bases. Together, in the dead of night, we boarded a Hercules and flew away from Helmand.

When we landed we were in Kandahar airfield, and we were taken by bus to a huge hangar, inside of which was a sea of camp beds. Two hundred of them, in fact. From each one you could reach out and touch at least two of your neighbours. I'd seen a photo exposé of the cramped conditions in Russia's most notorious prison in a magazine the week before, and this was worse, but you should always expect some turbulence when ascending – some up-currents and some down-currents, and at Kandahar airfield the up more than outweighed the down.

We had a day to waste on camp, so I called on a friend of mine, Alice, and within half an hour we were standing outside Tim Horton's, the famous Canadian coffee shop, franchised out of a shipping container.

'Can I have a cream cheese bagel?' I asked the pear-shaped waitress behind the counter.

'Sure, what type of bagel would you like?'

'A *cream cheese* one,' I repeated, trying to speak more clearly this time.

'Yeah,' she said tersely, 'but what type of *bagel* do you want? Whole-wheat bread, rustic, sesame seed or twelve grain?'

'Anything.'

I rode the up-current with Alice all afternoon, as we hung out in the café, sipping fruits-of-the-forest smoothies and shooting the breeze. But then a down-current caught me again. Night fell, the Taliban rocket threat went up, and I trudged back to the hangar with the camp beds to fetch my body armour.

Inside, on one of the beds, my six lads were watching porn on a laptop.

'What's on?' I asked.

'Chick in a gorilla suit,' one of them replied.

He was not wrong. The woman was middle-aged, her gorilla suit was crotchless, and she was slapping herself and making howling noises.

The camera panned in for an extreme close up of her genitals. As an officer – a responsible man in a position of authority – I was called on to settle the argument on which bit was which.

After that I called Jim, who confirmed that I would be mentoring the Afghan Army after my leave – happy days – and all of a sudden I was caught on an up-current again. The bus arrived to take us to the airfield, and we were off. We joined the phalanx of soldiers shipping out from the hangar of camp beds, heading for home, but still the ascent wasn't smooth. The bus dropped us off outside a huge, bright white departures room, where we sat for many hours, sipping at lukewarm tea from styrofoam cups, waiting for our flight.

Suddenly, and without warning, the RAF decided to play us a video. It turned out to be about the hazards we could expect to face when we arrived back in the UK. They worried that we might have convinced ourselves that we were invulnerable during our time in Afghanistan. This could lead us to drive recklessly, crash our cars and prove conclusively that we weren't. We also ran the risk of accidentally talking to the press, who would creep into our local pubs and get us to say something damning about the army in an unguarded moment. Finally, we might simply find it difficult to adjust to life back home.

'How many times do you think you'll hear this?' the presenter asked us.

The scene was a man in the pub with his mate.

'So what was Afghanistan like?' his mate asked. 'Did you kill any-one?'

The scene changed again. 'So, did you kill anyone then?' asked someone else.

Then it changed a third time. Now it was a man at the breakfast table with his infant daughter. 'Daddy, did you kill anyone in Afghanistan?'

Bollocks, I thought. No one's going to ask that. People aren't vultures.

The video whirred to its conclusion. We waited around some more. Finally, after another hour and a half, and several more cups of tea, it was time to get on the plane. From there to England everything else was a blur. I sat in my seat for half a day, as we wound our way slowly homewards. I snatched a few minutes sleep here and there, and other-wise I stared at the nylon upholstery in front of my face. When we finally touched down at Brize Norton, we were all in a stupefied daze.

We were taken through the arrivals lounge, handed our rail warrants and loaded onto a coach at the front of the terminal. More nylon upholstery. It took us over little roundabouts where gentle, bespecta-cled men peered up at us from their steering wheels, and then we were gliding along past fields and trees. Before we knew it we were standing in the mild summer sunshine, in full desert uniform, at Oxford train station. I could taste the humidity in the air as if it was something solid, and I could still feel the Helmand dust in the seams of my clothing. A small group walked over to the nearest cash machine, but then they realised that none of them could remember their PIN codes.

One of my soldiers was already on his phone, having an argument with his mum. She wanted him to come straight home after his four months in Helmand, but he wanted to go drinking with his mates.

This was it. We'd broken out at the surface. Strangely, though, something was still out of balance. The paraphernalia of Afghanistan had fallen away from us: the heat, the desert, the guns, the blast walls. They were all gone. Only our uniforms were left, and soon we would shed them too. But inside our heads we were still at depth. Me at my headquarters depth, and others much lower down.

I walked inside the station to convert my rail warrant into a ticket, and joined the queue. The station porter saw me and bent his arm upwards into a sort of salute. I don't know why. In the aisle next to me two boys, perhaps ten years old, stared intently at me as I stood there in my combats.

'Where've you come from?' one of them spat.

I hadn't seen a child for four months. Maybe they only sounded rude because I wasn't used to it. I was tired and dazed, and I couldn't remember how to talk to children. So I stood and looked at them, impassively.

'Where've you come from?' the same one demanded again.

'Afghanistan.'

The desert uniform, the deep tan, the smell of sweat; I could hardly deny it.

'Did you kill anyone?'

'No,' I replied, taken aback.

'I would have,' he said. 'I would have killed fucking loads of them.'

With that, they ran off, laughing and smiling at each other.

So that was that. Maybe you had to be at depth to realise what shits the people at the surface really were.

When the train to Birmingham came I boarded it with two soldiers, a Scottish corporal in the Logistics Corps and a calm, articulate private from the Parachute Regiment. We were borne northwards, and we carried a little bubble of Afghanistan along with us. As we walked down the aisle of the carriage, we made for a table for four. It was already occupied by a frail-looking woman in her forties but, as soon as we made to sit down beside her, she gathered her things together and scurried away down the carriage. We shrugged our shoulders and chuckled, unable to really care.

It was probably for the best anyway, because before long our table became steeped in the Afghanistan that we carried with us.

'We picked up this civvy last week,' said the private from the Parachute Regiment. 'He'd got caught in a mortar attack, and his skin had turned into fucking tissue paper. Shock of the blast. We tried to CasEvac him, but every time we touched him our fingers just went straight through and the blood came out, like breaking through the crust on a fruit pie.'

That's interesting, we thought.

There were children nearby, and I was an officer. I should have told the two soldiers to change the subject but I just didn't feel like it.

Fuck it, I thought, as I looked out of the window onto the lush English countryside. I couldn't believe how green it was.

We left the Scottish corporal at Birmingham. He was travelling all the way up to Glasgow that afternoon, and I said what a shame it was that he should spend his first full day of R and R on the train.

'Doesnae bother me, boss,' he replied. 'Just mair time for drinking on the train, isn't it?'

The Parachute Regiment soldier and I changed trains, and chatted pleasantly as we sped northwards. After a little while the ticket collector came ambling down the carriage.

'Where have you fellows come from?' he asked us.

'Afghanistan,' I replied, dreading the follow-up question.

'Would you like to go up to First Class? You boys are doing a bloody good job out there.'

I was amazed, and grateful. We picked up our things and walked down the corridor. He offered us all the free food and booze we liked, but both of us were too shy to accept it. In the end we settled for a small glass of orange juice each, and we were embarrassed when we took it.

My travelling companion got off at Preston, and I stayed on until the train reached Lancaster. As it pulled into the station I shouldered my Bergen in the doorway, as I had done on the ramp of a Chinook three days previously. I jumped down, and this time my boots landed on the familiar tarmac and peeling paintwork of the platform. I was home.

8

'Help me,' I croaked.

I was lying on my back, with soldiers standing over me, and I couldn't move. 'Help me,' I begged.

Mid-tour leave had been wonderful. I'd spent a week in Cornwall, climbing the sea cliffs with friends, watching my girlfriend get sunburned and turn pink, while the whole of the north of England sank under torrential rain. Then I'd returned to Lancaster for the wedding of one of my oldest friends and, miraculously, the sun came out there as soon as we started driving to the chapel. True, in between the two places I'd nearly been arrested as a vagrant in Bristol Parkway station, but I'd escaped without too much hassle and the wedding, in the end, was perfect. I drove to the chapel with the groom, as the last defeated rain clouds were rolling away over the purple hills.

'So, who do you think's going to cry first then?' I asked him, 'do you reckon it'll be your mum?'

'It might be me,' he replied. 'Did I ever tell you, I once cried at the end of *City Slickers*?'

He didn't cry at the wedding but his mum did, in bucket-loads.

Now I was back in Afghanistan, and I was in trouble. I was lying on the ground and I couldn't move. I thought I'd figured out what had happened. I was still in Kandahar, and I'd slept late into the day. My body must have been knocked for six by the return of the heat, and now I was so dehydrated I couldn't move a muscle. My limbs were so weak I couldn't even lift them.

So what could I do? I could see people walking around, but they were ignoring me. I'd waited for minutes, which seemed like hours, to see if my strength came back on its own, to try and avoid the humiliation of asking private soldiers for help in my weakness and vulnerability. But I wasn't getting any better. It seemed to me that I could either beg for help, or carry on sweating out water until I faded away and died. So I begged.

'Help me,' I whispered, but even my voice wasn't working properly. The words sounded like mumbled groans in my ears. Bollocks.

After that train journey home with the Parachute Regiment soldier, I had finally shed my uniform, and Afghanistan had receded further, so that it hid just below my skin. And there it had stayed, for the two weeks of mid-tour leave.

I'd put my uniform back on at the transit hotel in Brize Norton airfield, it was still sandy in the seams because I hadn't bothered washing it. Then I put on the familiar boots which pinched my toes because I'd never gotten around to exchanging them for half a size up.

So Afghanistan expanded again, from its home under my skin, to take up a small bubble all around me. After that it didn't take long for it to grow outwards and take up the whole world. I'd arrived at Kandahar, and gone to sleep listening to machine guns firing on the perimeter wall. Now I'd woken up, and I couldn't move. I was helpless.

'*Please* help me,' I asked the people walking past me, one more time.

Bang! I was awake, sitting upright in my camp bed, and gasping. The wonderful fresh air rushed into my lungs.

I hadn't been dying of dehydration at all. I'd been in sleep paralysis. It'd never happened before. It was scary, being able to see, being able to hear your own voice, but being unable to move. Maybe it was listening to the machine guns that had brought it on. Who knows?

CHAPTER 8

And who cares, even? It was just a rumbling from the subconscious, indicating that all was not well down there. But what use was the subconscious, anyway? It couldn't carry a Bergen or aim a rifle. Let it stay unwell, if it likes, as long as it does so quietly, and doesn't interfere with the useful parts of the machine.

After another day spent in Kandahar, I boarded the Hercules which took me bowling back to Camp Bastion, and Helmand Province, to take up my new job, mentoring the Afghan National Army – the ANA.

I was headed for Camp Shorobak, a small, square desert camp next door to Bastion. It was the main ANA base in Helmand – the headquarters of 3 Brigade, serving under 205 'Hero' Corps, and the home of all Afghan troops not deployed out in an FOB.

I was taking over the role of comms mentor for the brigade from a friend of mine who, after four months in the job, was swapping places with me to do his time in Lashkar Gah. Over the next few days I tried half-heartedly to convince him that he had plenty to look forward to. He didn't buy it but – ah well – fuck him.

At the crack of dawn I walked to the Camp Bastion shop to pick up the short-hop convoy to Shorobak. I waited around, as usual, and after a while a couple of 'Snatch' Land Rovers pitched up. A man climbed out of the back of one, took his helmet off, and a familiar mop of curly blond hair flopped out from under it.

'Eh up,' said Dabbers.

'How's it going, Staff?' I asked.

'Not bad,' he said, twisting his pudgy features into a smile.

Dabbers was going to be my right-hand man for the next few months, like Roachy had been, supporting me with advice, thinly-veiled criticism and a steady supply of profanity. I liked Dabbers, I knew him from back in England, and I was looking forward to working with him.

'Let's pile back in the Rover,' he said. 'We'll head back to Shorobak now, and we'll be just in time for the Afghan morning meeting.'

'OK.'

The route from Bastion to Shorobak only took ten minutes on a good run. Dabbers and I jumped in the back of the Rover and headed out into the thin strip of desert between the two camps.

'This convoy got bombed last week,' said Dabbers as we drove, by way of conversation.

'Yeah?'

'Yeah. Hit by a suicide bomber. This fella had a car rigged to go up, and he spent the whole morning driving up and down the approach road, looking for a target. They reckon it was a botched attempt, 'cos they found bits of two people in the car afterwards.

'Must have been one driver, and one guy in the passenger seat making sure he went through with it. The passenger was probably supposed to get out in time, but the driver must have lost his nerve too early 'cos he blew them both up. Stupid fucker. Anyway, they hit the front vehicle of the convoy and the blast was so big it blew the windows out in Shorobak, a kilometre away. But they screwed up again, 'cos there was no shrapnel in the bomb – it was just a blast. They were three feet away from the lead vehicle when they blew, and they didn't kill anyone!'

'Fuck me.'

'Yeah. But it was lucky there was a lot of dust in the air, 'cos the bomber only saw the front vehicle – which was armoured of course. The next vehicle was an open-topped truck with twenty lads sat on the back of it. They would have got blown to pieces if he'd have seen them. As it was, everyone walked away without a scratch, except for the top-cover gunner from the lead vehicle. He got his hands burned by the blast. You'll see him walking around with these two big rolls of bandages like clubs on the ends of his arms.'

'So are they beefing up security on the convoys now, then?'

'Yeah, we've got protective measures in place now, to make sure that sort of shit can't happen again. From now on, every top-cover gunner on this run has to wear gloves.'

CHAPTER 8

And with that Dabbers gave me one of those looks, which said 'It'd be hysterical if it wasn't actually true.'

We pulled into the front gate of Shorobak, past the Afghan sentries in their concrete booth, and then turned left through a little chicane towards the more formidable British defences. Ours was a camp within a camp, a walled-up little square at the corner of the bigger, wilder square owned by the Afghan National Army.

As we rolled inside the front gate, I saw a flat wooden figure by the guard room. It was a memento from a period when the Americans owned the base: a Wild West cowboy with drawn-on bullet holes and the inscription, 'Welcome to Camp Tombstone'.

We came to a halt in front of a spartan memorial for the fallen. Dabbers picked up my kit bag. I swung my Bergen across my back, and together we walked towards the accommodation blocks to dump my kit.

'Have you been briefed on what the job is here, then?' asked Dabbers, as we walked.

'Well we're mentoring the brigade comms cell, right? The guys who run comms for the brigade commander?'

'Pretty much. There's two guys in the brigade comms cell, Asif and Rohulla, captain and major. We're mentoring them, but we're also teaching radio lessons to the soldiers in the brigade comms squadron, which comes under a different officer, Captain Hameed.'

'Right.'

'Anyway, let's dump your kit and head down to the brigade morning meeting. You'll meet most of the important people there.'

'OK,' I replied.

At this point – about to meet some of the most important Afghan soldiers in Helmand, and feeling the need to make a good first impression – I was acutely aware that I had almost no knowledge whatsoever of Afghan culture.

Prior to this day, I could count on one hand the number of significant dealings I had had with the Afghan National Army. I had shared helicopters with them a few times, had helped an Afghan soldier to find a new handle for his screwdriver in Sangin, and had caused a soldier in Musa Qal'eh to burst into gales of laughter by saying 'Hello' to his friend through his walkie-talkie. Other than that, nothing. I needed a crash course.

'So, what are they actually like?' I asked Dabbers.

'They're OK,' he replied, noncommittally. 'Most of the time they just do their own thing. You know, we try to help them as much as we can but you can't teach them if they don't want to be taught.'

'What about pitfalls? You know, cultural stuff?'

'Not much,' said Dabbers, smiling. 'Just say *salaam alaykum* a lot and put your hand over your heart. It means "Peace be upon you". Oh, and don't fart in front of them – for some reason they hate that.'

'OK then,' I replied.

I may have had minimal dealings with the Afghans up to this point, and Dabbers wasn't shedding much light on them, but their reputation preceded them. According to some in the British Army, the Afghan Army was incompetent, lazy, cowardly, backward and gay.

The first four were to be expected. The ANA was only four years old, most of the soldiers had never even left their villages until they joined up, and even some of the officers barely knew how to read. It was a peasant army. You expected it to be shit.

It was the last one that intrigued me. The gayness. We heard stories about man-love Thursdays, when the Afghans partied in the evening before their day off on Friday. We heard about the younger soldiers walking around with painted nails all day on Thursday, and the British mentors clearing out and making themselves scarce once night fell – leaving the Afghans to whatever it was they got up to.

The gay stories weren't just hearsay, either. I'd heard plenty first hand from friends doing mentoring.

CHAPTER 8

I had a friend in the Logistics Corps, who mentored ANA convoys. Out in the desert a truck had broken down, and his whole convoy ground to a halt for two hours while it was fixed. They were in dangerous territory so the British mentors walked down the line of Afghan trucks to make sure no one was sleeping at their posts. My friend found half a dozen Afghan soldiers asleep, and then he came to a truck with no one in it at all.

He looked high and low trying to find the driver and his passenger, but he couldn't see them anywhere. Then he peered over the lip of the drainage ditch by the track. There they were, locked head to toe with each other in the 69 position.

That, I remarked, was something you just don't get taught at Sandhurst. You would creep through your platoon's position at night, pretending that you were defending the boggiest, rainiest corner of Wales from Russian invaders, and diligently check on your pretend subordinates' foxholes.

Glow-in-the-dark plastic sticks to denote your arcs of imaginary fire? Check.

Torch with red filter that you're not allowed to switch on anyway? Check.

Silver whistle, as sported by British Army officers in such notable conflicts as the First World War? Check.

'Now remember, fellows, it's important not to start fellating each other out here, or the enemy might be able to sneak up on us.'

Why had none of our instructors mentioned this possibility, as something to guard against in our future positions of responsibility? So much for Sandhurst.

A good chunk of the Afghan Army was certainly gay but, then again, not all gayness was created equal. The Afghans weren't going home after a six-month tour, like we were, to spend two years with their wives and children. Most of them lived up in the north, and they were down in Helmand for the long haul. If they wanted the comforts of the flesh then their options were decidedly man-orientated. Besides, it's not as if girls were that easy to come by – even when the soldiers did get their sporadic bouts of leave – at least not before marriage. Most of the young Afghan soldiers in Helmand had probably never got close to sex with a woman, and perhaps they had been turning to men instead long before they joined the army.

Besides, we weren't in a position to throw too many stones. The British Army's airborne forces liked a bit of man love. It was just drunken kissing, mostly, and it wasn't done for sexual gratification. It was male bonding. It was a shared camaraderie between us, the best and hardest brigade in the army. It was airborne. It was also a fuck-you to everyone who wasn't airborne, to the crap Hats and the fat fucking civvies. 'What's that you say, mate? You think that kissing blokes is a bit of a nancy thing to do? Well here's us, ten times harder than you are, and we're doing it, so stick that in your pipe and smoke it.'

Of course it only worked within the airborne forces. If you kissed a guy who wasn't airborne, that meant you were *properly* gay.

So the gayness of the Afghans was a puzzle to me, but not an intractable one. It was an interesting phenomenon, to be observed from a safe distance. But there was another, bigger question that troubled me about the Afghan National Army, and it was 'Whose side are they on?'

Even the most moderate of Afghans must have been a *bit* religiously bonkers, I reasoned in my ignorance. An impression prevailed that the majority practised a form of village Islam that they acquired in the Dark Ages, and then refined through centuries of mistrust of foreigners. And historically they had proven themselves to be, shall we say, on the hostile side towards the infidels.

Surely the Afghan National Army all secretly despised our immorality and heresy? Even if they didn't, the Taliban were their fellow countrymen. How could they really side with us in their hearts of hearts? Wouldn't the Afghan National Army turn out to be, fundamentally, a bunch of bitter and resentful quislings who plotted against us whenever they could tear themselves away from having sex with each other? I didn't know, but I was going to find out.

Dabbers and I arrived at the accommodation blocks. They were long, oversized half-tubes, like giant baked bean tins, cleaned out and laid sideways, stretching fifty metres from one end to the other. Down each side stood a row of camp beds, butting up against the exterior walls, and around every one was a sprawling mound of kit with a sleeping bag snaked on top. This was the young officers' hangar. It was deserted, because it was breakfast time.

I dumped my Bergen on an empty bed, into which a big, smouldering chunk of shrapnel had landed when the convoy got bombed the week before. Dabbers laid down my kit bag.

'Right then,' he said. 'Morning brief.'

We walked out of the British camp-within-a-camp, through a gap in the blast walls, and across a huge grey concrete helipad.

'So,' said Dabbers, as we walked, 'you've got four kandaks in a brigade, right? Each one is basically the same as a battalion. And each kandak has a logistics officer, an S4, who's a major. It's based on the American system.'

'OK.'

'And the brigade commander is called General Muhayadin. You'll meet him this morning – looks like a Bond villain.'

'Acts like a Bond villain?'

'No, he's just a bit mad. He went fucking ape-shit at the S4 from Kandak 3 in the morning brief yesterday. The S4 was supposed to get a consignment of tomato paste to his troops in Sangin, but it didn't arrive on time.'

'So what, it's only tomato paste. What happened to the S4?' I asked.

'See that, boss?' said Dabbers.

Beyond the enormous helipad, I could see a tent – not a large, angular military tent of thick poles and tough canvas, but the sort you might go camping in. Two armed guards stood outside it. They were young Afghan soldiers, with AK-47s slung over their backs.

'He's in there,' Dabbers grinned. 'Muhayadin's making him stay in the tent for three days as an example to the rest of them.'

Sure enough, as we passed the tent, there he was, sitting inside it, guarded by two embarrassed-looking private soldiers, with only a bottle of water and a piece of flatbread for company.

We rounded the corner from the punitive camping trip and came to the smart, American-built, brigade headquarters. Several Afghans stood around in the doorway, leaning against the whitewashed walls, smoking, staring and fingering their rifles. I felt a little unsure of myself – shy, even – and let Dabbers take the cultural lead.

'*Salaam alaykum, salaam alaykum!*' he yelled at the assembled crowd, taking his hand off his heart only in order to shake each one of them by the hand.

'*Salaam,*' they murmured in response.

'Who were those guys?' I asked, as we passed through the doorway. 'None of them were wearing any rank.'

'No idea,' said Dabbers. 'Probably just random hangers-on. You can't really go by rank too much anyway. Some of them don't bother with it at all, and others just put on the badges of a higher rank if they feel like they deserve it.'

We walked down a sparse, clean corridor and pushed apart the doors to the brigade briefing room. It was empty.

'Must still be having their fucking parade,' said Dabbers.

We walked back down the corridor, past the unidentified hangers-on with another round of *salaam alaykums* and out to the other side of the buildings, where a parade was indeed in progress. Two hundred wiry and bored-looking men stood on a huge expanse of stony ground which was girdled by a thick rope, like a cricket pitch. They faced a tacky-looking wooden podium. A few senior officers stood on it, and stirring

CHAPTER 8

military music played over a crappy Tannoy system. A disembodied voice rolled across the parade ground, giving an unfamiliar word of command.

The two hundred men lurched into action. They must have been given the call to 'get on parade'. I counted the steps with them.

One, two, three, four, five, six, seven, eight, nine, ten, eleven, twelve, halt, check, one-two! Ah, so at least drill was universal.

Most of the front few ranks tried to get their time from the music, but each man had a different idea of what the beat should be. When they came to the halt it was like watching camera flashes in a crowd. They jumped to attention sporadically throughout the front row. By the time the rear ranks got involved, the pace was so disorganised that they just gave up and jogged along behind, shuffling into their allotted spaces when they reached the right point.

Slowly, a hush came over the assembled masses. General Muhayadin, indistinct in the distance, began to speak. He gripped his wooden podium and discoursed at length in Dari to his eager subordinates.

After a few minutes of this we'd had enough, and we returned to the briefing room to wait.

We sat there as it filled up. Every few minutes more people – British, Afghan and American – filtered into the room and took up their seats. We waited.

Forty-five minutes later, General Muhayadin burst in through the door. The briefing began.

His round head was completely bald, and beneath his angular nose bristled a thick, dark moustache. His black eyes sparkled, hard and cunning, but on his face he wore a childlike smile. He used it to beam encouragement at all and sundry.

His duty officer briefed the room on the past twenty-four hours' events in Helmand, and then Muhayadin stood up in front of the map boards, pointed at an interpreter to come up and translate, and began to address us. He talked about the conflict that was going on in Marjah, a large swathe of fields and farms to the south-west of Lashkar Gah. The 4th Kandak had been deployed there for forty-eight hours to shore up the Afghan National Police against a Taliban uprising, but their mission was running on into weeks.

The previous day, an Afghan soldier had been injured in Marjah, and Muhayadin spoke passionately about him.

'We must not let this act by the insurgents go unpunished!' he said. 'I would be happy to take off my rank slide and go to Marjah myself, and fight alongside our soldiers and avenge what has happened to this man, but I cannot,' he sighed with a despondent flourish. 'I must stay here and lead the brigade.'

It was not the sober assessment of the day's events that I'd grown used to in British HQ, but I had to admire Muhayadin's showmanship. He made a few more comments about the situation in Marjah and then, just as abruptly as he had entered, he strode out of the room. This signalled the end of the morning brief.

Dabbers had to return to the British camp to run some lessons on the general purpose machine gun. I went with him, and we'd got as far as the huge, cracked helipad when we met a young lance corporal, Rich.

'Rich,' said Dabbers, 'meet Mr Lee. Boss, Rich is the young lad on the comms team I was telling you about. The team's you, me, him, and Sergeant Plows when he's around. Where are you going, Rich?'

'I've got to find Captain Hameed.'

'Do us a favour, take Mr Lee to see Major Rohulla at brigade HQ first, then you can go and introduce him to Hameed as well.'

'All right.'

Rich and I cut down a little alley of blast walls and barbed wire to the small compound where the interpreters lived – 'Terp Town.

It was a jumble of bits of wood and rusting old bed frames, secreted in the little walkways between squat wooden huts. There were nine huts in total, made of plywood, and Rich pushed open the door of the first one he came to.

The hut was dark and the air was heavy, and I could just make out three or four Afghans inside. One was sleeping under a brightly coloured blanket, and two more sitting cross-legged on carpets in the small piece of bare floor at the centre of the room. They were watching a pirated DVD, which looked terrible, and they glanced over at us impassively.

'All right, fellas?' said Rich. 'Is Tariq about?'

An apathetic silence.

'Tariq – you know, little bloke, beard, works with me?'

'I think he is Hut 3 now,' said one of the interpreters, and he went back to watching his DVD.

We stepped out into the sunshine, walked for ten yards, and ducked into an identical brown hut with a large '3' written on the door in permanent marker pen.

'Tariq, you there mate?' called Rich into the blackness.

'Rich, how you doing, man? You livin' the dream?' came a sharp Afghan voice.

A short, swarthy man with wide lips and a long, scraggy beard emerged from the darkness. He was wearing British desert trousers, a fake Tommy Hilfiger T-shirt which read 'Taliban Hillfighter', and a floppy blue hat. Rich introduced me and we shook hands. Then the three of us walked off, back across the massive helipad to the ANA buildings to track down the brigade's comms officers.

'First one you will meet is Major Rohullah,' said Tariq. 'He is Brigade S6.'

'Basically the brigade comms major,' said Rich. 'Dabbers reckons he looks like the Devil.'

'Next one is Captain Hameed, in charge of comms company,' said Tariq. 'He is one fuckin' dodgy bastard.'

'Yeah,' said Rich. 'He's a fat lazy shit.'

'And you will not meet him today,' said Tariq, 'but soon Captain Asif is back; second in command of brigade S6. He is very good man. Fuckin' diamond geezer.'

Working with the British Army was doing wonders for Tariq's English.

We passed the little green tent with the S4 major inside, who looked even more pissed off than he had at breakfast time, and walked beyond the brigade headquarters to another smart whitewashed building where Major Rohullah, the S6, had his office.

Rich went in first. The room was chock-a-block. There were at least four different groups of people coming, going, dropping off equipment or getting papers signed. In the middle, at a bare, low desk, was Major Rohullah, with angular features and a wispy goatee beard. He gestured for us sit on the row of plastic chairs which lined the wall opposite his desk.

Then, during a lull in the chaos, he looked up and spoke. Tariq interpreted.

'The major would like to know what he can do for you,' he said.

'I've taken over the comms mentoring team,' I explained, through Tariq. 'I've come to introduce myself to you, and to discuss any problems you have with your communications.'

'It is nice to meet you, and I look forward to us working together,' he replied, without enthusiasm.

'Are you happy with everything the mentors are doing for you, and is there anything you need help with that we are not doing already?' I called above the din in the room, trying to spark his interest.

'No,' he replied, 'everything is fine.'

I was expecting a little more than that – if not an avowal of eternal thanks and gratitude, then at least a cup of tea. Instead we shuffled out of Major Rohullah's office a few minutes after we had entered, and the press of people closed up behind us as we left.

The bottom line, as I would find out, was that Major Rohullah didn't need our help. He was bright, competent and perfectly capable. He'd also seen three British mentors in four months, knew that I would be gone almost before I'd arrived, and was probably quite fucked off with a string of people poking around his department trying to change things.

'You'll never get much out of him,' said Rich. 'We'll go and see Captain Hameed now. He'll keep us sat down for hours, the fat fuck.'

We stepped out into the sunshine, and crossed the parade ground with the cricket pitch boundary, passing a little kiosk selling cigarettes and Pakistani soft drinks to the crowd of Afghan soldiers in front of it, and arrived at comms company. It was another whitewashed building, this time with a flower bed and a lopsided metal archway at the door. We stepped inside. A moustachioed, leering man stood up from his desk to greet us.

'This is Captain Hameed,' Tariq announced, with resignation.

He clasped my hand in his as I introduced myself.

'Welcome, welcome,' he said in English, with a broad grin on his face.

His office was bare apart from a large desk which dominated a corner of the room and a radio on a chair which crackled to itself. A blue tarpaulin hid a little kitchen area, and in front of that hung a giant Afghan flag.

Captain Hameed waved us to the chairs in front of his desk, and sat back down behind it. He shooed away the handful of subordinates who had been milling around his room, and surveyed us with a jolly, rolling laugh which he pushed out through tight lips.

'I am very glad you are here,' he told me in Dari, smiling benignly.

'He says he is very glad you are here,' explained Tariq, in English, with the air of one who is slightly bored with his job.

'I look forward to us working together very much,' continued Hameed, 'since Afghan soldiers and British soldiers are like brothers. We may be in different armies, but we all wear a uniform, and that makes us like brothers.' He paused for a moment, and then warmed to his theme. 'And that means we must help each other as much as we can. We should always do things for each other, for perhaps in the future I have information on the enemy, and I hear what they are planning, I can tell you and then you will pass it on to your commanders and that will help us to win.'

This was a hundred per cent bullshit. Hameed was in charge of a radio company in a desert base twenty kilometres from the nearest mud hut, and he never left. How on earth was he going to hear information on the Taliban? I could tell where 'we must help each other as much as we can' was going. Perhaps Hameed sensed my hostility, because he decided to change tack.

'Do you have a wife?' he asked.

'No,' I replied, 'just a girlfriend.'

'I am married, and I have ten children!' he announced, with pride writ large on his face. Tariq translated his words, and Hameed held up all ten of his stubby fingers for emphasis. 'I wanted more, but after ten my wife refused to have another!'

'You love the jiggy-jiggy, right?' said Rich, a grin on his face.

'Jiggy-jiggy!' Hameed laughed, with a knowing wink. 'Jiggy-jiggy *hoobe-ast*!'

'He says jiggy-jiggy is good,' said Tariq.

'Yeah, fucking jiggy-jiggy *hoobe-ast*!' laughed Rich.

'Jiggy-jiggy *hoobe-ast*!' I joined in.

Back home, it would have been unimaginable for a young lance corporal like Rich to giggle with a senior captain about the latter's single-minded love of procreation, but then none of the usual conventions applied at the moment.

For a start there was the thorny issue of how to address each other. In the UK, as captains (I was a lieutenant, but I was wearing captain's rank to work with the Afghans because they wouldn't have listened to me without the extra pip), Hameed and I would have called each other by first names – except at work, with a lance corporal in the room, where we would probably have used 'mate' or nothing at all. Rich would have called us both 'sir', or 'boss' if he knew either of us well, and we would have called him by his rank and surname, or just 'Rich' if *we* knew *him* well. (First names for soldiers were still a bit dodgy, but 'Rich' was a shortened surname and not a Christian name, so there we were OK.) Tariq was a civilian so what he called the three of us would have been anyone's guess – probably 'mate', which would have annoyed me because it would have implied that it was possible to be mates with both a captain and a lance corporal simultaneously, and if that was allowed to happen then the whole army system would come crashing down around our ears.

But here, in Hameed's grubby office in the middle of the Afghan desert, everything was muddled up.

I still called Rich 'Rich', and he called me 'boss'; there we were on safe ground.

Tariq called Rich 'Rich', but he knew that Rich called me 'boss' so he didn't want to call me 'Graham'. Then again, he didn't want to call me 'boss', because I wasn't really his boss, so he just called me by my last name with no title.

Rich didn't want to call Captain Hameed 'boss' because he wasn't his boss, but he *certainly* didn't want to call him 'sir' because, in his eyes, Captain Hameed wasn't really a proper officer anyway; he was just a fat man with a moustache and a uniform who liked jiggy-jiggy. So Rich called Captain Hameed 'Captain Hameed', and so did I to make things easier.

What Captain Hameed called us I had no idea, because everything he said came through Tariq, who Rich and I both called 'Tariq'.

What Tariq called Captain Hameed, I was similarly clueless about. Captain Hameed was a senior captain, and I was really only a lieutenant pretending to be a captain, and Tariq deferred slightly to me, so going by rank he should have also deferred to Captain Hameed. Then again, Tariq was paid $600 a month for interpreting, which was as much as

General Muhayadin got, and was far more than Captain Hameed could ever hope to earn, so Tariq was in no mood to defer to him or to any other Afghan officer.

It was almost as if the whole Afghan war was a maze of contradictions and nonsense, but maybe that was an analogy too far. Either way, there was an easy solution, as there was with all the other contradictions in the war – just switch off the part of your brain that gives a shit.

One of Captain Hameed's soldiers returned, carrying a large Thermos flask and several damp-looking glasses. He laid them down on the table, holding a glass under the Thermos and pressing the plunger. Steaming, light-green chai poured out. The soldier filled four cups to the brim. Thick, dark pieces of tea leaf swirled in the liquid. Hameed produced a little saucer of banana-flavoured sweets in foil wrapping, and a jam jar half filled with sugar. Then he lunged for a heavy, side-handled near-pint jug, and dragged it merrily to his side of the desk. It seemed that Hameed had a *special* mug. He handed us our chai in the little tumblers and, sensing the good mood rising off the jiggy-jiggy conversation, he gambled on a return to the theme of us 'helping each other out like brothers'.

'We are very short of tables and chairs at the moment,' he lamented, through Tariq. 'Are you able to give us any?'

I prepared myself to disappoint him. We were trying to develop an Afghan National Army which could stand on its own two feet, and that wouldn't happen if we just went around solving all their problems for them.

'I'm sorry,' I said, 'but you'll have to go through your own quartermaster's. I can't get them for you through mine.'

Captain Hameed nodded his head resignedly, and shrugged. He changed the conversation back to our families.

'Do you have any brothers and sisters?'

'One brother,' I told him. 'He's in the army as well.'

'I used to have five,' Captain Hameed said, in a matter-of-fact voice.

'All the rest died in the war with the Russians, and now I am the only one left. I have a lot of nephews and nieces to look after.'

I thought I caught a flicker of sadness crossing his face, but then it was gone and he was talking again.

'But it is good that you are here, and I hope that you will keep coming here and we will sit and talk about our families and make happy times, and then we will not miss them so much.'

I said that I was glad to be here as well, and that I enjoyed us talking about our families together.

'My foot is very painful,' he digressed. 'Do you think you could arrange for me to visit the doctor in Camp Bastion to have it looked at?'

'I'm sorry,' I said, 'but I can't do that, either. You need to see the Afghan doctor, and if he can't do anything for you he'll write you a chit which you can use to see the British doctor in Bastion.'

I was sure he knew this already.

'I would do,' he sighed, 'but my foot hurts so much that I cannot walk across the camp to see him.'

I doubted it. He had seemed quite agile enough when he got up to shake our hands.

'Why not phone the doctor up and ask him to come to you, if you're too sick to move?' I suggested.

Captain Hameed sensed that he was getting nowhere, and abandoned the line of questioning. We drank our chai and talked on for an hour and a half about our families, our home lives and the finer points of jiggy-jiggy. He was in full flow, and only paused to draw breath and to send great wads of spit flying towards a brown and glistening corner of his carpet.

Every now and again I tried to steer the conversation around to the comms lessons which we gave his soldiers, but each time I succeeded it was only for a few seconds. Once the chai was exhausted the chat began to wind down, and Captain Hameed settled onto his final theme.

'We cannot fight the Taliban as well as you can, because we have no tanks and no planes,' he said. 'When the Taliban shoot at us, we have only our rifles to fire back at them with. If you gave us some planes, when they shoot at us, we could destroy them. Afghanistan would be at peace within two weeks.'

I don't think that this was an out-and-out request for me to produce some fast jets for the Camp Shorobak comms company. It was just a mindset. It was 'identify a problem and suggest a solution by which you get the maximum amount of stuff for free. Repeat ad nauseam.'

Captain Hameed finished up with another affirmation that we were like brothers, and that he hoped we would always come to see him and talk of home and make ourselves happy.

'I've enjoyed talking of home as well,' I replied. I was being honest.

He and Rich compared on their fingers how many times in a row they could have sex before falling asleep, and then we said goodbye to Hameed.

Rich, Tariq and I walked out through Hameed's garden, and made for the hangars which dominated this side of the camp.

'I'll show you the mobile TOC,' said Rich. 'Tactical operations centre. Headquarters on the back of a truck. We're building it for the Afghans.'

We crossed a tarmacked road. A company of Afghan soldiers drove past us in smart new Ford Rangers. Five men sat in the front cabin of each, and several more squatted on the dusty rear flatbed. RPG warheads clinked loosely together behind the passenger doors, and garlands of plastic flowers decorated every dashboard.

The Ford Rangers were a present from the Americans, like the M16 rifles which the soldiers carried, which replaced the old AK-47s. They were harder to use, but they were marginally better rifles, and they used 5.56mm ammunition instead of 7.62mm, which was a good thing because 5.56mm was harder for the Afghan soldiers to sell. Too much 7.62mm had been going missing, passed on to all the other AK-47 users in Afghanistan like, say, the Taliban.

CHAPTER 8

Across Helmand, the whole of 3/205 Brigade had a strange mix of ancient Soviet-pattern equipment and modern-ish hand-me-downs from the US. Every now and again, a new piece of American equipment appeared and out went the Soviet equivalent, but it never happened gradually. It was always a sweeping step-change across the board.

'Soviet D-30, 122mm,' Rich said, as we walked into the hangar. We were standing in front of a gigantic artillery piece from the 1960s.

'The Afghans have got six of them here, but they didn't have any sighting units. Someone tracked one down in a museum back in the UK and had it flown out here, so now what they do is line all the guns up, put the sighting unit on one gun, align it, fire it, and move on to the next one – just go down the line.'

'Brilliant,' I said.

'Anyway, here's the mobile TOC.'

It was a truck with a wooden box on the back.

'All right, mate?' Rich called, to the empty hangar.

'Eh up?' came a thick Geordie voice in reply. A pair of legs appeared under the chassis, and then they turned into a fully grown, wiry, shaven-headed man.

'Hello, boss,' said the owner of the legs. 'Corporal Hayes. You're taking over the comms mentoring, yeah?'

'Yeah.'

'Well, you've arrived just in time to take all the glory for the mobile TOC then,' he smiled. 'I've been working on this bastard for two months solid.'

'So what's the idea with it?'

'It came out of the push up the River Helmand in the spring. The Afghan brigade staff needed something they could work out of in the field, 'cos they were just milling around for the whole operation doing fuck all. The Yanks use mobile TOCs when their brigade staff deploy, and the Afghans are using American doctrine, so they get a mobile TOC as well.'

I had never seen an American mobile TOC, but I imagined it like something out of *Transformers* – a high-tech, deployable command centre with banks of radios and panels with flashing lights all over them.

I fancied the driver could press a button, and it would turn itself from a truck to a headquarters in the blink of an eye.

The Afghan mobile TOC looked like a school technology project.

I learned that Corporal Hayes had had several frustrating weeks of slow going with it, hamstrung by shortages of tools and building materials, but it was now nearing completion. Alas, it still looked shit.

It was a flatbed truck with a framework of light girders welded onto it, and plywood panels bolted on to those to make a cube. Apart from a couple of storage boxes, the interior was completely bare. No banks of radios and flashing lights. Whatever the Afghan brigade staff did with the inside of the mobile TOC, it was going to be up to them.

'Cheers then, Corporal Hayes,' I said, and we turned tail and left.

Rich peeled off, to track down some radios, and Tariq and I walked back to the British side of camp together.

After an hour and a half talking jiggy-jiggy with Captain Hameed, I was pretty sure the Afghans weren't all puritanical religious extremists who despised Western moral degeneracy. But I still had some important questions that needed answering. The biggest one was, 'Are the Afghans really on our side, and do they really hate the Taliban?' I decided I was just going to ask Tariq for a straight answer, but I warmed him up with a bit of general chat first.

'You're married, right?' I asked.

'Yeah, my wife lives in Kabul.'

'Any kids?'

He made an uneasy little sigh. 'Not yet. Maybe once I finish this job. It's too dangerous at the moment.'

'I guess your wife worries about you loads when you're out here,' I said.

'Not really,' Tariq replied, breaking into a sly smile. 'She calls me on my mobile, and I tell her I'm in Herat! I'm like "Yeah, it's OK here. A bit boring. We're just relaxing in town." '

I roared with an inordinate amount of laughter, and he went on.

'All the interpreters tell their wives they're in Herat. It's a problem, 'cos all our wives know each other, so no one can make a mistake or we are all fucked up.'

'And what's it like up in Kabul?' I asked, trying to steer the conversation around. 'Are the army doing a good job up there?'

'The Americans, man. They fucking crazy army. While ago, they kill about one hundred people in Kabul. There was a suicide bomber and the Americans just start shooting everybody. A lot of people angry.'

We talked about Kabul a bit more, and then I went for the jugular.

'So how do you feel about the Taliban?'

'A lot of the stuff they do is not good. Fuckin' IEDs, blowing people up for no reason. Ambushing people.'

'Yeah,' I replied.

'Just fuckin' dodgy bastards, ain't they?' Tariq surmised.

A few days later they ambushed Rabuka's patrol, in the Danish area of operations, and killed his friend the driver.

9

I got most of the story from Dabbers, but I wanted to see Rabuka to get the rest of it. We had a half-baked system at the time to assess soldiers for trauma after an 'event' like this, and it involved me interviewing Rabuka and asking him a list of questions along the lines of 'Have you started wetting the bed?'

Ultimately his answers would be filed away, handed to Jim the operations officer when we got back to England, immediately handed on to his replacement when Jim got posted out of the squadron as part of the normal rotation, possibly discussed with my replacement once I'd been posted on, then quietly shelved for want of a clear idea of what to do about them. But that didn't mean that interviewing Rabuka was useless.

The simple act of talking about what happened was supposed to help. It turned the events into a narrative, something that existed outside the head of the one who'd lived through them, and eventually something he could detach himself from. Well that was the theory, anyway.

I decided to find Rabuka when I heard that he was coming to Bastion to swap over some radios at the main store. I called up FOB Price and asked for the Danish detachment commander.

'Hi,' I said, 'do you know Sig Rabuka?'

'Yah.'

'I'm his troop commander. When he gets to Bastion, can you tell him to pop along to my old office, any time between 0800 hrs and 1000 hrs?

CHAPTER 9

I'll make sure I'm there … I'd like to see him, check up on how he's doing.'

'Yah.'

I took the short-hop convoy to Bastion and let myself in to the little tin-box room. I sat sweating at what had once been my desk, doing a bit of paperwork on the computer … 0830 hrs … 0900 hrs … then 1000 hrs, and still no sign of Rabuka.

I lost patience and thumbed a lift to the Danish area of camp, thirty minutes' walk away, and after some searching I managed to find their ops room.

'Did a little Fijian signaller arrive on last night's convoy?' I asked the Danish corporal who poked his head round the plywood partition wall.

'What does he look like?'

'Short, dark skin, curly black hair. You know, Fijian-looking?'

'I think so,' said the Dane. 'He came in here for some batteries. Try the accommodation tents.'

I walked out again across the rocky yard and, after a good deal more searching, I found the accommodation tents. Inside one of them was a single Bergen with our squadron colours painted on the back. Success. Kind of.

I still had no clue where Rabuka was, but at least I knew he was in the area. I thumbed a lift back to the British side and searched our tents, and the offices, and the café, and the cookhouse. The bastard had disappeared.

I gave up and wrote off the wasted morning, caught the midday convoy back to Shorobak and made straight for our cookhouse, de-feated, to take my lunch. I pushed open the greasy swing door and there was Sig Rabuka, sitting at a cramped table, chatting with his mates.

His face cracked into that friendly islander's smile when he saw me. 'Where've you been all morning, boss?' he said.

'Fucking looking for you in Bastion,' I replied, smiling back. 'What are you doing here?'

'I got a message that you were going to come to meet me when the convoy came into camp last night at 0100 hrs, but when we arrived there was no one there. I walked over to the British area to find you, but everyone from the squadron had gone to sleep.'

'The message was supposed to be that I'd meet you in the morning. You walked all the way over at 0100 hrs to try and catch up with me?'

'Yeah, but because everyone was asleep I walked all the way back again, and then this morning I couldn't find anyone either, so I caught the convoy over to Shorobak.'

'No worries,' I said. 'Now let's find somewhere quiet and have a chat.'

We walked out of the cookhouse, down past the long metal domes, and out to a little gravelled yard. We sat outside in the bright, beating rays of early afternoon, at a secluded spot where people came to sunbathe. Signaller Rabuka told me his story.

He had deployed in an armoured Danish patrol in the early hours of one morning from Armadillo, heading northward through the desert towards Attal. In a small dip, close to where we had watched the sun rise over the valley three weeks beforehand, the Danes had tried to play a trick on the Taliban.

They set off a large explosive charge near to one of their tanks to fool the enemy into thinking they had struck an IED. Rabuka and one other were sent away to a distance of a hundred metres to pretend to sweep a helicopter landing site for mines. This, the Taliban would assume, meant that the Danes had taken casualties and needed extraction by air. Sensing weakness, they would attack. Then the Danes could turn the tables, opening fire from pre-prepared positions and wiping them out.

As expected, the Taliban had attacked when Rabuka and his companion were sweeping for mines, but the Danes got more than they'd bargained for. The Taliban attack was incredibly savage. Small-arms fire, RPGs and 82mm mortar bombs started crashing around the two soldiers. They sprinted back to the tank with rounds splashing at their feet and clouds of dust shooting up around them. Two more tanks, which had been hiding behind a ridge, surged forward in support.

Then tragedy struck.

One of the tanks hit a *genuine* IED, and a very large one at that. It didn't penetrate the hull, but the driver's head smashed against the inside of the roof. It was the same driver who'd driven us to Attal three weeks beforehand, Rabuka's mate. Knocked unconscious, he slumped forward onto the controls. The tank lurched and accelerated, speeding downhill towards the deep wadi below. Men jumped clear in panic and landed with a thud in the dust, which churned around them with the detonation of mortar bombs. The tank dropped over a ridge and down into the wadi below. Everyone had jumped clear, except for the driver.

Signaller Rabuka ran out into the open towards the tank, the ground thundering around him with enemy fire. He'd crawled inside and seen the face of his friend, bloodied and disfigured. He couldn't reach him. He was called for by the command vehicle on the top of the hill to come up to them and fix a radio, so that they could talk with Armadillo. He ran up the hill again, under crippling fire, and fixed the radio. Then he turned around, and ran back down the hill to help his friend.

The Taliban bombs and bullets never let up for an instant. He did what he could for the driver in the cramped and bloody interior of the tank, until the Quick Reaction Force arrived from Armadillo. They extracted the patrol, and started to pound the Taliban with their own guns. Signaller Rabuka, with the rest of his comrades, was evacuated to a ridgeline. There he watched the battle progressing, powerless to help.

His friend was dead.

Sig Rabuka finished what he had to say, got up from the bench and turned away to fetch his kit bag. He was going back to Armadillo, to continue the grind of patrols and ambushes. I was his officer, and I was going back to the Afghan side of camp, for a cup of chai with Captain Hameed. I shook Rabuka's hand. It was all I could do for him.

****

Over the next few days I started getting to grips with the Afghan radios. They were hand-me-downs from the US Army, like all the rest of their kit that wasn't a hand-me-down from the Russians.

The Taliban used hand-me-down kit from the Russians as well, plus the occasional hand-me-down Lee Enfield rifle using a design copied from British India, because the lucky Afghans had a distinguished history of foreign military patronage.

The Afghan National Army radios were about fifteen years out of date, and unencrypted, but they were easy to use and reliable. In fact, they were *so* reliable that the Brits often borrowed radios off the Afghans they were mentoring when they couldn't get their own to work.

The displays were digital, and the only thing needed for comms was the right frequency for the network you wanted to join. Even an illiterate and innumerate soldier could match a few wavy lines and a decimal point, scrawled on a piece of paper, to the corresponding symbols on his radio dials, so it was happy days for Afghan comms.

Our mentoring team ran daily lessons in radio operation for anyone who would attend them, which was usually soldiers from the infantry kandaks stationed temporarily in Shorobak. At the beginning of our deployment the lessons had been structured like a British training class. They started with an introduction, a list of dos and don'ts during lessons, a clear statement of the session's aim, a breakdown of operating frequencies, temperature tolerances, effective ranges, power settings and more, and a question-and-answer session to ensure that everyone was paying attention.

By the time I arrived, after four months in the province, the lessons had been pared down to getting the radios out, showing the Afghan soldiers how to put a frequency in, watching them do it, and calling it a day. It was still an exasperating process. Dabbers used to moan about it chronically. He made it sound like chaos, where the best you could hope for was to fling some knowledge into the melee and hope that a little bit of it stuck to someone.

And, if we were trying to influence the Afghans, they were certainly influencing us. They rarely turned up for lessons in the afternoon, and we soon realised that it was pointless to schedule them in, but if we weren't teaching the Afghans we had very little else to do.

Gradually we took on their pace of life, because we had to, and the British enclave of camp became almost as sedentary as the Afghan one. We started to care less about timekeeping, and after lunch each day we came back to our bunks and lay side by side in our long green rows. Some people dozed, some read and some watched DVDs. July was rolling into August now, and the temperature was starting to drop slightly. In the mid-afternoons I usually went running, pounding the hard earth around the camp's perimeter. I ran around the chain-link fence at the edge of camp in the relative cool of 42 or 43°C, with buildings and hangars on one side and nothing but endless, barren desert on the other.

Idly, I toyed with the notion of crawling under the fence and running towards the horizon, free from the confines of camp, just jogging away into the desert until I died of thirst or was captured by the Taliban.

Every time I passed a sentry tower a listless Afghan soldier would thrust his head from the window, clap his hands and shout 'Yes, yes, very good! Faster! Faster!' or invite me in for a cup of tea. I never really felt that the Afghan National Army understood the concept of voluntary exercise.

Every morning I stepped out of the British corner of camp, crossed the giant helipad and took my place in the daily brief at the Afghan brigade headquarters.

Half a dozen British mentors sat in on the meeting, on plastic chairs, out of the way, while the Afghans formed a purposeful horseshoe around the map boards in front of us. There were mentors for every branch of the brigade: engineering, logistics, personnel, religious affairs, communications and all the rest. At the end of the meeting every day we broke off to find our respective staff officers, and talked to them about whatever problems they had.

'No problems at all,' was Major Rohullah's stock answer, and I had come to believe him. Occasionally, he might have a question or two about what was happening on the British side, or he might ask me to speak to one of the other mentors for him, but most of the time he was happy to just get on with his job without interference.

In early August he disappeared on his leave, replaced by his second in command, who had just returned from leave himself. In most normal armies a 2iC is someone to take the administrative workload off the boss – a helpful understudy, who ploughs through the tedious aspects of command, leaving his superior free to ponder the important decisions. In the ANA, a 2iC was more like a tag-team partner; if he was in camp you could award yourself home leave, and when you returned (whenever that might be) he could depart. Sometimes you would overlap in camp for a day or two, but then sometimes you would both go on leave at the same time and leave your department completely vacant. I suppose it all evened itself out in the long run.

This particular second in command was Captain Asif. He was the diamond geezer that Tariq had mentioned. I found him after the morning meeting, the day that Rohulla disappeared on leave, while he was locked in an animated discussion with an American major.

Asif was a small, thin man in his early forties with greying skin, and lips permanently bent into an anxious pout. He looked as though all the worries in the world were pressing down on him. I guessed what passed for a diamond geezer in Afghanistan was a bit different to back in England.

CHAPTER 9

The American he was speaking to was a fat guy, middle aged, with raw, pink skin, who bulged into the folds of his tight desert shirt. He had small, round eyes, and below them he wore a tight, hairy caterpillar of a moustache. I positioned myself at the far end of the table at which they sat, and waited to introduce myself to Asif.

They were debating the state of comms for the counter-narcotics kandak, the unit the American major mentored. It had just been drafted into the brigade to work in the Gereshk district. The kandak was a haphazard addition to the Afghan forces in Helmand, assigned to the province once the poppy season ended, and the counter-narcotics work dried up. They weren't trained for the infantry role in which they found themselves and, by all accounts, they were appalling at it.

The American called across the table to me. 'Say, are you this guy's mentor?'

'Well, I've never met him before,' I replied, 'but, yes, I suppose I am. My name's Graham, nice to meet you.'

I offered my hand.

'OK,' he said coolly. 'Well, I'm not real comfortable with captains calling majors by their first names, but I guess that's how you guys do things, so my name's Karl. Can you explain to Captain Asif here that I need two RT 7000 radios off of him by the end of today?'

Ah yes, the answer to all comms problems – get a bigger radio. After the first minute of conversation my intuition told me that Karl was an idiot and, what's worse, a bit of a dick, who'd decided on a comms solution and now he was steamrolling it through. Asif wasn't going to get a chance to put his case across, because his skin was olive brown and he didn't speak English. I was the middle man.

The four of us sat down together. We talked for an hour, through English and into Dari, and Dari back into English, and then English to English between Karl and me, while Tariq and Asif had their own conversation in Dari. Then Asif spoke to us, through Tariq, in English, and between Karl and me, then back to Dari. Once the hour was up, my intuition was well and truly confirmed. The conversation went *something* like this:

Karl: The counter-narcotics kandak commander in Gereshk has no comms to his entire unit, *god-damn it*. We need the extra power of those RT 7000s, stat!

Asif: But the radios which you already have give more than enough range to provide comms. I think the problem is that, when the counter-narcotics kandak charged through Shorobak on their way to Gereshk, they refused to be trained on the radios as a point of honour, and now they don't know how to use them. Let's send someone out to train them and then the problem will be solved, *inshallah*.

Karl (shaking head in exasperation): Well, if you want to arrange some extra training, then fine, but this problem can't wait to be solved on Afghan time. We need comms, and fast. The 4th Infantry Kandak have two RT 7000s they're not using, so you need to requisition them for us, you piece of crap.

Asif (despairing at the human condition): Well, if Major Rohulla was here then *maybe* we could get those radios off the 4th Kandak but, see, here's the thing – in case you haven't noticed, Afghanistan runs on power politics, patronage and tribalism. Major Rohulla is powerful enough to get those radios, but if I tried then the kandak commander would tell me to go screw myself. He'd rather throw them away than let the counter-narcotics kandak borrow them, because the rest of the brigade thinks you're a bunch of dicks. You'll be hounded out of Helmand soon, *inshallah*.

Karl: No, no, no, stop being so backward. That stuff's all in the past. We reformed your army in our image, remember? So now you don't have to worry about politics and petty rivalries, 'cos we've shown you a better way. You absolutely have the power to requisition those radios, because it says so in your Combat Service Support Doctrine Four-Point-Oh. And I should know, because we cut and pasted it directly from *our* Combat Service Support Doctrine Four-Point-Oh. I know no one in your brigade staff has ever read it, but if you have a look then it's all there in black and white, and that's the best kind of power there is.

Asif: Yes, well, we Afghans have a way of dealing with people like you. I'll just draw you out and bog you down with a few false leads, subtly broken promises and complex explanations that somehow get lost in translation, until you're so exasperated with trying to push your solution that it'll end up getting done the Afghan way, like I wanted all along. In the meantime, I'll despatch a sergeant to Gereshk to see what's wrong with the counternarcotics kandak's comms. If they need training, he'll train them. If they need bigger radios, he'll report back as much.

Karl: OK, I'll play along, but I already know what he's going to find; they need bigger radios.

Asif: OK, goodbye. Peace be upon you.

Karl: Yeah, whatever.

We stood up from the table. Karl shook our hands briskly, and strode out of the room. I turned to Asif, and introduced myself properly.

'It is nice to meet you,' he said, with genuine warmth. Asif had honest eyes, girdled by wrinkles of worry. He had shrugged off Karl, but the world was still pressing down on him. It looked like it had been doing so for years.

We chatted for a few minutes.

'I'm sorry, I have to go and inspect my soldiers now,' he said before long. Then he looked up at me shyly. 'Would you like to come for lunch at the Afghan officers' mess today?'

'Yes, I would, very much,' I replied.

'OK, OK,' said Asif, breaking into a childlike smile. 'One o'clock – see you then.' We exchanged a warm handshake and said our goodbyes.

I killed some time in the morning, correcting some errant punctuation marks in a document I'd sent to Lashkar Gah. The squadron second in command had found them running around inside his territory, became horrified, and expelled them back to Shorobak for me to exterminate.

Then, just before 1 p.m., I walked over to 'Terp Town and knocked on every door trying to track down Tariq. I found him after a few minutes, and he greeted me with a clammy handshake.

'How are you doing, man, you feeling well?' he asked. 'You feeling strong? Your family, are they well? You livin' the dream?'

'Yeah, I'm doing good, thanks,' I replied.

Tariq and I walked across the great, sparse camp towards the ANA cookhouse. It was a huge hangar, again brand new, and when we stepped inside it we saw endless rows of tables and chairs basking in a pale, blue light. Verses of the Koran were written on the whitewashed walls in black paint, in stanzas thirty feet high. Captain Asif was waiting for us in front of the lunch queue.

'Welcome, welcome,' he said in English, and then pointed at me. '*Hoobe-ast?*'

'*Hoobe-ast!*' I affirmed and then, pointing at him, '*Hoobe-ast?*'

'*Hoobe-ast!*'

My knowledge of Dari was coming on in leaps and bounds.

CHAPTER 9

Asif shepherded us into the short queue behind the high tables where lunch was being served. He held himself back and invited us to go before him, with a shy but theatrical wave of his arm. We came to the front of the queue, and Afghan soldiers handed each of us a neat stack of food. We sat down at one of the clean, steel tables and I examined my lunch.

There was a sort of base layer on my plate of tomato slices, cucumber and onions. On top of that was a square tranche of naan bread. On top of that was an eight-inch slice of melon, and another one of watermelon. Between the two slices was an apple, a small lemon and a can of the Pakistani soft drink, Mirinda.

I took my lead from Tariq and Asif and used the naan bread as a shipping pallet, carrying the rest of my food off the tomato and cucumber salad, and onto the table with the fruits still stacked on top of it. We ate our salad and chatted, and I nibbled at my naan bread and drank my Mirinda. Every now and again a friend of Asif's came past and he would laugh and joke with him in Dari. Then Captain Hameed came past to say hello, and Asif dismissed him coldly.

We finished our salads and made a start on the bread. 'Would you like some rice?' Asif asked.

I had plenty of food in front of me. I assumed that Asif was playing the good host, making sure that I had everything I wanted.

'No, thank you very much,' I assured him. 'This will do me nicely.'

'I will get you some rice,' he replied, in a tone of quiet determination. Two minutes later he returned with a large metal tray, with different compartments pressed into it, like you get in infant school.

It had a generous portion of lamb on the bone in tomato sauce, a mound of chopped okra in oil and a huge mountain of rice.

Fuck. I'd only been eating the starter. This was the main course. I stuck my fork into the rice mountain. Double fuck. There was *another* massive piece of meat inside it.

I fought my way through both types of lamb, and the okra, but I left a pathetically small dent on the rice. Tariq and Asif both finished off their entire meals and wiped the sauce up with the last of their naan. Then Asif went to fetch me another bowl of meat.

I guess it was a cultural thing. I felt like my very manhood was on the line. I took one more piece and then said:

'That was delicious, but I just can't eat any more.'

'If you are too full,' Asif explained, 'then forget about the rice. Just eat meat.'

I struggled on as best I could. After that final bowl of meat I gave up, and Asif relented. I was probably looking quite sick. I eased myself up from the table, we shook hands on a meal well fought, and I walked back to the British camp to sleep the food off.

Over the next few weeks I ate with Tariq and Asif many more times, and I was always dumbstruck by the size of the Afghan appetite. These were some of the skinniest, wiriest men I had ever met, and I physically could not eat half as much as them. And they didn't just do it for special occasions. They ate that much for *every single meal*. The only explanation I could think of was that they all had worms.

After three hours dozing on my bunk I roused myself, pulled on my shirt and boots, and walked off to find Corporal Hayes to see about progress on the mobile TOC. When I found him he told me, with a mixture of pride and relief, that after two and a half months of solid and lonely effort it was finally ready. This was good news indeed. I had had almost no involvement with the inception, design, sourcing of materials or with building the project, but I was now the leader of the comms mentoring team and, as such, I was prepared to take full credit for bringing the mobile TOC to its fruition.

It was almost literally useless but, somehow, it had a magical quality about it. Everyone who had a stake in it benefited from it somehow.

Once it was built, the American doctrine-writers could tell their superiors that they had delivered a key capability to the ANA at brigade level – a deployable command and control node that could move forward in support of manoeuvrist operations.

For us Brits, although we really did suspect that it was useless, it offered solid, tangible proof that we were actually doing something with our time.

The Afghan brigade staff liked the idea because they thought General Muhayadin would like it, and General Muhayadin liked it because he was looking forward to having his own personal War Caravan. He could kick the brigade staff out of it, deck it out with carpets and teapots and garlands of plastic flowers, and make his deployed life a damn sight more comfortable.

The next morning Dabbers and I walked with Corporal Hayes to the hangar where the mobile TOC lived and, with bated breath, we took it for a test drive.

We bumped it over mounds and rocks and dragged it through drainage ditches and, to our amazement, it didn't fall apart. Our excitement began to rise. We jumped down from the cab and examined the partial welds on the framework. They were still attached! We could sense the culminating moment approaching us. Finally, we were going to get this thing off our hands.

Dabbers trekked away across the gravel to warn Captain Asif of our imminent arrival. I jumped back into the cab with Corporal Hayes, and we began a slow traverse across camp. The TOC had already passed its test drive, and we were damned if we were going to let it fall apart on the way to HQ.

When we arrived at the brigade headquarters Asif was waiting there for us, expectantly. The mobile TOC rolled towards him. It was a shaky frame of tarnished steel and unpainted plywood. Corporal Hayes had worked tirelessly on it, but there was only so much he could do with the tools and materials available.

I thought that we were delivering the Afghans a genuinely shoddy piece of kit but, as we parked up in front of Asif, he looked delighted with it. Dabbers and I had hatched a plan to hand it over to him at the earliest opportunity, so he could Afghan-ize it: deck it out with whatever radios he wanted, put down some carpets, get a teapot on the go and throw around some garlands of plastic flowers. We knew that it'd be pointless for us to deck out the interior, because the Afghans would just screw around with it anyway. And, besides, we couldn't be bothered.

Once Asif had fitted it out we could present the finished article to General Muhayadin, give him a quick demonstration of its capabilities and wash our hands of the whole affair.

Asif had other ideas.

'*Hoobe-ast, hoobe-ast,*' he nodded, smiling, and then he mumbled something in Dari.

'Captain Asif wants to know if we can show it to General Muhayadin now.' said Tariq.

Why not, I thought, let him do what he likes with it.

We donned our berets, made sure our shirts were properly tucked in, and walked down a little dirt pathway to find the general. Asif disappeared into a narrow, glass-panelled walkway, and emerged a few seconds later with a beaming Muhayadin. Behind him strode the commanding officer of 1 Royal Irish, Muhayadin's mentor. He had a hard job, always trying to steer the aged Afghan general onto the least maniacal path he could, and it required a lot of skill – judging his mood, picking his battles, using whatever cards he had in his hand. He stayed behind Muhayadin, peering over his shoulder, probably wondering whose hand the mobile TOC was going to become a card in.

The two of them had been in a meeting, perhaps grappling with something important that would decide whether some men lived or died, but it was instantly overridden by the excitement of the TOC. We led them to where it stood, and I deferentially gestured for Muhayadin to enter the hulking box. His smile expanded, long and heavy, beneath his bushy moustache. He climbed up the thick metal steps and surveyed the interior with delight, reverentially brushing his hands against the coarse wooden surfaces.

'*Hoobe-ast!*' he chuckled. '*Hoobe-ast!*'

Muhayadin's satisfaction beamed from him, and it spread infectiously to the little Afghan entourage that had formed around us. The glow which he gave off enlivened his subordinates, and soon they were beaming enthusiasm as well. No doubt they would reap the rewards of his approval for weeks to come.

'Can we run power cables into the rear cabin?' Muhayadin asked, through Tariq.

'Yes, sir,' I replied, 'to wherever you like.'

To the radios *or* to the war kettle.

'And how much storage space is there?'

'All of these lockers, and room under the benches as well.'

He was sizing up the lockers. Cogs were turning. He obviously had something in mind. Something ingenious.

Muhayadin chuckled quietly to himself, and pottered out and down the steps. We took a photo of the group of us, with him posed magisterially above us on the vehicle's rear steps. Then he strode off contentedly with Commanding Officer 1 Royal Irish, on whose lips I could almost see the words 'Now you've got the TOC to deploy in, and you're in such a good mood, perhaps we could rethink your strategy in Marjah?'

I descended the heavy steps, and Captain Asif's hand stretched out to me in gratitude.

'Thank you very much!' he exclaimed in English, with a gentle gleam in his eye. He shook my hand for a minute or so.

'I'm glad the general liked it,' I said, aware that he wasn't letting go.

Eventually he turned away from the TOC, but as he walked my arm went with him. He pulled me down the little dirt path, across a stony yard and out past the billets of a company of soldiers. I wondered where we were going. I wasn't used to walking around camp holding hands with fellow officers. Still, I wanted to see how this was going to pan out.

After a hundred yards Captain Asif released my hand. We were standing in front of a cucumber patch.

Every accommodation block in Camp Shorobak had a little garden beside it to grow flowers, or cucumbers, or sunflowers, or whatever, but this was one of the most prolific. Water was life in Camp Shorobak, just as it was in the valley, but here it didn't come from the River Helmand. Here it was supplied courtesy of the United States Army. It was supposed to be for drinking only, but every billet and office in Shorobak had diverted the water into a garden out front. It came from a borehole, and maybe it was running dry, or maybe it wasn't. No one on the Afghan side of camp seemed to care. Like the good food, new buildings and M16 rifles, it was something to enjoy while it lasted, however long that might be.

Asif stooped into the tangled vegetable patch. He pulled up handfuls of long, thin cucumbers. Once he had all he could carry he picked his way over the miniature channels and dams of his irrigation system, and pressed them onto me and Dabbers. We accepted them, bemused but grateful, and he went back for more.

I didn't want a dozen cucumbers. I had nothing to do with them, but I was touched by the gesture, because it came from the heart.

We ate a few of them right there – Dabbers, Tariq, Asif and I – standing in the open in the middle of camp. They were incredibly moist and delicate, with an unusual flavour.

A few minutes went by.

'And now you come to my office for chai?' asked Asif.

I was half enthusiastic about the idea, but there were still some rogue punctuation marks to be chased up on the British side of camp.

'I'm sorry,' I said. 'I have to get on with my work.'

Asif's eyes sank a little. His lower lip curled in disappointment. He looked like he was stumbling into fog. Never in my life had I met someone so naked and unarmoured against the big bad world, or even someone who enjoyed drinking tea with their friends so much.

We made a little more small talk, but something had changed. The atmosphere had turned rotten. After a few minutes I cold take no more.

'I suppose we could squeeze in a quick cup of chai,' I ventured.

A smile crept across Asif's face. It worked its way out from his lips and crawled up his cheeks, ascending almost up to his eyes but not quite making it. His tiredness and sadness were in his eyes, and they always stayed there. But his smile was back, and that was something.

We walked back to Asif's office, and had a cup of chai. Then we had a second one.

Ah well, screw the punctuation marks.

Asif began pouring out our third steaming cup, and I took the opportunity to ask him some questions that interested me.

'Do you have much problem with soldiers smoking hash?' I asked. I knew it went on, but I didn't know how much, or whether it really affected the army's performance.

Captain Asif paused for a moment, thoughtful but concerned.

'Some problems, yes,' he said. I drew in breath to press him further, but he pipped me to the post. 'I think porn stars must all smoke hash, because there is no other way they could last that long at sex.'

I felt a bit like Winston Smith in the proles' pub, trying to get a straight answer. The porn star observation caught Tariq's interest, and the two of them debated it in Dari for ten minutes.

Dabbers and I sat and looked at each other.

'We both agree that all porn stars must be on hash,' Tariq announced, 'because they can carry on for half an hour sometimes. We both think that eight or nine minutes is the maximum time for normal sex.'

Subconsciously I started to put together a counter-argument about modern editing techniques, but I decided that it wasn't worth the effort.

'Yes,' I replied, 'I suppose eight or nine minutes is about the limit for normal sex.'

I was intrigued where the conversation was going to go from here, but then Karl burst in through the door.

He strode into the centre of the room. We sat on our chairs around the wall, inadvertently circling him, looking him up and down. He obviously had a shit on about something.

In deference to his rank I rose from my seat, to welcome him and shake his hand, but he didn't offer it to me. Dabbers, Tariq and Captain Asif stayed sitting down. I was going to be the middle man again.

'Would you like a chair?' I offered Karl.

'No, thank you,' he replied, 'I don't have the time. We need to get two RT 7000 radios from wherever we can, and get them to Gereshk. Preferably by tomorrow.'

He seemed to have forgotten our conversation from the day before. Karl stood awkwardly in the middle of the floor, with his chest puffed out and his wrists held tightly to his sides, almost to attention. Dabbers and the two Afghans reclined lazily in their chairs. I was trapped in no man's land. I couldn't sit down and leave Karl standing awkwardly on his own, surrounded by a ring of hostile faces, but I didn't want to stand up, shoulder to shoulder with him and make it appear to Captain Asif that I was taking Karl's side. I hovered above my chair, as noncommittally as possible.

'But Captain Asif has already sent a sergeant to Gereshk to try and find out what the problem is.' I said.

'Well, that's fine,' snapped Karl, 'but the kandak commander has no comms to his men and we need those radios.'

I was still on Asif's side. They didn't need those radios, they needed to learn how to use the ones they had already.

'Would you like a cup of chai?' said Asif.

'*No*,' said Karl, reproachfully, 'I'm too busy trying to get hold of these radios.'

All of a sudden I lost any interest I may have had in mediating for Karl. He had shown no respect for Asif, not even a cursory knock on the door. He was refusing to listen to what anyone else had to say and, what was worse, he was failing completely in his role as a mentor. Instead of

172

presiding over and guiding an Afghan solution to a problem, he was trying to steamroller through his own ideas. To cap it all off, he was just plain wrong.

There was a heavy pause. We were stonewalling him. Then he spoke again.

'Well, look,' he said. 'If you're not going to release those radios to me then I'm going to go and see General Muhayadin and see what he has to say about it.' There was a threatening gleam in his eye.

'OK,' said Captain Asif.

Karl bustled out of the room, with as little ceremony and as much disruption as when he had arrived.

As his footsteps grew fainter in the clean-swept corridor the tension evaporated. We exhaled, and smiled. 'Fuckin' dodgy bastard,' said Tariq.

None of us were worried about what General Muhayadin might have to say, least of all Captain Asif. The counter-narcotic kandak were outsiders, drafted in from another province, not really Muhayadin's men. They were so far down the pecking order that, as far as he was concerned, they barely deserved to have rations, let alone radios:

'Sort of an unloved ginger stepchild of a kandak,' as Dabbers put it.

We never heard from Karl again.

10

I spent the next few days trying to finish off the pile of cucumbers Asif had given me. I kept them by my bed, and would take a few bites between meals, even when I wasn't particularly hungry. It was pretty monotonous, but I couldn't bring myself to throw them away. A week or so in, when they had grown limp and tired-looking, I tried offloading one or two, but they wobbled alarmingly when proffered, and tended to induce a terse 'No, thanks.' I never managed to offload a single cucumber, and in the end the final few specimens had to go in the bin.

Meanwhile, our comms lessons were lurching unsteadily forward. Lesson attendance had sunk to an all-time low, and ranged from between four and five students to zero. Every time we asked what had happened to the rest of the twenty or thirty we had been promised, there was always a semi-plausible excuse:

'A convoy came in last night, and the soldiers were unloading stores until breakfast time, so now they must all sleep.'

Or, 'Today is a religious holiday,' – that we'd never heard of before – 'and we must pray all morning.'

It would have been easy to write this off as laziness, pure and simple, but there had to be more to it. ANA soldiers had no great love of physical exercise, but every time I walked through the camp to the morning brief I saw dozens of them on the PT Instructor course we ran for them. I stood and watched one morning, as a single, bald and sunburned British instructor stood in front of fifty or more Afghans on the huge helipad, and ground his hips at them as a warm-up exercise.

CHAPTER 10

A mass of camouflaged bodies ground their hips right back. They'd even got out of bed early for this, so why were the comms lessons failing so miserably?

I never taught the lessons myself because – according to the dogma of the British Army – it wasn't really 'officer' work.

I'd tried to sit in on one just after I arrived, but that was scuppered when no Afghans turned up to be taught. There had been some confusion over the times that we'd agreed, or so they said. After that I never quite got round to sitting in on another one, and I was secretly content to let Dabbers get on with whatever it was he did with them. My taking-of-the-back-seat lasted until about two weeks after I arrived, when Dabbers had to go on a resupply convoy to Sangin, and I realised that I would actually have to teach a week of lessons myself. Maybe I would find out why the Afghans could never be bothered turning up for them.

At 0800 hrs on Monday morning I walked over to 'Terp Town, notes in hand, to pick up Tariq for the day's lesson.

As usual he was sprawled on a sofa in one of the wooden huts with a handful of the other 'terps. He never seemed to sleep in the same one. I suspected that he moved from hut to hut to give his life a bit of variety.

'How are you, man? You well? You feeling strong? Your family, are they well? Livin' the dream, yeah?'

'I'm doing good,' I replied, 'and my mum and dad are well. I spoke with them last night and they're fine.'

'That's good,' said Tariq, without any real enthusiasm. I was beginning to think that I always took his stream of questions too literally – that he didn't really expect a reply and that he had absolutely no interest in how well my mother was. Still, that was how you greeted people in Afghanistan. Everyone has pointless customs. I changed tack.

'But I tell you what, Tariq, I'm getting pretty bored around here in Shorobak. I'm starting to wonder if I could blag my way up to Kabul to go and inspect the basic training programme for comms soldiers.'

His eyes lit up.

'Yeah, man, we'll go up to Kabul together. We can go to my house, my wife will cook us dinner, I can show you the sights!'

This was a terrible idea. I'd be putting him and his wife in danger, and there'd be no way on earth I'd be allowed to do it anyway.

'I'll see what I can do,' I said.

We walked across the helipad and arrived at the billets of the head-quarters company soldiers – adjacent to the cucumber patch – where the lesson was due to take place.

I leaned my head inside the bare grey room, expecting to see thirty-odd Afghan soldiers sitting patiently on the floor, eagerly awaiting the knowledge that they were about to receive.

Inside lay a single Afghan soldier, half-dressed, aimlessly vegetating on his bunk.

'Tariq,' I said, 'can you tell him to go and find his officer, and let him know that it's 0830 hrs and Captain Lee has arrived – as agreed – to teach the comms lesson?'

Tariq conveyed this to the lone soldier in a roundabout sort of way, and he roused himself from his bunk, finished off the laborious task of dressing himself, and sloped out of the room. Ten minutes later a few other soldiers started to trickle back in. Then a few more. Then a couple left again. Then half a dozen more arrived and at about 9 o'clock we had the manpower for a semi-respectable class of students.

We were still missing the radios that I was supposed to be teaching on. After some debate a young private was dispatched to go and find them, and after another fifteen minutes or so he returned, radios in hand, but looking rather sheepish.

'These radios have no batteries attached,' I pointed out, 'so we can't turn them on.'

'Yes,' he nodded apologetically.

There was a general discussion in Dari. Still no sign of an Afghan officer to sort things out. Tariq spoke up:

'They say they know there are no batteries, but these are the only 1077 radios they have. Comms company have taken all their batteries and they won't let them have them back.'

The soldiers shuffled their feet. I felt like they wanted the lesson to be a success, to please me as their mentor and make me feel like I was being useful. It was an endearing trait. After a while Tariq piped up again.

'They say that they have two 1099 radios with batteries, and perhaps we could do a lesson on them instead?'

I had planned to teach them the 1099 radio the next day, and that meant I had planned to learn about 1099 radios myself this afternoon. I had almost no idea how they worked but still, I thought, how hard could it be?

'Yeah,' I said, 'tell them to fetch the 1099s.'

Another young soldier got dispatched. He came back with two American-built high frequency 1099 radios in hand. Tariq told everybody to gather round and then – only an hour after I'd arrived – the lesson got underway.

My students sat or squatted on the floor, and I went through a dry preamble about the range and capability of the equipment, and about what situations you might find yourself using it in. Standard stuff.

Then I picked up one of the radios.

'This is how you assemble it and turn it on.' Tariq translated for me.

The demonstration began.

I was on shaky ground here. I had never touched a 1099 radio before. I had no clue how to assemble it or turn it on, but I was banking on it being extremely simple.

I picked up the radio and the battery and inspected them. There was only one possible way in which they could fit together – so far so good. I picked up the antenna and saw that it, too, had only one possible socket into which it could fit. In it went. The same with the headset. Now it was just a matter of trying a couple of switches and dials and – hey presto – the radio came to life. Success! I began to relax a bit.

'Now that the radio is set up,' I went on, 'this is how you put in a frequency.'

Mercifully, this too turned out to be remarkably easy to do. Why weren't British radios like this?

I stood back, victorious.

'OK, now it's your turn. We'll assemble the second radio and then you can form into pairs. I'll tell each pair a frequency and you need to talk to each other on it.'

The Afghans fell into pairs as if this lesson was a well-worn routine, which it probably was. They quickly assembled the second radio, and then the first two students programmed in the frequency I had given them. They picked up the handsets and reeled off the usual Afghan radio greeting, '*Salaam salaam salaam salaam*' – peace peace peace peace – and then … nothing happened. Neither one could hear the other.

I hadn't a clue what was wrong. I dived in and started playing around with the radios, pretending that I knew what I was doing. Half a dozen of the more experienced soldiers in the class had the same idea. Within a few seconds there was a little knot of us standing around, pressing buttons, playing with the cable fittings and shouting suggestions:

'Tariq, tell them to try moving the antennas further apart' – from me, or, 'They say we should try re-entering the frequencies' – from Tariq.

At least with the crowd I felt like the pressure was off me, but I felt my authority as the teacher slipping irrevocably away. Eventually, through some combination of poking and pressing and shifting, we managed to get the two radios to communicate with each other.

'Right,' I said, trying to reassert my control over the class, 'well done to those two. Now it's the next pair's turn.'

I nominated a frequency at random and two soldiers began to set the radios up. This time everything worked smoothly. They heard each other's voices in the receivers, smiled with pleasure and moved back into the crowd. Another pair came up, and then another, and I began to feel that the lesson was going rather well again.

We carried on like this for about ten minutes, until a gruff-looking soldier in his thirties came up for his turn. I nominated a frequency as usual and he seized the dials on his radio and started jabbing away in earnest.

He was pensive, mesmerised by the LCD display in front of him. After a couple of minutes of trying he still hadn't managed to arrive at the correct frequency.

'Perhaps he'd like to watch someone else have a go first?' I suggested.

The soldier mumbled something.

'He says it's OK, he knows how to do it.' Tariq translated.

A few of the other Afghans tried to pitch in with advice but he dismissed them. Sometimes they tried to muscle in but he shrugged them off with a dirty look or a jab with the elbow. He sat glued to the set, watching the numbers rise and fall on the screen. Tariq began to lose heart.

'Oh my God! What is he doing?' he groaned, and walked off to stand outside. I'd lost my interpreter.

The rest of my students were starting to look around for alternative entertainment. A few of them picked up the other radio and its carrying harness and started to fit them together. That was going to be the next part of my lesson but I guess they'd decided to skip ahead. They walked outside and practised patrolling with it, and about a dozen of the others went out to watch them, looking like it was the most fun they'd had all week.

I was uncomfortably aware that my control of the class had completely vanished, and I thought about shouting at them in English. They would get the message. I could tell the radio-hogger to get off the set and let someone else have a go, and I could tell the rest of them to get back inside and pay attention. Then we could do the rest of the class in a nice, well-ordered silence.

But, in the end, I decided against it. The whole thing had an air of primary school mentality about it, and I figured that I should just let them enjoy themselves. At the very least they'd get a bit of experience handling the kit.

Eventually we managed to dislodge the radio-hogger from his set. After twenty minutes of swishing the dials about he still hadn't succeeded in entering the correct frequency, so he gave up and sulked at the back of the crowd. Another gang seized his radio and started talking to the group who were patrolling outside. Then, once they got bored with that, I seized the opportunity to regain control.

I shepherded everyone back inside.

'Have you all had a go at entering frequencies into the radio?' I asked.

There was a general nod of agreement.

'OK then,' I surmised, 'so you can be proud of what you've achieved today. You've learned to communicate with the 1099 radio set, and added to your abilities to operate as professional soldiers in the field. You will now be even more effective on your next deployment.'

Now there was a general nod of satisfaction. I suspected the irony had been lost somewhere in translation.

'So that's the end of the lesson,' I carried on. 'Tomorrow, at the same time, I will teach you the 1077 radio.'

The group broke up.

The soldiers went off to wherever it was they went, and I fell into step alongside Tariq as we headed back to our side of camp. We walked in silence for a minute or two before he produced his overtime sheet from his jeans' pocket.

'Will you sign my sheet, please?' he asked me tentatively.

He was getting into the habit of asking me this. I'd got him to do some written translation for me and I'd agreed to sign it off as overtime. Now he was hoping to get overtime pay for teaching lessons as well. It had been a trying morning and I wasn't in the mood.

'But you're contracted for eight hours a day, and you've only worked for two hours today, so that's not overtime,' I pointed out.

CHAPTER 10

'So you don't want to sign it?' he said, looking hurt.

'It's not that I don't want to, it's just that you haven't done any overtime. It's 11 a.m. and now you've got the whole day off.'

We walked the rest of the way back in silence.

The next morning, just past 8 o'clock, Tariq and I walked back to the headquarters company billets for their lesson on the 1077 radio. Dabbers had been preparing for the resupply convoy to Sangin for the whole of the previous day and I hadn't seen him once. He'd left camp at 4 o'clock that morning and I was preparing myself for another three days of teaching.

This time, when Tariq and I walked into the darkened building which served as bedroom and classroom for the company, there were a dozen soldiers waiting for me. Even the company commander had turned up to make sure his soldiers attended.

We milled around for about ten minutes as a few more soldiers appeared, and then I said:

'Right, let's get started. Where are the radios?'

The company commander said something to Tariq.

'He says they only have one radio today and it is in the vehicle parked outside,' Tariq translated.

I could feel my enthusiasm waning.

'OK,' I said, 'let's go and have a look at it.'

I walked through the dirt yard towards a solitary Ford Ranger, flanked by Tariq and the commander of headquarters company with my class of soldiers in tow. The gate of the vehicle park was locked and no one had the key, so we climbed over the barbed wire fence. The Ford Ranger was locked as well, and no one could find the key to that either.

Someone located it after a few minutes searching, and I settled down in the driver's seat to teach my lesson. Of course, with only one radio I couldn't get the Afghans to communicate with each other, but I supposed that I could get them to sit in the passenger seat, one at a time, and practise entering the frequencies.

I turned the power switch to 'on'.

Nothing happened.

I gave the radio a cursory once-over.

'There's no power cable in the back,' I observed.

The company commander started to look worried. He paused, then spoke.

'He says, yes, he knows,' said Tariq, 'but there are no power cables available at the moment.'

'OK,' I replied, exasperated. 'Are there any other radios that I can teach on this morning?'

'He says that there are none.'

My exasperation was now tinged with relief.

'In that case,' I said, 'tell him that we'll have to call off the lesson for today, but that he needs to find some working radios for tomorrow's lesson.'

Tariq relayed the message. They had a mumbled conversation between them.

'He says that all of his soldiers will be busy tomorrow, and for the rest of the week, with deployments.'

My exasperation was still there, but the sense of relief was undeniably growing.

'Fine,' I said, 'we'll have to finish off the course some other time.'

Just like that, my teaching career was over.

I spent the rest of the morning wondering what was going wrong with our comms lessons. Of course, we were battling the general Afghan chaos, but there was also something deeper working against us.

Basically, I didn't think we were teaching our students anything worthwhile. After all, I had mastered the 1099 radio as I was in the process of teaching it, and Tariq had translated Dabbers' lessons so many times that he could almost give them himself. It hardly required

British expertise to teach Afghans how to put frequencies into radios, and there was an air of 'just trying to keep busy' about the way we plugged on with the comms lessons.

Nevertheless, we mentored a crucial aspect of the operation of a 7,000-man strong brigade, and I wondered if there was something we could hit upon that would genuinely improve the way they did comms.

Communications security, COMSEC, was something that interested me. ANA radios were unencrypted and it was simple, at least in theory, for the Taliban to eavesdrop on them. A lot of Afghan soldiers believed that by changing frequency they could avoid Taliban attention, or that their radios operated outside the range that could be intercepted. They were wrong, and I wanted to know how much information ANA soldiers gave away on their radios, and what could be done to stop them. I'd heard that sometimes, when the Taliban came up on an ANA radio net, the two sides even baited each other over the air as if they were in a school yard:

Taliban: Where are you fuckers? Tell us where you are and we will come and fight you!

ANA: Bullshit, come on then, we'll fucking kill you!

Taliban: So tell us where you are then, you bastards!

ANA: OK, we're in the desert five thousand paces north of the main irrigation ditch, fight us here!

And then a British mentor would wrench away the handset.

Perhaps we should have been teaching lessons on COMSEC, and letting the Afghans teach each other how to use their radios.

Chewing this over took up the rest of my morning. Then, when I walked into the Camp Shorobak cookhouse for lunch, I saw Dabbers sitting at a table, grimy and kitted out for war. He was sharing a table with the rest of the mentors who were supposed to already be halfway to Sangin.

'What happened to you?' I said.

'Don't fucking ask, boss,' Dabbers smirked.

'No, seriously,' I asked all the same, 'what happened?'

'We met the Afghan convoy at 0400 and – fuck me – they were actually on time for once. We lined the vehicles up and had the brief, and told them what the route was. They were all like, "Ah, yes, yes, there will be no problems with this route, *inshallah*." Anyway, you know we were supposed to rendezvous with the Americans at 0600 in Camp Bastion, right? Well, as soon as the convoy got out of the gates of Shorobak, five minutes into the move, all the Afghan vehicles fucked off to the left instead of to the right and headed out towards Highway 1. The Americans were all waiting in Bastion ready to go but we had to spend the next three hours driving up and down in the desert trying to round the Afghans up, and by the time we'd got them all back to Bastion the Yanks had had to leave – they were getting too far behind schedule.'

'So you all just came back here?'

'Yeah, we didn't have enough force protection without the American escort.'

'So when's the convoy going again, then?'

'It's not. There's not enough days now to make it there and back before they're on to the next job.'

'So what about all the food and ammo for the Afghans at Sangin?'

'They're just going to have to make do with what they've got. Poor fuckers. How were the comms lessons?'

'Yeah, all right,' I said. 'They're quite … hard work, aren't they?'

'Welcome to fucking mentoring, boss. It could be worse – I heard someone had to discipline two of the Afghans he was mentoring yesterday, up in Musa Qal'eh, when he caught them fucking a donkey.'

Dabbers grinned the grin of a man taking pleasure in another's misfortune. Now I was broken in he was obviously looking forward to me taking some of the teaching load off him. What he didn't know was that I had a card up my sleeve. After chewing over the COMSEC problem, I'd started thinking about sweeping changes we could make to our mentoring, and in the process I'd hit upon an idea to get out of camp.

Later that day I would tell my superiors that I wanted to join the 4th Infantry Kandak on their upcoming deployment to southern Helmand. The 4th Kandak were taking over from the US Marines in the town of Garmsir, and I was going to explain that I wanted to deploy to assess ANA COMSEC implementation in the field, their corporate knowledge and skills base and its implications for the robustness of their comms structure. From my findings I could redesign their training programme in Shorobak and create a meaningful uplift in comms provision throughout Helmand.

Pitching it to them was the evening's work. First I wanted to test the water by trying my idea out on Dabbers. I explained it to him.

'Right,' he said, 'so you're going off on a fucking jolly, and leaving me to teach all the comms lessons!'

'No I'm not!' I lied. 'This is a chance to have a real impact on ANA comms. It's the last big thing we can do before the end of the tour.'

He was sceptical, and quite rightly so. When I explained the idea to my superiors they were also sceptical. Happily, though, they assented after a brief campaign of persuasion. That was the advantage of being largely superfluous; no one missed you when you left.

For once, my plans came together as smoothly as clockwork, and before long, one morning in mid August, I walked across camp to my last morning brief before leaving for Garmsir.

I was early, and I crossed the room to talk to Asif.

'I'm leaving for a few weeks,' I said. 'Dabbers is going to look after the comms mentoring until I come back.'

'OK.'

I didn't explain my plans to Asif, because he wouldn't have understood. I was a warlike man from a peaceful country, and he was a peaceful man from a warlike country. Since I'd started to mentor the Afghans, I was no longer feeling the burning pain of the British rear echelon. I had an interesting job now, and I was learning stuff, but I still wanted to find the war, and going to Garmsir was my last good chance.

Asif wouldn't understand why I was going, but he'd seen many young British and American men disappear off on these little trips before. I think he just accepted it as a fact of life, like the clouds moving across the sky.

Asif wasn't built for the army. He had joined up in 1985 to fight against the Russians (or for the Russians – he was always evasive about what side he'd been on), and since then his life had been based on conflict, but he was not like the warlike young men who came to Helmand, willing to gamble their lives for a bit of excitement and armed with a cynical comment for all occasions, as I was.

He was a family man, ageing and tired, and a small, passed-over fish in a large and vicious pond. If he'd been born in almost any country but Afghanistan he would have probably worked his whole life as a second-hand bookseller or a mender of bicycles, but instead he was an officer in the Afghan National Army. I liked him a lot, the poor bastard.

The staff settled into their chairs, and we waited for the meeting to start. It promised to be a corker. The previous day, without warning, General Muhayadin had ordered his men to build three checkpoints on Highway 1. He'd decided he was going to replace the Afghan National Police checkpoints on the highway, which did nothing to stop the Taliban, extorted bribes from every driver, and were generally worse than useless.

Overnight, nearly half a kandak of soldiers was scraped together, pushed out the gate, and sent to fill Muhayadin's three new checkpoints. A deployment which would have taken weeks of planning in a British brigade headquarters was achieved in less than twenty-four hours, though of course no one knew how the checkpoints were going to be supplied or maintained, or even built. Right now the soldiers on the highway were living out of the same squalid hovels that they'd kicked the police out of, except they were much more crowded. Nevertheless, Muhayadin was preparing to present his deployment to Highway 1 as a tactical masterstroke.

We waited for Muhayadin's entrance onto the stage.

It didn't come immediately. No one seemed to know where he was.

In the interim we had the update from the duty officer on everything that had happened in Helmand the day before. It seemed that the Afghan National Police, the ANP, were not showering themselves with glory in any corner of the province. The duty officer stood gingerly by the huge map board which dominated the wall behind him, and gestured to the area called Nad-i-Ali, a few kilometres to the south of Lashkar Gah.

'The Taliban are very strong in Marjah. Now, close by in Nad-i-Ali, also growing strong. Because of this, ANP have made ceasefire deal with Taliban.'

The terms were that the Taliban would stop attacking the ANP and, in return, the ANP would close down their checkpoints and leave the region. I had little experience of police methods, but this seemed more on the lines of a surrender than a ceasefire. Still, what did I know? Besides, the police chief had vanished into Helmand and no one could find him, so there was no opportunity to scrutinise his decision-making.

The duty officer finished his brief. Muhayadin was still absent, so we were treated to a further preamble. A wizened, severe-looking ANA major stood up to address his colleagues.

'Our soldiers in Sangin have not been paid for nearly a month now,' he growled. 'Soldiers need their money to send home to their families, and to buy themselves clothes, and when they speak to their wives in Kabul or in Kandahar on the phone, they need money for that as well. It is important that we must pay our soldiers.'

He rumbled on for several minutes, gathering momentum and warming to his theme. Then he concluded with an ill-tempered flourish. 'You are not fit to call yourselves officers,' he shouted at the room in general, 'when our soldiers in Sangin have not received their pay.'

This was typical fare for the morning brief – an impassioned speech about some grave injustice that was going on, which managed to completely skirt around why it was happening or how it could be fixed. The accusations of incompetence began to fly back and forth between the Afghan staff. Everybody abhorred the incompetence of which everybody stood accused, but nobody was to blame – and the soldiers in Sangin got no closer to receiving their money.

After several minutes more shouting, the American mentor of the administration branch stood up and cleared his throat. 'If I could just speak for a second,' he said, brushing aside a lock of greasy hair, 'The reason those soldiers haven't been paid is because the pay team haven't left Musa Qal'eh for Sangin yet. They had two flights out which they could have taken, but they missed them both. It seems like they're quite happy putting their feet up in Musa Qal'eh and don't want to get on with their jobs just yet.'

Suddenly, it wasn't the fault of anyone in the room. The Afghan staff settled down grudgingly, and at that minute General Muhayadin strode in through the door.

We stood for him, chairs scraping backwards across the rough, tiled floor, and he smiled and gestured for us to sit. He loomed over us, his presence dominating the room, his black eyes sparkling with cunning beneath his bald pate. He may have lacked something when it came to substance, but no one could say that he was short on style.

He needed it. He had attended staff college in Moscow, and fought for the Russians against his countrymen throughout the 1980s. In the 1990s he had fought against the Taliban with the Northern Alliance. Now, in the twenty-first century, he was still fighting, as a general in the ANA. Most of the staff officers in front of him fought against the

Russians with the Mujahideen, and would have gladly killed him back then if they'd been given the chance, but they all took it as a bit of a joke these days.

The general addressed us. It was time for his explanation of the removal of the ANP from their checkpoints.

'The ANA are established in all three checkpoints on Highway 1, and the ANP have been thrown out.' He paused for dramatic effect, and then plunged onwards. 'This morning, a man drove up to our new checkpoint, and in his hand he held out 500 Afghanis for the soldiers to let him past' – about five quid – 'but the nearest soldier looked at him and said "No! We are the ANA! We will guard this road because it is our duty, and you do not need to give us bribes. Keep your money!" and the man in his car looked at the soldier and he said "Thank you! I am so glad now that the ANA are here!" '

The general grinned at us emphatically, glowing in the knowledge that his soldiers had improved the lives of the citizens of Helmand, at least within the confines of his own mind.

He gathered his thoughts, and launched into a triumphant conclusion. 'Now that the ANA have improved the security on Highway 1, we must ask the British to fulfil their role, and build up our checkpoints and keep supplies flowing to our men.'

With that, he fixed his wily stare on the row of British mentors who lined the partition wall, off to one side of the room. The ball was in our court, or so it seemed.

We worked hard to look impassive. How the *hell* could Muhayadin just throw his soldiers out onto Highway 1 without a scrap of planning? It wasn't our job to build their checkpoints, or to bring supplies out to them, or to do anything other than mentor the things that they did themselves. If they wanted to stay on Highway 1, then they should have thought it through and taken more than twenty-four hours of rations with them.

Then again, Muhayadin probably knew exactly what he was doing.

In the end we *did* ferry rations out to the ANA, and our engineers *did* build their checkpoints for them, because otherwise it wouldn't have got done. By throwing his soldiers out of the door with nothing to sustain them, Muhayadin got exactly what he had wanted all along – three checkpoints, up and running, with the least possible effort expended by himself. Fair play to him, the cunning old shit.

The morning brief broke up to the sound of general mutterings of disbelief, and I went to find Captain Asif again to tie up some loose ends.

We exchanged a bit of small talk, but for once the conversation dried up early. Our eyes turned to the fuzzy little television screen in the corner of the room. On it, the Russians were fighting in Georgia. The news report showed some footage of soldiers setting off a multiple-launch rocket system, and the missiles streaking away towards their victims.

'That's a Katyusha, isn't it?' I asked Asif.

'I do not know,' he replied through Tariq, 'we call it a Repeater. When one rocket fires, its flames start the fuse on the next rocket, and that on the next, and so on.' He paused, and looked at the screen silently with his moist, sad eyes. 'What strange things human beings are,' he said, 'to invent something like that.'

I watched the bursts of yellow flame as the rockets screamed away into the air. I tried to think of something equally profound and yet easily translatable to say.

My mind was blank.

'Yes,' I replied.

11

The alarm went off at 0430 hrs. I rocked gently out of my camp bed and my bare feet sank down onto the cool concrete floor. Everything was black. My hand went out and found my Bergen. I pulled back the top flap and stuffed my sleeping bag inside. Then I found my body armour. I slung it over me and wriggled until it settled down comfortably on my shoulders, then I slunk out of the hangar into the night.

I went to breakfast. I sat down in the cookhouse with Ed, the commander of the mentor company for the 4th Infantry Kandak, with whom I was going to Garmsir.

'Morning,' I said, sleepily.

'Morning, mate,' said Ed, in his Cockney twang. 'You ready to do the business? Looking forward to Op Wongle?'

'Op what?' I said.

'Operation Wongle – it's what we've called the convoy move down to Garmsir. We got it from the *Viz Profanisaurus*. It means 'the act of rubbing your member between your wife's buttocks, in an attempt to wake her up for intercourse.' We figured that no one would want to get killed on something called Op Wongle, so it was a good incentive for the lads to stay alive.'

Ed was a youngish major with fresh, clean features, a shock of blond hair and a permanent sardonic smile. He'd been more than happy to take me on when I asked if his company could host me down in Garmsir for a few weeks, with only the vaguest of assurances that I 'wanted to have a look at the Afghan comms'. The bottom line was that he was

191

chronically short of manpower. The mentor company came under the command of the 1 Royal Irish battlegroup, but the soldiers and officers who comprised it had been scraped together from right across the army. They were a rag-tag bunch – twenty-eight men in total, whereas a normal company would hold upwards of ninety, and they always seemed to be last in line for extra men and equipment. Another unloved ginger stepchild. Ed was happy to take on anyone who was willing to tag along with his company and 'do the business' with them.

This suited me just fine, Op Wongle or no. When Attal was built, in the spring, it was Ed's company, and their Afghans, who deployed there to patrol in the valley below. I'd heard about them before, when sitting on the Danish tanks and watching the sun rise. It was they who'd nearly got annihilated in the crossfire when the hated company of ANA from Sandford rolled through the gates of Attal.

When Marjah erupted, in the height of summer, it was they who'd been sent in to secure it. Their 48-hour operation, for which no one had brought any spare clothes, dragged on and on for six weeks.

One day, in Marjah, the Territorial Army SAS radioed through to them and requested an escort into the region. It was too dangerous for them to drive into alone, they explained. Ed's company escorted their SAS charges with two lightly armed WMIK Land Rovers, which was all they ever patrolled with because it was all they had available. The SAS had *seven* WMIK Land Rovers in their convoy, with heavy machine guns and automatic grenade launchers. Nevertheless, they still requested the escort. Once they had done what they came to do in Marjah, they radioed the 4th Kandak mentors and requested an escort out again.

Ed's company had a habit of landing in the shit, and Garmsir promised to be no different. Finally, I was going to see some action.

When I arrived in Helmand in March, the countryside around Garmsir was off-limits to all but the Taliban. The few patrol bases that we held down there were marooned in hostile territory. They were battered by swarms of poorly trained fighters, sent up from Pakistan, given an AK-47 and told to sell their lives cheaply.

In the spring, and the early summer, the American 24th Marine Expeditionary Unit rolled through Garmsir and smashed the Taliban to pieces. I had seen them at work from Lashkar Gah – they advanced until somebody shot at them, worked out where they were being attacked from, annihilated the position with artillery and fast jets, and continued to advance until they were shot at again.

A good way to kill the Taliban it was, but a way to win hearts and minds it was not. Or so I thought. I imagined every local down there was going to hate our guts. The Americans were leaving soon, and an ANA kandak couldn't match their firepower. The Taliban knew what was happening. Would they try to retake Garmsir from us, as soon as we got down there? Who knows? We were going to find out.

We finished up our breakfast.

'Jump on the Pinz,' said Ed. 'We'll drive over to the Afghan camp, pick up the kandak, then we're heading over to Bastion to meet up with some Americans. They're going down this morning as well, and we'll stop at FOB Dwyer tonight, in the desert, then tomorrow we'll go to FOB Delhi, in Garmsir bazaar.'

I walked out of the cookhouse and across the yard to the Pinz, which was a sort of olive drab Volkswagen love bus, but with no roof and with tractor tyres. It was the baggage wagon. I threw my Bergen in the back of it with everyone else's, and then climbed on top of the mound. As I balanced myself, I noticed that one of the vehicle's armoured panels was yawning out of its brackets. It was a metre square Kevlar sheet, and it was about to fall off.

We drove the half kilometre to the ANA camp and parked up, and I got out a penknife and tried to screw the armour plating back into place. After ten minutes' hard work I managed to secure one side of the panel, but by that time I couldn't be bothered to do the other. I shouted for a roll of gaffer tape, and plastered the other side of the panel onto the Pinz with Green Friendly.

I guess this was always the way the British went to war. Mel Gibson had his manly nods and stirring music, and even the real-life Americans had Operation Enduring Freedom and unmanned aerial attack drones. We had Operation Wongle and armour plating held on with gaffer tape.

The sun hauled itself up into the murky dust of the horizon. ANA vehicles fell into formation around us. First it was trucks full of firewood for the cooking pots of the soldiers in the field, then pickups with eight men in each, then open topped 5-tonners with two dozen Afghans squashed in the back of each one. Some of them wore their helmets, and others just wore bandanas.

Once every Afghan truck had fallen into line we fired up our engines, and the roar spread over the assembled vehicles like a wave of anticipation. The second British Pinz refused to start. We unravelled a towing strap and attached it to the front of the stricken vehicle to bump start it. The Afghans stared at us. Their American-donated vehicles never had any trouble starting up.

We rolled out of the front gate of Camp Shorobak, behind an open truckload of Afghan soldiers who were already trying to get back to sleep among the dust and fumes and noise. When we entered Bastion we turned our engines off and waited for the US Marines, who were travelling to Garmsir to resupply their own men. They only had a few more weeks to serve there before they handed it over to us.

Ed came over.

'Hello, mate. You're a comms geek,' he said, 'you can be liaison officer with the marines. Here's your radio.'

'Cheers,' I said. 'What do I have to do?'

'Sit in one of the Yanks' Humvees. Press the transmit button on the radio when you want to talk to us.'

I found the button I had to press, and my transformation into liaison officer was complete. I jumped down from the Pinz and went to find the Americans.

They were about a mile away, getting their vehicles ready.

'Hi,' I said, to the first marine I saw, 'I'm the British liaison officer. Where's the convoy commander?'

'Right there,' he said, pointing to a small, plump female officer who was flitting from truck to truck with a clipboard. I walked over to her.

'Hi, I'm the British liaison officer.'

'OK,' she said. Her lips contorted below a thin, downy moustache. 'I didn't know we had one. You can ride in the lead Humvee, up there.'

Happy days. 'Lead' meant that we were going to be the first vehicle in the convoy. 'Humvee' meant that we were going to have air conditioning.

I threw my kit onto the back seat, and shook hands with the four marines inside. I got comfy, and half an hour went by.

My radio earpiece crackled into life. It was Ed.

'Hello Charlie Four-Four Delta, this is Charlie Four-Zero, over.'

'Charlie Four-Four Delta,' I said.

I'd made my call sign up on the spur of the moment, when Ed handed me the radio.

'What's happening? When are we moving?' Ed said.

'Don't know.'

'OK mate, let us know when you do.'

Another hour went by. Then the trucks started up, and finally we thundered out of the front gate of Camp Bastion.

We drove out into the desert, and everything around us became totally, maddeningly flat. Precisely half the world was grimy blue sky and the other half was stony pink desert. On the desert half, scrubby bushes were scattered about, six inches high every three or four metres, repeated with military precision as far as the eye could see.

We were like ships, ploughing through the vastness of the ocean. No points of reference, and death if you got separated from your vessel.

Midday happened. Thereabouts, two dark, misshapen blobs popped up on the horizon. We drove closer, and we saw a broken-down tractor with a shattered water bowser. I wondered what had happened to the driver. Rescued by friends or died in the desert?

The tractor and its bowser floated past on our right hand side, and a few minutes later they were swallowed up by the desert again.

Two or three times we saw local trucks on the lip of the horizon, visible for a few minutes before disappearing, sailing on a different course to ours. Then, in the mid afternoon, a low, wide blur appeared. It looked like a gang of men.

'What is that up ahead, man?' shouted the turret gunner.

'I don't know, we'll go take a look, you ready to rip up there?' shouted back the driver, over the engine noise.

He put his foot to the accelerator and we pulled away from the convoy, speeding towards the men in the distance. The big blob turned into several little blobs, three tall ones and two dozen short ones.

'I think they're fucking shepherds!' shouted the driver. 'We'll go take a closer look, but don't shoot any of them.'

'What?' the turret gunner bawled.

'He said don't shoot them!' yelled the man opposite me, smiling.

'OK!' replied the turret gunner.

They were goatherds, three stick-like old men watching over their flock, which looked even hungrier than their owners, wandering in the desert. They carried no water. Perhaps they couldn't afford the bottles.

The men acknowledged us with a feeble wave, and we waved back and drove on, letting the desert swallow them up.

We rolled onwards. Since we'd left Camp Shorobak, the Earth had rotated through a hundred and eighty degrees, and the sun was heading to the horizon again. Just as it was setting we saw, out in the dust, a thin square line of blast walls. We'd reached FOB Dwyer.

CHAPTER 11

Dwyer was a desert base, a logistics hub supporting FOB Delhi in the bazaar.

It was a rest stop for military convoys, but it also played host to private contractors' trucks – ferrying fuel, food, water and other supplies to the American troops and sustaining the battle to win over the people of Garmsir.

The American military, mighty as it was, did not have the resources to supply itself with everything it needed, so the contractors were an essential component of the fight for hearts and minds.

Alas, however, it seemed that every action in Helmand was dogged by an equal and opposite reaction. Sustaining the soldiers came at a heavy price. $15,000 per truck for a run to Dwyer, or thereabouts.

The money went to the handful of trucking companies prepared to drive the route, who nevertheless complained to the US Department of Defence that they were making precious little from it, because all of their profits were being eaten up by bribing warlords not to attack their convoys.

Two years later it would transpire that a man called Abdul Wali Khan was behind many of the protection rackets. And he, as it happened, was currently the Musa Qal'eh chief of police, despite his own boss, the district governor, accusing him of having orchestrated mass killings of civilians and of taking $20,000 a day in opium taxes.

The US Marines had fought and died in Garmsir that summer for Afghans' hearts and minds, in heat which touched 60 degrees. Then, when they wanted to quench their thirst, they had had to drink bottled water which was tainted with the blood and poppy of Musa Qal'eh. As the fight in Garmsir rolled on, the money flowed steadily to the warlords who drove Afghans in Musa Qal'eh against us, and whose hearts and minds would need to be fought for all over again.

For our part, the British had forced Abdul Wali Khan from Helmand in 2006, saying at the time that 'all our good work could be undermined by the baggage he brings with him.' Then President Hamid Karzai pressured us to take him back in 2008, so our PsyOps team was now giving him a PR makeover: putting up posters of him tending wounded civilians and ignoring the allegations of mass murder. And so the fight for hearts and minds went on. And on.

We slept in Dwyer for a night, then continued to the green zone.

We were travelling in close convoy now, so the marines didn't need a liaison officer. I went back to the beat-up old Pinz, and climbed onto the mountain of Bergens in the back. I spotted with satisfaction that my gaffer tape repairs to the armoured plates were still holding, but the other Pinz was doing worse. It had lost a panel somewhere in the desert between Bastion and Dwyer. No one had even realised it was gone, until the driver saw his Bergen in the mirror, being dragged across the ground by a bungee cord.

Now there was a big square gap in the vehicle's rear compartment, exposing exactly one-third of it to small-arms fire, supporting fire, indirect fire and improvised explosive devices. The armour plate was lying somewhere in the desert, swallowed up like the broken-down tractor and the hungry goatherds.

I sat on our Pinz, which was the good one, and the driver came over. He was a sergeant with wide features and long, square shoulders, and he made for the passenger door. The cab had no roof, so I was looking straight at him from on top of the Bergen mountain in the back.

'I thought you were driving,' I said.

'I am. The driver's door doesn't open from the outside, so you've got to go in through the passenger's door and shuffle across.'

'Really?' I said.

'Yeah, and the passenger door doesn't open from the inside, so when you get out everyone's got to shuffle through the driver's door.'

He climbed in and sat behind the wheel.

'Handbrake doesn't work either. Neither do the electrics, even the lights. And watch this – when you put the key in you've kind of got to force it up and round, and give it a little jiggle half way, otherwise it won't start.' He thought for a little while. 'It's pretty shit, really.'

Pretty shit indeed.

What if someone lobbed a Molotov cocktail into the cab while we were driving through the bazaar that afternoon? It wouldn't be hard, because the cab didn't have a roof. Suppose the guy in the passenger's seat couldn't get out because his door handle was broken, and the flames swallowed him up before he could shuffle over to the passenger side?

Or what if the driver got wounded, and we needed to get away but we couldn't, because no one else knew the special way of turning the key in the ignition? Then again, at least we were better off than the other Pinz, which was missing an armoured plate and couldn't be started without a tow from someone else. Imagine that – having to extract under fire and running around with the tow strap trying to bump start your vehicle.

At the time, the media were having a field day over shoddy British Army equipment. It was a hack's wet dream – 'If only this soldier had been carrying piece of equipment X, he might have avoided getting shot by the Taliban.'

Their outrage didn't ring true for me. There's no doubt that the Pinzes were awful but, then again, this was war and awful things were happening all the time. The Pinzes were an aberration, thrown up by the currents of general chaos that swirled around us. They were the same currents that killed Rabuka's mate, when his patrol was pretending to get hit by an IED and he drove over a real one instead. They were part and parcel of war.

When the MPs' expenses scandal broke back home it was a double wet dream for the hacks. Our equipment was woefully inadequate, we were told, by people who had never used it, and instead of buying better stuff for us our parliamentarians were squandering money on duck ponds, but it was all bullshit at the end of the day. The majority of British Army kit was very good and, besides, it wasn't a soldier's job to ride into warzones sporting the very latest in high-tech gear. It was a soldier's job to make do, in whatever circumstances he found himself.

Even conflicts have budgets, sometimes supply chains get screwed up, and soldiers are always more of a danger to themselves than shoddy kit ever can be. I touched on two high-profile death-by-equipment-shortage cases in my time as an officer, and both could have been avoided if bored soldiers hadn't decided to go off on jollies. But, since the dead men left families behind, it wouldn't be right to talk about them here.

The bottom line is that war is chaos, and if chaos is going to be unleashed then people are going to get killed, sometimes quite stupidly and pointlessly. It was an idiot's game to pick a single dead soldier, a single piece of poor kit and a single luxury duck pond on the south coast, and string them together and spin it out as a grand abandonment of our boys in the field. Soldiers are only abandoned when they're called on to fight wars that aren't sensible, and that has little to do with what they drive and what they carry while the war is in progress.

Happily, we in the British Army knew how to tell the difference between a sensible war and a foolish one, because many great and clever men had mulled the matter over already. They wrote the Principles of War, and all we had to do was learn them. If you followed them, then your war was sensible. If you didn't, then your war was foolish, and these people knew what they were talking about. Tally any historical war up against the Principles, and it was always the ones that didn't correspond too well that had turned out badly.

'Officer Cadet … Lee!' Captain Jordan-Barber shrieked at me after five weeks at Sandhurst. I stood to attention on the parade square, looking like a nervous wind-up toy soldier.

'What is the first Principle of War?' he asked.

'Selection and maintenance of the aim … sir!' I stammered back at him.

CHAPTER 11

'Correct. Fall out!'

I turned smartly to the right, and marched myself off the square. I'd passed basic training, and I was ready for the serious stuff.

Selection and maintenance of the aim was the primary and over-arching principle of war. Clausewitz, who was the greatest and cleverest of all military philosophers, had this to say about it: 'No one starts a war – or rather, no one in his senses ought to do so – without first being clear in his mind what he intends to achieve by that war and how he intends to conduct it.'

Good advice, which every officer cadet knows, but the men in West-minster who sent us to war – and they were almost all men – had never stood to attention on the parade square at Sandhurst, and had never stammered 'Selection and maintenance of the aim … sir!' and turned smartly to the right and marched themselves away.

Some had selected the aim of destroying a terrorist network, while some had selected the aim of freeing the Afghans from tyranny, and some had even selected the aim of cleaning the heroin off Britain's streets, and so on and so on. Some people had maintained their aims as the war ground on, and some had changed their minds and switched their aims. Then some people had got voted out, and new people had come along with still more new aims.

A lack of good kit was unfortunate, but a lack of a clear aim was indefensible, and far more deadly.

It was true that every now and again we found ourselves under-resourced in terms of kit, but every day we found ourselves under-resourced in terms of thought. Before the Afghan ground was trodden by the boots of men in desert fatigues, it should have been trodden by the minds of men in suits and ties, but it wasn't. The boots were breaking the ground, and the suits couldn't even decide on a point for them to aim for.

Our American cousins were no help in our search for an aim. In October 2001 President Bush had described our incursions into the country as 'carefully targeted actions … designed to disrupt the use of Afghanistan as a terrorist base of operations and to attack the military capability of the Taliban regime.'

Ten years later, US Under Secretary Robert D. Hormats described the point of the mission as a prosperous Afghanistan, and 'millions and millions of more men and women working on the next great product, or scientific advancement, or medical breakthrough. And it will mean increased hope and security for generations to come. That's the vision we have been sacrificing for – and that's a vision to which our commitment endures.'

Of course! We'd finally figured it out. The war wasn't about terrorists at all, as misguided President Bush had thought. In reality, somewhere in rural Helmand was the next Steve Jobs, and we were fighting to ensure he could escape from poverty and start making us more great products.

Naturally, we had difficulty understanding such grand strategic visions from our vantage point in the Helmand desert, but then we were simple soldiers and knew little of such things. *Ours was not to reason why, ours was but to do and die.*

We left the British part of FOB Dwyer, and drove in convoy to the Afghan side.

It was 300 metres square of raw desert, surrounded by a blast wall. On the inside it was completely empty, apart from a row of ANA vehicles in the sand and a shorter row of coloured blankets butting up against the wall, where the Afghans were still asleep. Last night they'd jumped down from their wagons, unrolled their bedding in the dust, and lain down immediately under the stars. They didn't get an evening meal that night, because no one had thought to organise one.

This morning it took them less than ten minutes to stow their kit and jump on the trucks. They put on whatever they had to protect themselves from the desert – a pair of British goggles, a set of fake Oakley shades or just a cloth – and we nosed out of the gate and joined the American convoy as it lumbered past. Our two columns of vehicles knitted together to form a mile-long snake slithering across the desert.

After two or three minutes we plunged down a steep slope into the barren, flat plain beneath FOB Dwyer. We were to the rear of the convoy, and the line of vehicles ahead of us stretched out nine-tenths of the way to the horizon.

We climbed up a little rise, and found ourselves on another ridgeline. Now the view below was a tangled sprawl of greens and greys – the Helmand River valley. We were much further downstream than Sangin or Musa Qal'eh, and the river wallowed on its floodplain, spreading out into shingled marshes and disappearing into a myriad of irrigation channels.

We turned left and traversed the ridgeline for perhaps half an hour before the track took us downwards again and into the wide, flat valley whose far slopes, if they existed, lay beyond the horizon.

Rock gave way to sand, and our surroundings began to resemble dunes on a beach, with tufts of hoary green bushes sprouting up from golden yellow carpets. Strange buildings began to appear on either side of us – mud-brick domes with sides pared away until only a few crooked legs remained, like drunken daddy-long-legs. Perhaps they were shrines.

We ploughed into a sand pit. The tall American trucks got through it without a problem, and then the Afghans crossed, and most of them got stuck and had to be towed out. Then it was the Brits' turn, and the Pinz stalled right in the middle of it.

There was a farm nearby, so a small group of locals came to watch us pull it out. It wouldn't start on its own, so we rolled a WMIK back to it, towed it out of the sand, and then towed it for fifty metres more as it bumped and spluttered back into life. I wondered if we were impressing the farmers with our Western technological mastery.

Next we came to a narrow concrete bridge, which was another

remnant of foreign patronage in the 1960s or 70s. It was about two hundred metres across, built on stilts and balanced ten metres high over the Helmand River. We crossed it, passed a ramshackle police checkpoint and a hut with two ancient petrol pumps, and parked up in a dirty little village.

Ed's WMIK turned around and came roaring back down the column. 'FOB Delhi's just behind these buildings,' he shouted to us. 'We'll go to the patrol bases and drop off supplies first, though.'

He was like a circus ringmaster, charging around, trying to push his elephants and lions this way and that. He never planned too far ahead, but he always kept just enough control to save the whole thing from falling apart. The trucks rolled onwards. A hundred square, mud-brick shop fronts began to close in on either side of us, all with identical metal shutter-rolls suspended just below the roof, and each shutter was locked down.

We swerved around the pits in the once-tarmacked road. Then, after about five hundred yards, the scene began to change. We drove into a thriving bazaar. Dried-out old men went about their business as our vast column thundered past. A few of them gave us cheery waves. We passed vegetable shops, general stores and motorbike repair shacks with piles of spare parts spilling across the ground in front of them.

Then we passed tea houses, where strangely shaped kettles bubbled over little wood fires, and naan bread sizzled over a hotplate in the street. Men stood around outside them, drinking their drinks and passing the time of day.

After a couple of hundred yards the shops gave out, and the shuttered-up boxes lined the route again. Then it was just scrubby desert on either side of us, and a steep metal bridge in front leapt over an irrigation canal. Our engine revved, and we hauled ourselves over it. When the Pinz dumped itself heavily on the track at the far side we were surrounded by the long, low fields of the green zone.

We turned right, and then left, and all of a sudden we were lost in the endless network of dirt tracks, bushes, crops and irrigation ditches. Every few hundred yards we came to a cluster of mud huts, and a dozen or so small children stood waiting for us by the side of the road.

'You give! You give!' they shouted up to us in English, their hands bent into cupping positions as we stared at them impassively over the sights of our rifles. One boy, perhaps eight or nine years old, was more determined than the rest.

He chased us, shouting, like a dog whose territory we had entered and then passed through. He stood among the weeds and stones, legs spread wide, and screamed something venomous in Pashtu.

'You know he just called you a boy-fucker?' smiled the private soldier next to me.

We drove until the land opened up again. Several herds of camels and goats drifted across a wide green plain. We passed an ancient man in long black robes, holding a nylon string which looped around the neck of a single, scrawny sheep. He was walking it like a dog, and it was nibbling the roadside grass. The man looked up at us with hungry eyes, and flashed a smile which did not spread out beyond his three or four teeth. That single sheep must have been his only possession in the world, and his only source of income. He must have been starving.

We came up to an ANA patrol base at a T-junction, turned right, and began to bowl along a straight, narrow track running parallel to a deep irrigation ditch. Two or three kilometres disappeared behind. Then another ANA base. A couple more kilometres down the track, then Strongpoint Bravo – a large camp, built by the Americans and now shared between them, the ANA and the British mentors. This was as far as we went.

Chaos reigned in the camp for an hour. We were dropping off a bunch of the Afghans, and most of the Americans, and trucks broke ranks and started tearing around the compound at will. Stores got unloaded. People had arguments about who owned which bit of camp, and then stores got packed up again. They got driven around to another part of camp, and unloaded for a second time. The arguments flared up again because half of the drivers hadn't understood what was agreed. Then they upped sticks and moved a third time, then got caught in a traffic jam with trucks trying to cross to the opposite side of camp.

After a while things settled down, everyone got to where they were supposed to be, and a much smaller convoy slipped out of the front gate to return to FOB Delhi, escort duties accomplished. Even within the convoy, men and kit had been reshuffled. Now I was riding top cover on the WMIK, sitting behind the GPMG in the rear turret above the heavily armoured Land Rover chassis. The only other British machine gun in our miniature convoy was on the bonnet of the same WMIK, and mine was the only one that could swivel through a full circle. There were half a dozen Afghan trucks behind us, and they had their own machine guns, but they hardly counted.

All of a sudden, I was the best weapon the convoy had.

We drove back the way we'd come. We passed the 'boy-fucker' gang, and then passed a little clearing where a child was herding sheep and goats. He was about seven years old, and was alone. We crawled slowly past him as he stood, immobile, by the roadside. We were no more than ten feet away, and he stared straight into my eyes with a hard but inscrutable expression. I leaned into the butt of the machine gun, the ugly black metal of its body extending from my arm and pointing straight at him. The safety catch was off and my finger was resting over the trigger-guard.

I could remember seeing British soldiers in Northern Ireland when I was a boy on holiday, driving past them and watching them look down on our car from behind their guns. They'd seemed like a horrible bunch of bastards. Now it was me behind the machine gun, encased by armour and uniform, with the little boy in rags standing in front of me, the muzzle of my gun covering half of his tiny body. How strange life is, I thought.

We tumbled back over the steep metal bridge, through the little bazaar, and this time we pulled a right before the River Helmand, which took us into FOB Delhi. The heavy metal door swung closed behind us as we pulled a sharp left. Then we were facing a long, square shell of a building, which was going to be our home.

We parked up. A few feet in front of every bumper, mud-brick pillars rose from the ground to support a kind of colonnade. From this, a flat roof drew backwards towards the main body of the building – a single row of square rooms, opening out into the yard in which we stood. The building had once been clad in plaster, but most of it was gone, some chipped away by shrapnel and bullets, other parts crumbled into dust through age and heat.

I climbed down from the Pinz, and walked inside. It was dark and dusty. The company quartermaster sergeant, Den, a tall, sinewy warrant officer with a permanently sour expression and thick, greying hair, walked in behind me. His expression soured even further.

'Fuck me,' he spat, 'this is shit.'

'Yeah, we might need to do a bit of uninvited borrowing from the rest of camp to make it a bit more homely,' said Ed, pulling the belt of ammunition from the WMIK's machine gun. 'That bazaar was pretty heaving, wasn't it?'

'Yeah,' I said. 'Everyone seemed pretty friendly as well.'

'I was speaking to some of the marines this afternoon. They said when they rolled in here in the spring there was only one shop open. There must be at least twenty now.'

'So what's the threat like in the area?' I asked.

'IED-tastic. Bombs dug into the roads everywhere. But, other than that, basically nothing. The Americans have already killed anyone who's likely to shoot at us.'

For fuck's sake. *Still* no chance of action. I was relieved and disappointed in equal peculiar parts.

'Right,' said Den, 'let's get a brew on the go, and as soon as night falls we'll go round camp and get on the fucking rob.'

12

FOB Delhi was a hodgepodge of local mud buildings and shipping containers, tucked away behind the Garmsir bazaar. It was garrisoned by the headquarters of the 2 SCOTS battlegroup and a company of infantry soldiers, and we began to steal from them mercilessly.

Every day Den skulked around the camp, eyeing up kit which looked as though it'd been forgotten about, or left unguarded.

Every night he would disappear with a young soldier in tow, and return half an hour later with tables, chairs, polythene sheeting, strip lights, and once even a barbecue set. We kept that one hidden, biding our time until we could build an outdoor screen to hide it behind, so that the 'bastards couldn't pinch it back off us'.

Each time Den came back with a new piece of ill-gotten kit, it had a different excuse to accompany it.

'Shouldn't have to do things like this, but that's the way it is.'

Or, 'They've got fucking loads of tables, anyway. Looks like they've been hoarding them, the thieving fucking Jocks.'

Gradually our living quarters took shape. We pulled the cobwebs down from the ceiling and swept away the worst of the fallen masonry. We climbed the exterior walls and hammered antennas into the crumbling mud and straw of the roof. Polythene sheets went up between the crooked pillars and closed us off from the outside world, giving us a sort of communal eight-man privacy. We borrowed a hammer from the ANA, found some crooked nails on a windowsill and created a bench, a coffee table and some partition walls. We even made a wooden toilet cubicle, in which you sat on a plywood board over a half oil-drum as the stench of everyone else's deposits rose up around you in the midday heat.

Within three or four days we had transformed our shell of a building into something almost homely, and Den was looking for bigger and better projects. He wanted to build a partition screen around our stores dump, after someone took a few bottles of water from it one night.

'We've got to do something to stop those dishonest fuckers,' he said, without a trace of irony.

The ANA kandak headquarters occupied the rest of the building, and their view of what made a home was very different from ours. The Afghans swept their floors until there was not a single speck of masonry dust on them, and then soaked them with water from the camp well to keep the dust down. They unrolled their bedding on the smooth, clean floors, and that was that. A few of the officers had British camp beds and mosquito nets, more as a sign of status than anything else, but the Afghan soldiers showed almost no kit-stealing tendencies. This was probably just as well; Brits stealing from Brits was good honest thievery, but had the Afghans got involved it would have been an abomination against international relations.

On our second day in Delhi I crossed into the ANA rooms to find the kandak comms officer, Captain Dawood. Our company interpreter had wandered off somewhere, so I was accompanied by one I'd grabbed at random as he walked through camp.

We ducked under a patterned drape. On the other side was a small room, filled up by a bed and a radio, and on the bed lay Captain Dawood. He was a well-fed, jolly man with a small moustache and long, mousy hair. I introduced myself and, with a flourish, he called for chai. I had come across his type before, I thought: plump, moustachioed, overly friendly. It was Captain Hameed all over again. I decided to test the water with a bit of comms talk.

'How has the set-up gone?' I asked. 'Can you talk with all the patrol bases in the region now?'

'Yes, yes,' he replied. 'This radio, very strong. We talk to Shorobak as well, no problem.'

Fair play, that was actually quite impressive. It would have been a tall order on the equivalent British radio.

A soldier poured us out two cups of chai, and then poured a third cup for himself. We talked for a few minutes and sipped our drinks. The soldier pulled out a razor, dipped it in his tea, and started to shave himself. He looked at me and muttered something.

'He says it's a bit scrapey,' explained the 'terp.

I nodded in sympathy.

'I am very glad that you are here to help us,' Captain Dawood cut in. The alarm bells started to ring.

'I have a problem. My side is very painful here.' He gestured and arched his back, wincing for effect. 'Do you think you could get me to the British doctor here?'

Why not? I thought. I'd turned down Hameed in Shorobak because there were Afghan doctors there to look after their own, but there weren't any Afghan doctors in Delhi – and, besides, all that would happen was that he'd be given a box of ibuprofen and get sent on his way.

I set Dawood up with a doctor's appointment that afternoon, and took him to the med centre. Fifteen minutes later he came back, ibuprofen in hand.

'I told the doctor what was wrong, and he gave me these!' he grinned.

'Ah, they're the best ones!' I reassured him.

From then on, Captain Dawood and I were firm friends. I'd got him wrong when I compared him with Hameed. He was a likeable guy and a competent officer, who'd just happened to have a pain in his side. The next day he told me how much better he was feeling, now he had some pills, and the day after that he told me so again. He never asked me for anything else the whole time I knew him.

CHAPTER 12

We settled into a routine in Delhi. We went out on patrol most days – half a dozen Brits in the WMIK and the Pinz. Our usual excuse was that we needed to resupply the mentors at Strongpoint Bravo, or the two checkpoints in between, but it was mostly just because we were bored, despite Ed's warning that the route was IED-tastic.

We played a cat-and-mouse game with the Taliban. They never showed themselves, but they were always there, in the shadows. Sometimes they left wires sprouting from the middle of the track, connected to nothing, to have a look at our tactics when we discovered potential IEDs. More than once we drove up to Strongpoint Bravo and came back to find that some other patrol had unearthed a device on the track we were returning by. The Taliban were watching us, and they knew that if we drove up the road we'd be heading back down it an hour or two later, so they dug in some surprises for us.

One morning I was on top cover in the WMIK, preparing to roll out of the gate towards Bravo. As we were firing up our engines, a soldier came jogging down from the 2 SCOTS ops room.

'Some Afghan foot patrol's just found an IED on the road,' he said.

We were going out as lead vehicle. As top cover I would have been on the lookout for stray wires in the dust or freshly dug earth – telltale signs of an IED. But that's hard work when you're ten feet high, speeding along in a vehicle. Had we decided to drive out of the gate ten minutes earlier, and got to the IED before the foot patrol did, would I have noticed it in time? Who knows?

At the time it didn't even seem to matter that much. It was just par for the course. Sometimes people say that war is unreal, but perhaps it's real life that's unreal, and war that's the normal way of things – closer to our primal nature, the simple struggle for existence.

It felt OK, cruising around Garmsir, dodging the IEDs. The big war was here at last, or at least it was on the roads and in the villages. Inside Delhi the small wars still reigned. First and foremost there was Den's small war, nicking stuff, but even I had found myself a small war to be getting on with. I was at war with an ants' nest.

It sat a few feet from the entrance to our living quarters. It was a single, innocuous hole in the ground but all day huge, dark ants scuttled in and out of it. One day I poured an entire jerrycan full of water down the hole to try and drown them out. The water vanished into the depths, and the ants kept coming.

The next day Den suggested I try pouring diesel down instead. It cost the MoD around $400 a gallon to get diesel to us in FOB Delhi, some of the money going to Abdul Wali Khan, but no one had told us that at the time, and we had enough for our needs. I poured it down, and it worked stupendously. As soon as it touched an ant the creature ran around frantically for a few seconds, and then curled up stone dead. I poured half a gallon down the hole, or $200 worth, and in an instant the swarming stopped. Victory. Now the hole was just a hole, damp and crumbling in the sunshine. I packed a shovelful of earth on top of it, and wetted that with diesel for good measure, and then I retired, basking in the knowledge of a job well done.

The next morning another hole had appeared, three feet from the first one. The ants had been busy overnight, tunnelling up again from their underground fortress. Obviously a stubborn enemy. I went to fetch the diesel can. I was about to pour it down the hole when I heard a voice behind me:

'You should warn them three times before you do that!'

It was Slumdog, our interpreter.

'Why should I warn them three times?' I asked.

'It is a religious tradition,' he explained. 'On the first morning you must say to the ants 'Go away, you are not wanted here!' On the second morning, if they have not gone, you must say the same thing again. On the third morning you must warn them a final time. On the fourth morning, if they have still not left, then you have given them a fair chance and you may kill them.'

CHAPTER 12

'So can I warn them in English, or do I have to get you to warn them in Pashtu?' I asked.

'Our religion doesn't say anything about that,' Slumdog laughed. 'Perhaps you should just warn them in English.'

'If it's all the same to you,' I said, 'I'm going to keep pouring diesel on them.'

I finished off the jerrycan, and put a shovelful of diesel-soaked sand on the hole, and then the two of us sat down for a cup of tea.

Slumdog was tall and muscular, with an oversized foppish hairstyle, sparse designer stubble and two neat rows of pearlescent teeth that could launch a thousand low-budget romantic thrillers. That and his sharp eye for not-quite-Western fashion gave him his nickname, appropriated ironically from Danny Boyle's blockbuster. When we mocked his appearance he took it with unfailing good humour, and for this I liked him. He even played up to the stereotype, dancing around our bombed-out building with his hands clenched into fists and his first and little fingers raised in the air, singing 'I am the Slumdog!'

He was a Helmand local with wealthy parents, who'd studied for a computer science degree in Iran. He'd learned his impeccable English at a private school, but he was always on the prowl to improve it further. He would open up a packet of dry brown biscuits from our ration packs, munch one, and try to describe it in the most flowery way possible: 'Mmm ... De-*lic*-ious ... de-*light*-ful ... ex-*quis*-ite!' He was just eccentric enough to be entertaining, but deep down he was as normal as they come.

I was always interested in how our interpreters – in fact, any Afghans who worked with us – coped with going home. We were inserted into the country for six months at a time, did our jobs and then got extracted again. When we ventured outside our camps it was always on an operation: a patrol, or a convoy, or an attack. We were a landing party on an alien world. When Slumdog, or the other interpreters, or the ANA, walked out of camp, they might just be going home, or to the shops. How can you be fighting a war one minute and visiting your auntie the next? It didn't compute. I tried to take the subject up with Slumdog.

'Is it dangerous for you to live in Afghanistan, doing what you do?'

'Yes,' he said, in a matter-of-fact tone of voice. 'It is especially dangerous for me. Most of the other interpreters live near Kabul, where it is quite safe, but my family are in Lashkar Gah and it is very dangerous.'

'Are your family in danger because of what you do?' I asked.

'Mostly they are OK, because Lashkar Gah is cosmopolitan and there are not many Taliban there. People are better-educated, but travelling on the roads is very bad. I had another friend who worked here as an interpreter. A few months ago, he was driving from Gereshk to Kandahar and the Taliban captured him. They cut out his eyes, and cut off his ears and nose, before they beheaded him.'

'Have you been threatened by them?' I asked, slightly taken aback.

'Yes,' said Slumdog, 'they nearly captured me once as well. I was taking a taxi to Lashkar Gah to see my parents, and there were two of us who wanted to make the trip – me and one other man I didn't know. The taxi driver says, "OK, I will wait to find two more passengers, and then when the taxi is full we can go." So we waited for about half an hour and then he says "OK, I have found two more men so now we will go to Lashkar Gah."

'We all got in the taxi and started driving, but once we were on the road I realised that the two new men were Taliban. They started to ask me lots of questions, like, "Where are you going?" and "What do you do?" I told them that I was a computer science student studying in Iran and I was coming home to Lashkar Gah for the holidays. Then they started telling the driver to take a diversion off the main road, so that they could take me to a Taliban checkpoint in the villages. I thought I was fucked but then the other passenger started shouting. He said that it was not right to take people away like that, and the driver said that yes, he agreed, and he would not go to the Taliban checkpoint.

CHAPTER 12

'They all argued for about ten minutes but the driver refused to do what they wanted. In the end the two Talibans told him to stop the car and they got out and refused to pay him the money for the ride. They shouted at me that I was very lucky they did not have any weapons with them, or they would have killed me right there in the open.'

'How did they know you were an interpreter?' I asked. 'Could they tell by your clothes, or your accent or what?'

'I do not know. They might not have known I was an interpreter. Once they had got out, the taxi driver told me I should not have said I was a student, because they associate that with the Westerners. Maybe that was why they wanted to kill me.'

Slumdog looked at me impassively. I wanted more.

'So what do you want to do in the future?' I asked, intrigued.

'I want to go to Britain and study a degree,' he replied without hesitation. 'I don't know exactly what in, but perhaps engineering. Then I can come back to Afghanistan and help build the country up to be better than it was.'

'Will the British government let you do that?' I asked.

'I would need to work to fund myself, and at the moment I cannot get a work visa for the UK. It's a big problem, because the interpreters who work for you in Iraq can come and live in Britain afterwards, and my friends who work for the Americans can go and live in the United States, but we cannot go and live in Britain.'

'That's awful,' I replied.

'Yes. When Des Browne, your defence secretary, came to Shorobak I asked him about it. He said you have a problem in Britain, because the country is already full. Hopefully for 'terps this might change soon, he said, but he could not make any guarantees.'

Throughout the whole of Helmand, there cannot have been more than a hundred Afghan interpreters working for the British Army. Even if they all decided to move to the UK in a single week, it would have caused an undetectable ripple in the flood of new migrants. That year –

2008 – more than half a million people emigrated to the UK. How could we justify keeping out men who had risked having their eyes cut out for serving alongside us? Months later, once I'd left Afghanistan, I emailed the Home Office to ask them exactly that. I never received a reply.

Slumdog rose from his makeshift wooden chair, and left to pray with the ANA soldiers. I got up as well, and walked over to where our small group of British mentors was sitting.

I caught Ed mid-story.

'So we were under contact by the Taliban up near Attal, and the lads were talking to the fast jet above us. We wanted to pass the grid reference of the Taliban position up to the aircraft so they could drop some bombs for us. Anyway, the RAF keyword for the day was 'Boulevard', you know, for the grid references, so the lads were trying to code the grid up but no one knew how to spell it. It was the middle of a fire fight and everyone was shouting back and forth "How do you spell *boulevard*?" '

We laughed together, but then our little gathering broke up just as quickly as it had formed.

I went to sit in the sunshine, and read an ancient newspaper. After about an hour the company sergeant major, Scouse, came over to me.

'We're OK to roll out the gate in fifteen minutes, yeah?' he asked.

'Er, yeah,' I said, with an expression which must have read, *Why are you asking me?*

Scouse paused for a moment. 'You know you're patrol commander this afternoon, right?'

Until he'd walked over, I hadn't even known we were going on a patrol.

'Yeah, of course,' I said. 'By the way, where are we going to?'

'Just dropping off some stores at Strongpoint Bravo,' said Scouse, in a tone which made me think my bluff had failed. He was a good bloke, Scouse. Miniature proportions, a bald head and a kind demeanour. Never one to make you feel bad, just because you might be about to get him killed through your own ignorance.

CHAPTER 12

Fifteen minutes later we were rolling out of camp, with me in the passenger seat of the WMIK as patrol commander. Den was driving, and Scouse was following up behind us in the Pinz. The three of us, the top-cover gunners and Slumdog made seven men in total.

We drove through the bazaar as usual, scouring the press of bodies for anything untoward. It would have taken less than a second for a suicide bomber to rush up to us from the crowd and detonate himself. Den held the steering wheel in one hand and his pistol in the other. I kept my fingers hovering over the trigger of the GPMG and my pistol lay, with a round chambered, on the dashboard. Everything seemed calm.

We emerged from the swirling crowds of the bazaar and bumped over the steep metal bridge at the far side, heading out into the rural farm tracks. We passed the feral group of children with outstretched hands, and rounded the corner into the next tract of fields.

All of a sudden, I noticed that something was very wrong.

'Stop!' I shouted.

Den slammed on the brakes.

The wheels bit and the WMIK lurched. In a second we were stationary. Five yards in front of us, sitting on a wall and facing the road, was an 81mm mortar bomb. It was a foot long and as wide as a fist. What was it doing there?

It was exactly like the improvised roadside bombs we used to find in training exercises. In fact, it was *too* much like the bombs we found in training – it looked like the directing staff had left it in plain view so that we could find it quickly and they could go home and have a cup of tea.

Had the Taliban placed it there, to detonate as our vehicles drove past? Unlikely. It was so obvious they must have known we would find it. But they also knew what we would *do* when we found it. They knew that someone would have to get out of a vehicle and take a look at it. Perhaps it was on a command wire, and they were watching us. When someone approached the bomb they could detonate it. Perhaps the bomb was a decoy, and they were ready with a machine gun to open up on whoever went forward.

I thought about whom to send out to have a look at it. There was one obvious choice, and it was Signaller Thompson. He was a young soldier from my troop back in the UK. As chance would have it he'd ended up with the mentor company down here in Garmsir, providing comms. Now he was sitting in the back of the Pinz. He was the only man in the convoy who wasn't a commander, a driver or a gunner. If he went out, and the Taliban opened up on him, we could still function effectively as a patrol. He was the casualty we could afford to take. He was the right choice to send forward.

'Sig Thompson, go and have a look at that, will you?' I *should* have said, but it wasn't an order I could bring myself to give.

'OK,' I actually said, turning to Den, 'I'm going to go up and have a look at it.'

A slight pause.

'All right,' he said to me, and then turned to the top-cover gunner with agitation in his voice. 'Keep him covered, yeah?'

I got out of the WMIK, leaving my pistol on the dashboard. I don't know why I left it. Maybe I felt like I'd need my hands free. I walked a few steps forward, unarmed. Then I had a thought. *Check for a buried command wire.*

I turned my head backwards.

'Pass me down the metal detector,' I yelled to the top-cover gunner.

He dipped his head into the rear compartment and cast his eyes around. Then he popped back up. 'We left it back at camp,' he said.

'Oh well,' I thought, 'fuck it.'

I took a few more steps forward. Another idea popped into my head.

'Slumdog!' I shouted towards the Pinz behind us. 'Reverse back to where we saw those kids and ask them if they know anything about this mortar bomb. They might have seen something.'

I stepped forward again, gingerly, like a cartoon character trying to sneak up on someone. My eyes were transfixed by the ground, imploring it to give me some clue about the bomb on the wall – a wire, a footprint, anything.

Was I about to die? I wasn't sure, and I wondered why I didn't feel scared. I was six feet from the bomb now. Everything was still. I inclined my body so that I could look around it without stepping any closer. The wall behind revealed itself; on it was a neat row of seven or eight smaller shells, muddy and rusted. This was a good thing. The smaller shells must have been pulled from a field. The way they sat, in an ordered line on the wall, told me the kids were responsible for them. I turned away from the bombs, and at that very instant Slumdog called out to me.

'The children say it was they who put the shells on the wall. They'd been playing with them!'

Of course they had, the little fuckers. We ran our errands and returned to camp, where I reported the bombs to the 2 SCOTS ops room. Later on they would have to send out an unexploded ordnance team to clear it – a UXO team, a squad of highly trained experts, to deal with the lethal little packages that the children of Helmand used as toys.

We unloaded our kit from the vehicles, back in FOB Delhi, and Sig Thompson called over to me.

'Not bad for first time as patrol commander, eh, boss – getting a UXO find?'

'Yeah,' I laughed. 'Back of the net!'

By now I had been in Garmsir for nearly a week, and I felt like I was getting a good idea of how Afghan signallers operated. I was starting to put together a coherent set of ideas for reforming the comms training programme back in Camp Shorobak, mostly through long conversations with Captain Dawood, but I still wanted to get some experience of Afghan comms at the lowest level. I made arrangements to spend a few days at Strongpoint Bravo, where I could join in with their rural foot patrols. Of course the plan served a dual purpose, because I also wanted a bit of a walk around the villages.

The next day two more soldiers arrived in FOB Delhi, which eased Ed's chronic shortage of manpower. Before they arrived I'd been an essential part of the team at Delhi, because each patrol needed a minimum of six British troops, and one man had to stay behind in camp to operate the radio. So, even though I was a temporary add-on, Ed found that he literally could not do without me if he wanted to deploy anyone outside of camp. When the two new soldiers arrived I was able to leave for Strongpoint Bravo without him having to cancel his patrols.

We were due to make a run to Bravo that afternoon, but in the morning we attended a meeting, or *shura*, in the regional police headquarters, set one street back from the bazaar. To be more exact, Ed attended the *shura*, with Slumdog translating for him. The commanding officer of 2 SCOTS attended, as did the Afghan commanding officer of the 4th Kandak, the local chief of police and the heads of all the villages in the surrounding region. The remainder of us in the mentor company sat in the yard outside and enjoyed the sunshine.

I leaned my back against a low mud wall, and one of the newly-arrived mentor company soldiers came to join me. The meeting which was about to start was a big deal, locally, and a mortar attack by the Taliban was a very real threat. The piece of wall I'd chosen to sit against was near to a low mud outbuilding. I'd picked it so that if we got mortared we could dive inside it for protection. We removed our helmets to let the breeze blow over our sodden hair, but we kept our body armour on.

The soldier who'd joined me was short, tattooed and Irish. His name was Corporal Murdoch. He had a wide nose, thick lips and a hard stare, and was a minor celebrity in the company for having decided, on a whim, to serve five years in the French Foreign Legion before enlisting in the British Army. He lit himself a cheap Afghan cigarette and pulled a deep drag through it.

'This meeting's gonna go on for fucking ages,' he said, staring into space. 'We'd better think of something interesting to talk about. I fancy stirring up a bit of controversy. What do you think of the death penalty?'

'I've never really thought about it too much,' I replied. 'Give me a couple of minutes to chew it over.'

We sat in silence for two minutes. Then two more minutes ticked by.

'Well, have you got an opinion yet?' said Corporal Murdoch, smiling. He lit up another cigarette. 'I can feel a typical fucking officer cop-out coming on.'

'Let me think about it some more,' I said. 'You want a genuine answer, don't you?'

Another two minutes elapsed.

'All right,' I said, finally. 'I suppose I'm not in favour of it. Since we've got no way of knowing what happens after we die we are, by sentencing someone to death, condemning them to an unknown punishment. I think we have a moral right to sentence someone to time in prison, because we have an idea of the seriousness of the punishment we've inflicted. If we send someone to their afterlife, whatever it might be, then there's no way to gauge the punishment we've inflicted on them, and I don't think we have a moral right to do that.'

'All right, boss,' Corporal Murdoch said. 'But what if some guy raped your sister? You'd want to kill him then, wouldn't you?'

'I don't have a sister,' I replied.

'Well what about your mum, then? What if somebody raped your mum?'

I wasn't entirely comfortable with the way the conversation was going.

'Well, it's the principle that counts,' I muttered, in what probably was a bit of an officer cop-out.

Corporal Murdoch thought for a moment, and lit another cigarette, his face pensive. Then he brightened up, 'OK, what do you think there was before the Big Bang?'

'I've no idea,' I said.

'Well you must have an opinion.'

'Why?'

'All right,' he drew in his breath. 'I reckon that before the Big Bang there was another universe and that collapsed, and once it had gone into a little ball it exploded again and that made our universe.'

'But that's not an explanation at all,' I said, 'because then you could just ask what was before the Big Bang which created the universe before ours, couldn't you?'

'Ah,' said Corporal Murdoch, grinning slyly, 'but get this. That universe was created from the collapse of the universe before it, which was created by the collapse of the universe before *that*, et cetera et cetera. You see?'

'But that still doesn't answer the basic question of creation, does it? I mean, what set this chain of collapsing universes in motion in the first place?'

Corporal Murdoch and I paused for thought and, at that point, an Afghan policeman staggered over to us, and put his arm around me. He opened his mouth to say something, but he was too stoned to speak. He lolled his head and let out an incoherent moan. His AK-47 swung limply on his back. I wondered if the safety catch was off or not.

'I can't understand you,' I said to him, coldly. He tried to speak again. Another moan came out, and he leant into me so that our bodies were touching right down to our feet, and I could smell his breath.

Corporal Murdoch leapt onto his feet. 'Eh, pal!' he shouted, with venom in his eyes, 'Fuck off!'

The policeman lolled his head upwards without understanding.

'I said FUCK OFF!'

Somewhere, through his drugged haze, he realised what was going on. He sloped away and rejoined his friends at the doorway, behind which the *shura* was taking place. Scouse, the company sergeant major, walked over to us to see what was happening.

CHAPTER 12

Corporal Murdoch shook his head, indicating nothing to worry about. 'Eh, Scouse,' he said, 'what do you think there was before the universe?'

'Just colleges, wasn't it?' said Scouse.

'No, the universe,' Murdoch corrected him. 'What came before the universe?'

Scouse paused. 'I don't know,' he said, abruptly, as if he had just become aware of a serious gap in his professional knowledge. 'Anyway, I'm going to go to the bazaar for a can of pop, do you want one?'

That sounded like insanity.

Behind us, in the police headquarters, everyone in the region who was worth assassinating was sitting down in a meeting. It was highly likely that there was a suicide bomber, or some other surprise, waiting for them in the crowded bazaar beyond the high mud walls of the compound. Walking into it for a can of pop was deeply stupid.

Then again, I thought, *I do fancy a nice cold Mirinda.* If Scouse was going to go and risk his life getting cans, then I couldn't exactly let him go on his own and still drink them when he came back.

'I'll come along and back you up,' I told him, picking up my helmet and cocking my rifle.

We walked out to the gate, past a handful of Afghan policemen lazily watching the bazaar, and into the crowd of local men. About thirty yards in, Scouse dived into the first shop he could find. Inside it were trestle tables stacked with potatoes, tomatoes, onions and melons. It was doing a roaring trade.

I stood in the doorway, the butt of my rifle in my shoulder, my finger hovering near the trigger, scanning the crowd outside. Scouse went to a wrinkled old man on a small wooden stool, said 'Mirinda' and held up ten fingers. The man reached into a shabby chest freezer, and pulled out ten ice-cold cans of fizzy orange, putting them in a thin plastic bag.

Scouse didn't bother to negotiate a price. He handed over ten US dollars, which was more than an average week's wages in rural Afghanistan, and the same amount the donkey owner had been beheaded for when I was in Lashkar Gah.

The old man grinned in thanks. Scouse picked up the cans and walked briskly back out into the sun. I followed him, walking backwards to cover the two of us as we left the bazaar. We spent two more hours in the dirt yard outside police HQ, until finally Ed and Slumdog emerged, blinking, into the outdoor sunshine.

The village elders were still going strong, but Ed had sat through all he needed to. We mounted up our vehicles and returned to FOB Delhi, and as we left we saw the wise and elderly men of Garmsir still sitting around inside HQ, cross-legged on the floor, quietly debating among themselves. I asked Slumdog how the *shura* had gone.

'Not bad, man,' he said. 'The elders were happy that the ANA's here to provide security, and pleased that so much trade was returning to the bazaar.'

'Yeah, but they'd say that anyway, wouldn't they? They probably tell the Taliban how happy they are to see them.'

'I do not think so,' said Slumdog. 'The chief of police was there, and they told him to his face how much they hated the police force. They accused the entire force of being corrupt, in front of everyone in the room, and then they listed all the bad things the police have done. Someone said "We want the ANA here, but you must understand that if the police arrest a man in my village for no reason, then the next day that man's brother will join the Taliban, and there will never be peace." You know, they weren't afraid to say what they thought.'

We nipped back to FOB Delhi, grabbed a quick lunch, and then headed off towards Strongpoint Bravo, where I was to spend the next week. Our route took us back through the bazaar, quiet and subdued now after the excitement of the morning's *shura*, and out into the fields of Garmsir.

We came out onto the long gravel road, parallel to a deep irrigation canal, and every man tensed up. The next two kilometres were IED alley. Since we'd arrived, no one had got blown up, but we knew it was only a matter of time. The WMIK was the most heavily armoured vehicle, so it was in the lead. I stood in the back of the Pinz which followed, looking out into the fields with my rifle in my shoulder, trying to see through the billowing clouds of dust we kicked up.

Through the haze, a figure appeared by the roadside, not ten yards away – a young man in dark green robes. Weird – we never saw anyone but small children and wizened old men. All the young ones were gone.

As we drew closer, the first thing I noticed was his eyes. There was something not right about them, something malevolent. *He's up to no good*, I thought.

The next thing I noticed was his stance – expectant and animated, with awkwardly placed feet and forward sloping shoulders, like he was poised for something.

The third thing I noticed was – fuck! – he was holding a box in his hands, with an antenna sprouting from its middle.

Fuck.

He wasn't just holding his little metal box. He was *gripping* it, with his thumbs curled inwards as if it were a set of controls. Our eyes met.

Should I shoot him?

He's probably about to blow us up, so yeah, I should definitely…

Oh, fuck, we've passed him already.

The dust swallowed him up. My mind was tumbling. Should I have pulled the trigger? I didn't know. I didn't even get time to decide. By the time I'd taken in the angry eyes and the hands gripping the box with the antenna, the moment had passed.

If he was controlling an IED, it'd be armed by now. By the time I'd shouted down to Den in the driver's seat, and he'd radioed through to the WMIK to stop, it would be too late. There was nothing to do except keep on driving and see what happened.

I felt cheated by my own slow wits.

We drove, and the blast never came. I said nothing until we reached Strongpoint Bravo, when I leant down towards the driver's cab.

'There was a fella back there with a small box with an antenna coming out of it, Den,' I said, feeling like I was making something out of nothing. 'It'll be worth keeping an eye out for him when you drive back that way.'

Den looked at me. I could tell he was wondering why I hadn't shot the guy. He picked up the radio and told Ed what I'd seen. Ed's voice came back, scratchy but equally concerned.

'Right, we're gonna need to go back and have a look for him,' he said.

We screeched round in a U-turn and streamed back out of the front gate of Bravo. We drove up and down the gravelled track for ten minutes before I spotted the man in the green robes again, standing at a different point in the roadside, now talking to his mates.

He still had the box with the antenna in his hands, but now music was coming out of it. It was a fucking radio!

I felt stupid for making a fuss. I kept on feeling stupid until a few weeks later, when I was telling the story to a couple of sergeants from the Signals squadron.

'Fuck me,' said one of them. 'Did you shoot him?'

'Nah, I decided not to,' I lied.

'I would definitely have shot him.'

Perhaps the man in green robes owed his life to my slow wits that afternoon.

13

We arrived at Strongpoint Bravo for the second time in fifteen minutes. Along with my bags I unloaded a 24-can pack of Mirinda. It was a sort of hospitality offering for the six British mentors in the camp, like bringing a bottle of wine to a party. I left my Bergen in the dust and ducked through a low mud archway, into a darkened ops room.

'Mirinda, nice one. Can you stick them in there?' said a bespectacled corporal who was sitting on the radio set, gesturing to a small inner room. I squeezed into it through a gap in the mud wall, and I searched for a vacant space between the stacks of American ration boxes. In the corner I saw six bottles of Zam-Zam, the tangy, lurid orange soft drink, Mirinda's cheaper cousin. The bottles looked familiar, because they'd pinched them from us at Delhi.

The lads from Bravo had come over to Delhi a few days ago, to attend the repatriation service for a 2 SCOTS soldier who'd been killed near Gereshk. The infantry soldiers in Delhi were 2 SCOTS as well, so the dead man had a lot of mates on camp.

The whole base had turned out, and we'd gathered around in a clearing. Half a dozen Fijians sang us a song of remembrance from their homeland. Then one of the dead man's friends took two paces forward, and said a eulogy. He spoke quickly, which I took to be a sign of nervousness. Then he pulled out a crumpled piece of paper and read out a message that the man's wife had telephoned through from England.

His voice faltered, and I realised he wasn't nervous at all. He was fighting back tears.

'Well done lads,' he read. 'You're doing a great job out there. Keep your chins up and your heads down.' And with that his voice broke, and he turned away from us, seeking refuge in the crowd.

The 'Last Post' played.

'Fall ... out!' said the sergeant major.

We walked back to our corner of camp, and the lads from Bravo climbed into their vehicles and rolled out of the front gate, homewards.

Ten minutes later Den realised that they'd been into our stores and stolen all of our Zam-Zam. He fumed for three full hours, then decreed that no one from the outlying bases could ever again come within ten feet of our billets, unless they were under escort by one of us.

I set the Mirinda down beside the Zam-Zam, and walked outside to meet up with Stubs, a captain and a friend of mine. Twelve months previously I'd spent a few days with him on the glaciers around Mont Blanc. We were both quite a bit hotter now.

Stubs was in charge of the six-man mentor team at Strongpoint Bravo, overseeing a company of eighty ANA soldiers and officers. He was having a shit time. The company commander he mentored was weak, selfish and lazy, to the point of disbelief. He had shown his colours on the first day they arrived at Bravo when he'd demanded a personal shower and toilet cubicle, and insisted that it was the mentors' responsibility to build them.

Stubs had disabused him of this idea, and ever since, for a week or more, the company commander had been in a sulk. He was not interested in patrolling with his men, or in doing anything other than praying. When, occasionally, he was coaxed out onto patrol, he moped around dejectedly and complained about the heat. His behaviour would have been bad for a private Afghan soldier, but for the company commander it was indefensible, and just as in the British Army, or in any other army, a bad man at the top produced bad soldiers all the way down the ranks.

His uncooperative spirit infected his platoon commanders, his sergeants and his soldiers. Earlier that very day Stubs and one of his men, Junior, had nearly been shot by the Afghans they mentored. They had been on patrol in one of the nearby villages, and three or four Afghan sergeants had piled into a little shop to buy drinks. The remainder of the patrol waited for them, patiently, but after ten minutes the sergeants were still in there.

Junior walked up behind them and called '*Ali-kat!*' which in mangled British-Dari meant 'hurry up', but they ignored him. He called again, and they kept on ignoring him. Finally he put his hand on one man's shoulder, and gave it a tug. The Afghan sergeant flew around in a rage, and started jabbing Junior in the chest with the muzzle of his M16 and shouting at him.

Stubs ran over to calm the situation down, and the Afghan patrol commander ran over simultaneously. He was just as highly strung as his sergeant.

'You do not touch my men!' he screamed at Junior. He was waving his rifle around as well, but unlike his sergeant he had made a point of removing the safety catch first.

'Put the safety back on your rifle,' Stubs asked him, 'and then we can discuss this.'

'No!' he refused. 'He tried to push one of my men!'

The argument carried on for several minutes, until everyone was calm enough to lower the muzzles of their weapons and continue the patrol. Nothing was resolved, but the immediate danger had passed.

I had come to Bravo to spend a few days patrolling with the mentor team, and to see how the Afghan radio operators performed in the field. For the next few days, this is exactly what I did. We patrolled around the surrounding villages in a strange multinational coalition of Afghans, Brits and US Marines. The latter were hanging around in Bravo to ensure that the handover of the area to Afghan control was as smooth as possible. They joined us on patrol to show us the ground, tell us about the surrounding villages and bolster the numbers of non-Afghan troops. Each patrol comprised twenty or thirty ANA soldiers, half a dozen US Marines and two or three British mentors.

The marines ambled along at the rear, content to take it easy after the months of hard fighting they had endured in the area. The Afghans went up front with British mentors mingled in among them, and every time we reached a village it was the Afghan patrol commander who stopped to talk to the locals.

A typical patrol took us out of the mud-brick and HESCO sprawl of Strongpoint Bravo, into the network of farm tracks or towards the sparse desert scrubland which surrounded the camp. We searched the horizon for the enemy, and scoured the gravel for the tell-tale signs of an IED, but everything between our feet and the skyline was peaceful.

When we were not patrolling, the six of us Brits sat about on home-made wooden chairs and benches in Bravo, under the shade of a stolen parachute canopy. We read and talked, and when darkness fell we crowded around a little fire of hexamine fuel, and warmed up our foil-wrapped rations in an ancient, soot-blackened kettle. The fire had a wall of mud bricks around it, and the sight of its flames was the nearest thing we had to a television. Once everyone's rations were hot we kept the fire going to make relentless waves of tea in the same soot-blackened kettle. Then, when we couldn't drink any more tea, we kept throwing fuel blocks onto the fire anyway, just for the diversion that the flames provided.

The toilet we used was less luxurious but much better smelling than the oil drum in FOB Delhi. In Bravo we used the cubic wire cage of a HESCO block, with a rough felt lining to shield us from view. It was about a metre tall, and the same in width and length, and to enter you pulled open a little wire swing door and backed yourself inside. Then, crouching, you shat into a small green bag. Or, if you wished, you could take advantage of the stack of hardcore pornography which stretched almost to the ceiling. Once you had finished, you walked straight out of camp with your little green bag in hand. You stepped out of a narrow gap in the baked mud compound walls, and walked through scrubby grass to the burn pit. The whole countryside stretched out in front of you, right up to the local Afghan huts in the distance. Sometimes goatherds came within yards of the pit, and the only thing that separated them from you was a single coil of barbed wire, laid haphazardly on the long, hard grass. No one bothered to wear body armour. Perhaps if there was a sergeant major on camp he would have forced people to wear it, but there wasn't one.

Of course, all it would have taken was a man with a rifle and a good aim in one of the compounds across the field to pick off a soldier walking to the burn pit. But, then again, it was a lot of effort to get your body armour on. It was heavy and unwieldy, and it scraped against your ears unpleasantly when it went over your head. Besides, there were all the millions of Velcro straps you had to do up. It hardly seemed worth it, just because there was an outside chance that someone might shoot at you. And if no one else bothered with it then you'd look stupid if you were the only one getting your body armour on, just to go out and throw a bag of shit onto a fire. It seemed much more sensible just to risk your life instead.

Three days after I arrived in Strongpoint Bravo, Ramadan started. For the next month the entire ANA would not eat a morsel of food or drink a drop of water while the sun was in the sky.

We held a vague notion in the British ranks that Muslims were permitted to break their daytime fast if they were fighting jihad. We also gleaned that the war with the Taliban was grounds for fast-breaking, as long as the ANA mullahs declared that it was so.

Alas, they weren't going to do that, and this was partly because the Ramadan fast was a perfect excuse for *not* having to patrol, at least not in the daytime. There was no way that fasting soldiers could be expected to travel for miles on foot in the heat of Helmand and so, in the absence of jihad, Ramadan meant one dawn patrol a day for the Afghans, and no more. Sometimes it was only one every other day.

Whether or not the Taliban were going to observe the Ramadan fast was a source of great speculation. Of course many of them were devout, but many of them were also drug takers and prostitute users. Their moral stance on fasting seemed to us as nebulous as their moral stance on everything else. As far as we were concerned, we would just wait and see what happened. Perhaps the Taliban would stay subdued over Ramadan, or perhaps they would finally launch the one-off spectacular we had been waiting for, to end their fighting season with a bang.

On the first day of Ramadan the duty watch-keeper woke us up at 0430 hrs, to walk out of the gate at 0530 hrs with our Afghan comrades for patrol. Everybody but me stayed in their sleeping bags, happy to rise just in the nick of time to don helmet and body armour, oil weapons, check magazines and walk out of the gate. I was always afflicted with a raging hunger as soon as I woke up, and this morning was no different. I got out of bed and set about making myself some breakfast.

I fumbled for my head torch in the blackness. I was sleeping outdoors, in a camp bed beneath the stars, and by their faint glow I could just about see my way around. As I pushed away the folds of my sleeping bag a faint chill in the air brushed over me, and I reached for a second T-shirt to put on. The extra layer of thin cotton tipped a delicate balance, and all of a sudden I was warm again. How easy it was to keep yourself warm in the bone-dry air of Helmand. I lit a small hexamine fire under the kettle to brew up some tea for the rest of the lads when they awoke. The firelight illuminated the detritus from the previous night's orgy of tea, corned beef and instant mashed potato: packets, powders and dirty plastic cutlery strewn all over the desert sand. Slowly, the remaining British mentors began to emerge from their sleeping bags.

CHAPTER 13

'Did you hear that explosion last night?' Junior asked, pulling on his boots.

It had been impossible not to hear it. At about 0200 hrs I'd been jolted awake by a monumental bang which rumbled around the hills and valleys, echoing for several seconds. I should have jumped out of bed and donned helmet and body armour, in case it was a mortar attack, but I was drowsy. Instead I rolled over, settling for the next best thing – the protection of my sleeping bag.

'Yeah, I heard it,' I said. 'What do you reckon it was?'

'No idea. IED emplacement gone wrong?'

It could well have been.

We didn't pay it any more heed, and instead we set about getting our things together for the patrol. We shuffled to and fro around our corner of camp, all the time taking long pulls on our cups of hot, sweet tea.

I had recently become the proud owner of a red phosphorous grenade and a high explosive grenade, which were now bulging reassuringly in one of my side pouches, but because of them I couldn't fit all my rifle magazines onto my body armour. I settled for storing two of them in my right-hand trouser pocket. Into my left-hand pocket I slipped a large bag of boiled sweets from a ten-man ration pack, to hand out to local children.

The sweets looked like coloured frogspawn. They may also have tasted like frogspawn but I didn't know, because I'd never felt the urge to try one. As far as I was aware, neither had anyone else in the British Army, but I was sure that the children of Helmand would appreciate them. What a perfect allegory for counter-insurgency warfare, I thought: one pocket full of sweets, the other full of bullets.

I thought on it some more, and realised that I could take the comparison one step further. The sweets were shit, and a token effort; the bullets were precision engineered, well understood, and I'd even been trained in how to use them. I loved the smell of a good allegory in the morning.

Five of us left the British camp, and walked in the pre-dawn twilight towards the long mud huts in which the ANA slept. We found twenty Afghan soldiers waiting for us with their weapons slung lazily over their shoulders. A few minutes later six US Marines came to join us, and we fell into a loose sort of line and made for the front gates of Strong-point Bravo. No one gave a set of orders like the ones we had practised giving and receiving in training, and no one talked through our contingency plans. We just walked out the gate. It was a stroll in the countryside, with guns.

Our multinational band stepped onto the long dirt road which connected Bravo with the rest of the world. Each man chambered a round as he passed the outermost sentry box. We crossed the wide irrigation ditch at the front of camp, and filed onto a narrower track between two vast maize fields.

All across Helmand the maize crop was growing tall. Near Attal, right now, the patrols were forging through the fields with their bayonets fixed, in case the green stalks suddenly parted and disgorged a Taliban soldier within stabbing distance.

We kept our bayonets off, and followed the track in front of us to a nearby village. A few days previously its headman had been killed by the Taliban for his supposedly pro-Western attitude, so the man's son had told the patrolling troops that he did not want them in his village anymore. Now we were paying him another visit, to see if he'd changed his mind.

We walked up to the knot of mud huts. The sun was just beginning to break out from the dusty horizon and play on our backs. Americans, Brits and Afghans entered the tiny hamlet, passed through it and then fanned out into a 360-degree arc, covering the routes of approach. The Afghan patrol commander stood at the dusty crossroads, at the epicentre of our lethal halo, and the old men of the village walked out to meet him. They talked, and Stubs stood close behind them. I lay in a ditch, with a clear view over the fields beyond, leading to a small cluster of compounds in the distance. A thick-set American sergeant walked over and kneeled down beside me. He breathed steadily, in contemplation, studying the houses beyond the fields.

'We bombed the shit out of that place when we arrived,' he remarked, by way of an opener. He scratched his close-cropped sideburns meditatively.

'Then someone shot at us from that compound over there,' he continued, shifting his gaze, 'so we called fast jets in on it.'

'Yeah,' I said, 'I was in Lash when you guys arrived down here, so I saw the contact reports. You dropped a fucking lot of ordnance.'

'We landed just the other side of what's now Strongpoint Bravo,' the American sergeant went on, 'and pushed up to where we are now. It took about a week to fight through to here.'

We had just walked the same distance in about thirty minutes.

'Every time we came within sight of a compound they'd open up on us,' he explained, 'and then we'd drop something big on it, and then we could advance maybe a hundred yards or so before we got opened up on again.'

I looked around at the village men behind us. The ones who had had the shit bombed out of them. They were chatting away with the marines happily enough.

The ANA patrol commander shook hands with the village elders, and he slowly turned away. As a single entity, the rest of us struggled to our feet under our body armour and shook ourselves off.

We pushed out of the village, at a sharp ninety degrees to the direction from which we had entered, and strode onto another narrow dirt track. I dropped back to speak to Stubs.

'What did they have to say for themselves?' I asked.

'They were pretty on-side,' Stubs said. 'The guy whose dad got killed is doing much better than a few days ago, I think he's coming round to the idea that it wasn't our fault. The thing they're most pissed off with is the police. They said the ANP have shut off the water flow to the irrigation ditches, and won't turn it back on unless they pay them.'

I couldn't take the ANP seriously, with their badly fitting boiler suit uniforms, crap haircuts and drugged-up yokel grins. In my mind's eye I pictured them like impish Bond villains, standing over a sluice gate and cackling maniacally as they turned an enormous wheel and the canals ran dry. The reality, however, was failed crops one year, and starving children the next.

'I'll report it up to Delhi and they can put some pressure on the chief of police,' Stubs said.

We both knew that this would achieve absolutely nothing.

We paid a visit to another small village, where crowds of joyful children ran out and mobbed us, but we didn't stop for long. We lingered for just enough time to allow the ANA patrol commander to shake hands with every man in sight, and then we were off again. This time our track dwindled into a single pathway, just wide enough for two boots side by side. It ran under a long row of hoary trees, with a maize field looming up on one side and an irrigation channel falling away on the other. Every now and again we had to leap over gaps in the path, where diesel-powered pumps were sucking water from the ditch and spewing it around the maize roots opposite them. I was walking close to the American sergeant again. He looked at a large compound, pressing up close to the far bank of the irrigation ditch.

'We stopped at that place a couple of weeks ago,' he said. 'There were two guys in the compound and we asked them their names. Then we looked them up on the database. They both came up with no entries but someone must have fucked up somewhere, because when we got back to camp and checked again it turned out one of them was on the Most Wanted Men in Afghanistan list.'

'Seriously? So this guy was some sort of high-ranking Taliban commander, and you just asked him his name, and he *gave it to you?*'

'Yeah, man,' said the American sergeant, laughing, 'and then we let him get away!'

I shook my head in disbelief, and my gaze drifted forward.

CHAPTER 13

There were two Afghan soldiers walking ahead of us. The one straight in front of me was young and gangly, and he stumbled along as if he was in a dream, singing quietly to himself. He had the belt-fed PKM machine gun, and if the Taliban ambushed us we needed someone on that gun who wasn't going to cock it up. He didn't look like the man for the job but, then again, he was obviously the youngest and most gullible man in the platoon, and the PKM was a heavy piece of kit, so in a way it made sense for him to be carrying it.

He swung it over his shoulder, letting it loll around as if it was a pitchfork. When he turned around he noticed that I was holding my camera, and he lunged forward to tell his friend in front of him. Was he angry? I recalled some brief or other in which we had been told never to take photos of Afghans without their permission. He spun his friend's head around, and pointed at me. They muttered something between themselves in Dari. Then, purposefully, they strode off into the maize field together and started to pull down great handfuls of leaves. The soldier with the PKM stuffed his leaves into the front of his body armour, in between the four bullets he'd already put there.

What on earth were *they* there for? He had a machine gun. Once his belts of ammunition were exhausted, was he planning to load and fire his last four rounds individually?

He turned to his friend, stuffed maize leaves into his body armour as well, and then stood and looked at me expectantly. I noticed he had awarded himself four rank stripes on his helmet, even though he was a private soldier, and there was no such rank as a four-stripe anyway. I took a photo and they continued with the patrol, satisfied.

Before long we had walked in a complete loop, and we were nearing Strongpoint Bravo again. We didn't finish the patrol there. We walked past the base and out into the scrubby desert on the far side, drawing away from the life-giving network of irrigation canals. We were going to pay a visit to the 'poor' area of Garmsir, where the pleasant green fields gave way to dust and sand, and the people scratched a living in whatever way they could. Perhaps half a kilometre away, the barren, rocky hills rose up from the level plain, signalling the end of the River Helmand's valley.

We walked across hard ground, where weeds sprawled erratically back and forth, and arrived at a third tiny village. The huts and compounds were well spread out, because there were no ditches and fields to constrain them. Again we fanned out, while the patrol commander talked with the old men of the village at our centre point. We blossomed into a flower of steel and camouflage, opening up as the sun rose over the valley. The day was starting to come alive.

People were moving back and forth on the tracks, on foot or on bicycles, and sometimes on motorbikes. When they drew close to one of us we would raise our hands and shout for them to stop. Then, turning the palm upwards and raising the wrist, we signalled for them to lift up their robes. They might have been suicide bombers. They smiled good-naturedly at this affront against their dignity, perhaps appreciating the ridiculousness of the scene – a kneeling British soldier, pointing his rifle at the bare, emaciated belly of a bow-legged old man, whose robes were hitched up around his nipples.

A few minutes went by, and then a gaggle of children rushed out of the nearest compound towards me. There were half a dozen of them in total, all between five and ten years old. They stood a few feet from me, fascinated, and I lowered the muzzle of my rifle to the ground. I was not interested in becoming a source of entertainment for them. It put them in danger. I looked for some method of distraction, and saw two ANA soldiers squatting not twenty yards from me. I remembered the bag of frogspawn sweets in my trouser pocket, took it out, and displayed it with a flourish to the children, before throwing it across the sand for the Afghan soldiers to catch. The kids followed the sweets with a whoop of excitement and began to crowd around the two ANA men, who broke the bag open and began to distribute the dubious treats inside. At least the ANA were less of a target than us Brits.

One child was still standing in front of me. He was seven, or eight, barefooted and clad in a single layer of filthy grey cloth. His whole body was shivering and his mouth hung open, exhaling constant, silent gasps. He had obviously been cold all through the night, and was now waiting patiently for the sun to rise up high enough in the sky to warm him. He was too shy to speak so he just stared at me, transfixed. I must have looked very strange to him – a huge alien, or a monster, impassive and utterly inscrutable. After a few minutes a slightly older boy grew bored with the sweets and came over to join us. He looked like the small, shivering boy's brother, but he was much bolder.

'Oooh!' he moaned at me, contorting his whole face around the circular 'O' of his lips. I scrunched my features up in imitation of him. The two boys squealed with delight. The older one tried a different face, and I copied him again. They burst into gales of laughter. We carried on the game for a few minutes, until I got bored and began to ignore them. The older one grew bolder still.

'Eh!' he hissed. I looked on, impassively.

'Eh!' his voice grew into a shout. I still refused to acknowledge him.

'Eh!' he spat, a third time. Then something else came out of his mouth, slurred but recognisable, and in English:

'Eh! Goh hoome. Goh hoome.'

I was surprised, and a little taken aback. They didn't look like they wanted me to go home. They looked like they wanted me to stay, and contort my vast, pale features for their entertainment. I didn't even think that their parents would have told them to say such a thing. Even if their friendliness towards us was a sham, where was the logic in the adults being nice to us but encouraging their children to do the opposite?

I reckoned the boys were saying it to bait me, to try and make me react to them and carry on their game. But how did they know what to say? Perhaps the Taliban had taught it to them.

Anyway, they soon got their wish. The ANA commander finished up his business with the village elders and we rose from the ground and trudged back to camp. When we arrived at Strongpoint Bravo a report was written on the patrol, to be passed back to the British headquarters in Shorobak and Lashkar Gah. It should have encompassed all the subtle shades of feeling we encountered: the resigned acceptance of the son with a murdered father, the smiling embarrassment of the men who had to lift up their robes, the excited children who hissed 'go home', and hundreds more looks and smiles and scowls besides a thorough assessment of how the battle for hearts and minds was going in this corner of Helmand.

But there were thousands of grieving sons and embarrassed men and playful children in the province, and the battle had to be simplified somehow, into a manageable nugget that could be transmitted on the radio and briefed in meetings. And so it was.

When the report was written for that morning's patrol, the battle for hearts and minds was summed up as follows:

'Atmospherics: Good.'

It was 0830 hrs, and we had already finished our work for the day. We peeled off our sweat-soaked body armour and laid our rifles down carefully, and soon I was back in my sleeping bag and dozing. I slept, on and off, until about midday, when the sun moved round enough to beat down on my legs. The heat inside my mosquito net became unbearable in about fifteen minutes.

I got up and walked over to the camp well, where I drew a bowl of cool, clear water and washed myself. After lunch I took my turn on the radio set for two hours, and then I spent the rest of the afternoon reading a book and trying to keep the pages from falling out with the heat. The rest of the mentor team was just as productive as I was.

It wasn't until the sun was setting that we got together as a group again. We sat around the hexamine fire and cooked up stolen American rations for our dinner. Six of us sat facing each other: me, Junior, three other young soldiers and an acting sergeant with lean, broad shoulders, who for some reason everyone called 'the Colonel.'

'I found out what that explosion was last night,' he said.

'Yeah?'

'It *was* an IED emplacement gone wrong. A patrol went to have a look at it this morning and found a crater in the middle of a road about three kilometres away. The hole was three and a half metres wide and a metre and a half deep,' he said, in that precise way that soldiers have of relaying information.

'The bomb must have been fucking massive,' he went on. 'They reckon the guy digging it in messed it up somehow and blew himself to pieces. One-nil to us, then!'

We smiled at the man's death; one less IED layer, and zero effort expended by us. One-nil indeed.

In the centre of our circle, the tea water was starting to boil. A young Afghan soldier walked towards us across the dusty yard, with the look of a dogsbody about him. He sidled insecurely up to the edge of our group. We lounged in our seats with legs splayed as he stood uncomfortably in front of us, gagged by our lack of a common language. He pointed at our fire, and mumbled a few words in Dari.

'You want some hexi?' asked Junior, lifting up a few of the blocks.

'Mmm!' he nodded enthusiastically.

'No problem, mate, just wait there and I'll fetch you some,' Junior said. The Afghan waited patiently for a few minutes, and Junior returned with a handful of hexamine packs.

'Nuh,' the ANA soldier shook his head.

The packs were wrapped in brown paper. Maybe he didn't realise it was the same stuff.

'It's fucking hexi, mate, take it,' Junior said, forcing the packs into his hand. Then something strange happened.

The young Afghan flew into a rage, throwing the hexamine down at his feet. He turned away from us, raving in Dari, and stomped off towards the ANA billets. The Colonel flailed his arms and shouted 'Ohhgaaboogghhaahhhaahhha!' by way of taking the piss out of him, and the lad walked away with our laughter raining down on his back.

We had just humiliated him, and he was probably about to get humiliated some more by his friends for not bringing back any hexamine. I was expecting him to come straight back with his rifle set to automatic and machine-gun us to pieces.

'They're a bunch of fucking dicks, aren't they?' said one of the lads. 'I'd love to get in a full-on fucking scrap with them one day. Hey, how many of them do you reckon you could take on your own?'

'With them coming all together, or one after the other?'

'All together.'

'At least three or four of the scrawny fucking cunts. Then the rest would probably shit themselves.'

'Yeah, probably.'

We never got a chance to find out, because the Afghan soldier stayed on his side of the camp for the rest of the evening. Instead, after the second round of tea, two US Marine scout-snipers came over to join us. Their names were Ben and James and they were both young, easy to get on with and – contrary to the stereotype – they had an acute sense of irony.

They'd just been playing with the camp dog, Kilo, rolling around with him in the sand until he got pissed off. He'd snarled at them, and bit James's arm, and then freed himself and scampered off across the camp. James and Ben ran after him shouting 'Hey, come back here! We bought your freedom for you, you ungrateful fuck!' and once they'd got bored with that they'd come over to our side of camp.

'How's it going?' said Ben, sitting down on a camp chair.

'Not bad,' said Junior. 'Thank fuck it's getting a bit cooler in the evenings.'

'Tell me about it, man. We were here back in June. Fifty-nine fucking degrees! Some of our guys got in a firefight, and we took six casualties, but get this – one of them was a gunshot wound, the other five were heat stroke!'

'Bad times,' said Junior.

'Yeah, this place is worse than Iraq, and that was pretty god-damn bad.'

'Thank fuck we don't have to go back there again,' said the Colonel.

'Too right,' said Ben, in his urbane West Coast tone of voice. 'Everything started getting better over there once we let the police do whatever the fuck they wanted. They knew the neighbourhoods where all the insurgents hung out, so they would just go in there, pull all the men they could find out onto the street, take them away and shoot them.

'We were in this sniper position once, and the police burst into this house down the street and they dragged this guy out. They had him kneeling down with his hands on his head and someone was coming up behind him with a pistol. We were all looking down to see what would happen but then this police guy looks up and sees us, and he tells his buddies, and then they don't shoot this dude, they just take him away instead. I guess they thought we were gonna report them or something if they'd have shot him but we were just watching because we were like, "yeah, this is gonna be fucking *ill*, man!" '

The story, terrible as it was, rang strangely true. A reign of terror and injustice and, in its wake, something resembling peace. It squared with what I'd seen in Garmsir over the past few weeks. Here we were, in the aftermath of an apocalyptic offensive by the US Marines, and the bazaar was flourishing, village elders were standing up and saying they were glad that the coalition had arrived, and British soldiers could throw their faeces onto a fire, in full view of the outside world, and live to tell the tale.

I thought a great deal about why this should be so. Perhaps what the people of Garmsir had really wanted was just for someone – anyone – to finally and decisively win and put an end to all the fighting. Maybe they couldn't care less about the Taliban, or their new government in

Kabul, or us. They just wanted someone to finish the war, and the marines had done so for them.

On the other hand, maybe they were afraid. Maybe they acquiesced because they were bowed by military might. I thought about their plight in terms of economics, and the cost-effectiveness of fear. A man could spend years trying to influence another man by making friends with him, but he could influence him by making him afraid in seconds – 'quieten down or I kill you' works much faster than 'why don't we try to get along together?'

Maybe fear was the only economically feasible way that a tiny force could control a vast population. It was vile, but it had worked for the Romans, it had worked for the British Empire in India, and it had worked for the Taliban in Afghanistan.

They'd started as a small band, who rose from obscurity in the 1990s, swept to power, and pacified most of Afghanistan in just six months. Six months! And here we were, struggling away for nearly a decade. The Taliban brought some things which people could get behind, like an end to corruption and an end to civil war, but mostly they brought fear: beatings in the street, beheadings and death by firing squad. Horrible as their reign was, they had won.

Of course we aspired to do better for Afghanistan than the Taliban had done. We cast aside fear, and championed instead the doctrine of hearts and minds, but there was some crack, some flaw in the system which was defeating us at every turn.

Maybe we shouldn't have tried to win Afghans' hearts at all. We should have concentrated on their minds instead. Winning someone's heart, of course, was not the way to peaceful co-existence. If a man is murdered, the most likely suspect is his wife, and vice versa. When things go wrong, hearts are where the hot, sour rage of betrayal flows out from. 'We're here to help', we said to the people of Helmand, 'trust us'. But then we didn't help, we just fought. What did that leave in their hearts for us?

CHAPTER 13

My thoughts went to Clausewitz, the great military philosopher, who had cast conventional war as a process of interpersonal violence – a slugging match in the street, multiplied up to the scale of armies. Maybe our new type of war could be thought of as an extension of that, as a complete relationship between two people, which might at times involve violence, and might at other times involve building trust, or offering a helping hand, or coercion, or dislike and disappointment, or whatever.

Seen in this light, our war was different from the traditional type in an important way. Instead of waging a war in which people had to suppress their human foibles, for the sake of being violent towards one another efficiently, people's humanity was now part and parcel of the war effort.

The problem was that each of us was dysfunctional in our own way, and none of us were simple to deal with. We each fought our own small wars. Sometimes we worked for the common good, and sometimes we worked against it, and that made our engagement in Afghanistan, as people, as a nation and as a coalition, unendingly complicated.

This was not to say that we couldn't achieve anything in Afghanistan by this method, because all human relationships are unendingly complicated, and yet people still manage to relate to each other constructively and get stuff done. Relationships, I reasoned, could be tangled and complex, and yet still productive, as long as basic tenets are followed – like being honest with the other person, and making sure you understand where they're coming from – but unfortunately we were not doing either of these things in Afghanistan, or at least not with any sort of consistency.

In some places we were managing to follow these ideas, like with our engagement with the ANA, at least at kandak level and below. There were enough of us to mentor effectively, and mentoring low-level military tactics was not too complex, so we understood our partner in the relationship. We were also honest with them, because all we wanted was to train them up to be decent soldiers, and we were happy to convey this aspiration to them.

Above kandak level the honesty was still there - we still just wanted them to do well – but our understanding of our partner started to flag. We didn't know the mindset of the Afghan staff officers well enough to write effective doctrine for them. What we needed was someone to write doctrine for the ANA which they could get, but no one had. Instead we had pasted in American doctrine, which was ridiculous because America is one of the most developed countries in the world and Afghanistan is one of the least. When you try to run the Afghan Army on American doctrine you get aberrations like the mobile TOC, a twenty-first century command node transformed into the general's war caravan, but of course that was only the tip of the iceberg. There were much more serious, albeit subtler aberrations to be found everywhere.

Outside the army, both understanding and honest engagement were practically non-existent. We said that we wanted ordinary Afghans to be free from tyranny, but we didn't understand what that meant and couldn't be bothered to think it through, so instead we propped up the Afghan National Police, who were a disgrace. They received almost no mentoring, and they were usually little more than a militia serving the whims of their local warlord. Some of them were great drug takers, like the stoned man with his AK-47 at the meeting with the elders. Some were extorters, like the band that turned off the sluice gates for the irrigation system up the road. And some were rapists, who often had a penchant for young male children.

Two months beforehand, the Taliban had scored their only major tactical victory against us that summer. They'd assaulted Sarposa Prison in Kandahar, the largest jail in southern Afghanistan, and freed all the inmates there – 600 common criminals and 400 captured Taliban fighters. Many of the prisoners had been held without trial for months, or years. Some had gone on a gruesome hunger strike, sewing their own mouths shut as a protest. The rule of law simply did not work in

CHAPTER 13

Afghanistan, and the Taliban's assault on the prison was seen as a victory for justice, not a defeat.

At the same time as the Taliban were building themselves up as champions of justice, we were diverting millions of dollars to Afghanistan's warlords. Dwyer was not the only base for which our civilian contractors had to bribe the nearby forces to gain safe passage. It happened all over Afghanistan.

Further up the chain of power things just got worse. At the highest level we had failed from the very outset of our nation-building enterprise. The political structure had been set up to channel power into the hands of the president, Karzai, because he was our man. Now Karzai was presiding over a huge system of political patronage, pay-offs and back-handers, through which his inner circle – usually members of his own family – wielded the apparatus of the state in order to enrich themselves.

We granted Karzai the remit of a despot, and then got upset when he rigged elections. We told the Afghans that we were on their side, then propped up chiefs of police who raped their pre-pubescent sons, and scratched our heads in confusion when they didn't buy in to our message.

The situation reminded me of Europeans landing in the Americas, and trying to buy the favour of the natives with a few glass baubles - counting on their simplicity and naïveté. Our modern-day baubles were strings of words like 'trust us' and 'we're the good guys', and they were just as worthless as the glass trinkets of old.

It's sad for us that this may be the legacy of our latest war in Afghanistan, but it must be infinitely sadder for the Afghans, whose country we've sleepwalked into, stumbling around with our bombs and guns and mumbling the mantra 'we're here to help, we're here to help.'

I wonder if they'll ever forgive us.

The fire died down, and its light faded. None of us could be bothered to build it back up again so Ben, James, the rest of the lads and I went to bed.

The next morning I got a message, passed on the radio net from HQ in Shorobak. They wanted to know how my comms field assessment was getting on. Or, reading between the lines, they were nagging me to come back to Shorobak and get on with my real job, because they thought that I was on a jolly. I hitched a ride back to Delhi, where I wrote them a terse email pointing out that their suspicions were way off the mark. I had to lay it on a bit thick, because really they were absolutely right, but I was damned if I was going to admit it.

Whether I convinced them or not, it was obvious that my days in Garmsir were numbered. I decided to return to Shorobak before I annoyed HQ even further, so I booked myself a seat on the next convoy to Dwyer, the first step in the journey northwards.

I stayed in Delhi just long enough to say my goodbyes to everyone, including Captain Dawood, who greeted me with a dusty bear-hug because he was elbow-deep in a bowl of naan flour at the time. As well as being kandak comms officer he also doubled up as the camp chef.

My convoy to FOB Dwyer was with the US Marines, and I was hitching a ride with them in the back of an armoured truck. Just before we were due to depart, Ed came to find me. He had a 'terp with him.

'Hi, mate,' said Ed. 'This is Khalid. He says he's too old for all this stuff and he wants to go back to Shorobak so he can quit. Can you just make sure he gets back there all right?'

'No worries,' I replied.

Khalid and I sat in the back of an American troop carrier and bumped and juddered our way to Dwyer. And there we stayed, for a while. It turned out there wasn't a convoy going northwards for another three days, which was a shame, because Dwyer was a shit hole. Still, at least it was a shit hole with a DVD player. I spent the three days watching films back-to-back in the tiny, sweltering TV suite, which was a box the size of a living room made out of blast walls four feet thick.

Khalid didn't care about the delay, because it postponed his resignation for three more days, so it improved his finances. On the first day I kept an eye on him, to see how he was coping with the Ramadan fast. Even though the summer was ending and the temperature only got up to about 40 degrees now, I figured it must still have been hard for him not to drink all day. As I was leaving Strongpoint Bravo one of the ANA soldiers had got so dehydrated that he'd started hallucinating. His comrades thought he'd been possessed by the Devil, and asked for a mullah to be sent to exorcise him, so I wanted to keep as close an eye on Khalid as possible.

That evening I asked him how he was coping.

'Not bad,' he said. 'I've started drinking in the daylight – it's too hot to do without water.'

'Fair enough,' I said, and wandered off to the DVD room. I tracked him down again the next lunchtime, to ask him if he wanted a portion of food from the cookhouse, so he could save it until sunset.

'No, no, not necessary,' he said. 'I am eating lunches now. It's too hot to fast.'

It was cooler than it had been for weeks, but for Khalid's sake I maintained the polite fiction of a sudden heatwave. He was practically the only Afghan in the camp, and he must have been relishing the opportunity to break Ramadan without the stigma. On the third day he decided that the heat was so intense he was going to have to take up smoking as well. Then, when the two of us finally got on our American transport to return to Bastion, he eyed my box of water bottles sceptically.

'I think we need more for the journey,' he said. 'I'll get another box for us. Nice cold ones from the freezer in the DVD room!'

Khalid emptied the freezer of its water, and we boarded the armoured truck we were riding back to Bastion.

At 1400 hrs we set off in a huge convoy. We did not arrive in Camp Bastion until 2100 hrs that night. For the seven hours in between, Khalid and I lay on the floor of an empty troop carrier, with rags pressed over our faces.

'These things tend to let the dust in,' the driver had said when we set off, and he was not proven wrong. Every twenty minutes or so I got up and shook off the inch of sand that had settled on me. Then I readjusted the rag over my mouth and nose and went back to lying on the floor with my eyes closed.

It was nearly midnight by the time we made it to Camp Shorobak. My lungs ached from the dust. I walked to the shower block and shampooed my hair five times before the water stopped running brown into the plughole and, as I washed away the grime, I thought about Garmsir.

We'd had a few near misses with the IEDs, playing a cat-and-mouse game with the Taliban on the single track linking Delhi to Strongpoint Bravo. I'd been lucky, but it was a game which could only end one way – sooner or later.

Five days after I arrived back in Shorobak, it did just that.

14

It was on the usual run to Strongpoint Bravo that the IED went off. The WMIK detonated it, since it was the lead vehicle as usual. The blast was so powerful that it ripped the engine block from the Land Rover chassis and hurled it twenty yards into the irrigation ditch. By some miracle, no one was killed.

Scouse – the sergeant major I'd followed into the bazaar for ten cans of Mirinda – was in the driver's seat. He got the worst of it. The shockwave blew upwards from the foot well, smashed his ankle, shattered his leg bones and twisted his foot through a hundred and eighty degrees, so that his toes pointed behind him.

Scouse had been lucky up to that point. I remembered the boot he used to wear. It had a neat cylindrical groove in the sole, where a Taliban bullet had passed through it. He'd been caught in a firefight on patrol, and the Taliban were so close that he'd switched from his rifle to his pistol. Then his pistol had jammed and he'd dived to the ground to try and clear it under a hail of fire.

Once the shooting was done he'd walked away without a scratch on him, but he had a clean half-pipe bullet hole in his boot. What I remembered was the way he used to just walk around in it, as if it wasn't some magical artefact from the very brink of mortality, as if it was just something that you wore on your foot, but with a bit of wear and tear.

This time his luck had run out. He was helicoptered out of Garmsir, patched together in Camp Bastion and flown back to the UK to begin the months of slow and painful rehabilitation.

The top-cover gunner escaped with a shattered thumb – smashed by the shockwave because he'd been resting his hand on the roof when the bomb went off. The third victim, in the passenger seat, was Ed's new second in command. He had arrived in Garmsir the day before, and that patrol was his first introduction to the area. His time in Garmsir ended a few minutes later, when he was helicoptered off to Bastion with a broken leg.

The WMIK had been annihilated. The blast had taken off the entire front of the vehicle, and all that was left of the cab were two seats – the driver's and the passenger's – suspended over thin air. A few pieces of twisted metal, snaking off into nothing, were the only evidence that there had ever been a dashboard, a steering wheel, a bonnet or an engine.

There was a rumour going round that the Taliban called us 'the blessed', because they couldn't understand how else we kept surviving such catastrophic explosions. You had to hand it to the WMIKs, they could take an IED-ing.

Back in Shorobak I walked down to Afghan headquarters for the morning brief. It was my first one since returning from Garmsir, and it was going to be epic. Things had been going badly recently and General Muhayadin had taken it hard. So hard, in fact, that he had had a heart attack. He was still alive, and in command of the brigade, but he was frail and he was behaving even more erratically than usual.

His heart attack had been brought on by a Taliban resurgence. They had been subdued in Sangin and Musa Qal'eh, and pushed out into the rural backwaters. The US Marines had flushed them out of Garmsir, but still they were refusing to lie down and be defeated.

Now the Taliban were spreading out to the south and west of Lashkar Gah, into the Nawa and Nadi-Ali districts, which were huge swathes of rural land. The police had left the areas completely, and both the Afghan and British Armies were too overstretched to counter the uprising. There were small coalition outposts in both districts, but they were like the Sangin and Musa Qal'eh district centres had been two years previously. They were strongpoints under siege, in which ANA soldiers and their mentors sat and repelled attacks. The Taliban seemed like a bubble in a sheet of plastic. Every time it was squashed down in one place, it just popped up again somewhere else.

Even some of our successes from the summer were beginning to tarnish. Patrol Base Attal, whose construction had been the crowning achievement of May's push up the Helmand valley, was practically locked down. The Taliban were back, moving about freely within a few hundred yards of the camp. The ANA soldiers there were refusing to patrol because it was so dangerous. The British mentor team ventured out occasionally, on their own, but there were only a handful of them. They couldn't go more than half a kilometre before the Taliban forced them back.

Now Muhayadin had keeled over with the stress of it all, and we were sitting on our hard plastic chairs in the briefing room, awaiting his arrival – back from his sick bed. Commanding officer 1 Royal Irish, Muhayadin's mentor, had of course been saddened by his protégé's brush with death, but then again every cloud has a silver lining. In Muhayadin's absence he'd been able to speak to the next man in the command chain, the brigade executive officer, who, unlike Muhayadin, he did not consider 'dangerously irrational'.

Commanding officer 1 Royal Irish had given directions to the British staff, and as Muhayadin recuperated they'd busied themselves with the Afghan staff, rewriting the brigade's strategies under the auspices of the executive officer. Without Muhayadin it was easy to shape the Afghan plans to the way we wanted them. The idea was that, when the general returned, the staff's plans would be so well worked out, and so obviously sensible, that Muhayadin would have no choice but to say 'Yes, good work, that's what we'll do.'

Twenty minutes passed in the whitewashed briefing room. Then Muhayadin pushed open the wooden swing door and strode in. We rose from our chairs and stood to attention. He waved us to sit, beaming magnanimously, every inch his old self – the smooth, bald head, the thick moustache and the shining black eyes. Showmanship radiated from him. It was just like old times, except we all knew from his aide that he'd just spent twenty minutes in his office sweating and shaking before he could summon up the strength to address us. This was going to be interesting.

'I wish to thank the executive officer and his staff, and the British mentors, for doing so much planning for the future while I was sick,' he proclaimed to us. This sounded promising. Maybe the plan was going to work. We stared at him like a strange specimen in a tropical fish tank, and he went on. 'I am very appreciative of all your hard work, and it is nice to know that the brigade was in safe hands while I was absent.' He smiled, reassuringly, clearly under the impression that he was not a tropical fish but rather a father figure to us all.

'However!' his tone hardened, 'my plan for Helmand is the *opposite* of what the executive officer has devised!

'In my absence you have planned to strengthen our smaller bases up the Helmand Valley, so that we may send more patrols out into the rural areas. I do not see the point in patrolling these places. I believe we have only one purpose, and that is to *kill the enemy*. Whenever we are not killing our enemies we are wasting our time. My plan is to draw back from our patrol bases, and collect everyone around FOB Price,' he said, gesturing to the base in the centre of Helmand. 'From there, we can sweep up and down the valley' – he waved his ruler around vaguely on the map – 'and once a month kill all the insurgents in the countryside. For the rest of the time, we should stay in FOB Price. The difficulties in maintaining all the small bases are too great. Now, as I have already said, our only priority is killing our enemies, so from now onwards all leave is cancelled.'

He turned to face us and grinned. Perhaps at that moment he mistook the disbelief on our faces for looks of reverential awe.

CHAPTER 14

We didn't say anything just then. We bided our time. We knew that Muhayadin's plans would never become reality, because things that Muhayadin said hardly ever became reality. There were plenty of tools of persuasion and subterfuge that could be brought to bear against him. All that his proclamation heralded was another bloody mess to sort out but, in the end, it cleared itself up pretty quickly. Two days later Muhayadin took to the podium again to speak about his soldiers' leave.

'The welfare of my men is my number one priority,' he stressed to us. 'They fight very hard, and home leave is crucial for their wellbeing. From now on, you must ensure that every soldier gets as much leave as possible!'

So leave was back on and, within a few more days, Muhayadin forgot all about his plan to close down every patrol base in Helmand. Life went back to normal in the brigade. Commanding officer 1 Royal Irish welcomed the change and, I fancied, prayed that Muhayadin would either make a full recovery or else decline swiftly and terminally. Happily for Muhayadin, he managed to do the former.

He calmed down, and his erratic behaviour faded into the general background of chaos. It had plenty of other stuff to compete with. Around that time we got reports that Karzai wanted to get rid of Joe Mangal, provincial governor, and replace him with his predecessor, Sher Mohammed Akhundzada, who was more popular with the voting public, but unfortunately was also a narcotics baron. Then there was the mess around Haji Khan Mohammed, who we heard had just bought the position of chief of police of Gereshk for $100,000. The outgoing chief of police was not a big fish, but his deputy was, and we expected him to leave with his boss, taking a chunk of the police force with him. Then he would be another local strongman to deal with: a powerful person with no official position and a private army.

Like Mullah Abdul Salam, in fact – the governor of Musa Qal'eh. The one who had defected from the Taliban at the start of the year, possibly over a deal gone sour on his irrigation ditches. We suspected that he'd wanted Karzai to split Helmand Province in two, and give him the entire northern half. It hadn't happened, and now he was pissed off all over again. Chaos aplenty in Helmand.

Still, it could have been worse. One of the provincial reconstruction teams in a different province had just found out that their local road-building contractor was controlled by the Taliban, who for months had been blowing the road up with IEDs, then taking our money, repairing the road, blowing it up again, and asking for more money to repair it again.

Such was the way of the war in Afghanistan. It would likely go on like that for years and decades to come, with the international coalition playing its part for a while, and then the Afghans carrying it on among themselves, and then God knows what happening.

At least I, unlike the Afghans, could walk away from it all. My tour of duty was coming to an end, and it was time for me to tie up all my loose ends before saying a final farewell to Afghanistan. I wrote my recommendations for the comms training package in Shorobak, based on my findings in Garmsir. It made a nice report. I highlighted a few simple measures that would improve operating practice and I argued that a step-change in Afghan Army communications skill would only be achieved on the back of a comprehensive literacy training package. Put simply, teach the Afghan radio operators to read and write before you can expect them to do anything more advanced than they're doing at the moment.

My report was read by a few people in the British HQ at Shorobak, and broadly agreed with, but we were all going home soon and no one wanted to think too hard about overhauling comms training to include a comprehensive literacy package, so it was put to one side for the new lot to deal with. They probably looked over it and had their own take on my analysis, but didn't have me around to discuss it with them, and so the whole thing was quietly shelved.

Still, this was not my concern. I busied myself putting the comms team's affairs in order, and after a few days my replacement arrived, to mentor ANA comms over the winter season.

He was a great lump of a warrant officer who laughed like Lenny Henry, radiated enthusiasm and went by the name of Carl. He was several years older than me, but he had a youthful gleam in his eyes. He wanted to make a difference. On his first day in Shorobak we sat down to have a chat, and he asked me about our daily routine in the comms team.

'We generally work about two or three hours a day,' I said. 'There's the morning brief on the ANA side, then you might go around the guys we mentor and make sure they haven't got any major problems. After that, an hour of comms lessons if you've got them scheduled in, then you're free for the rest of the day.'

Carl looked at me as though I was a lazy wastrel, a sponger on the army's resources. It was probably the same look I had given to Dabbers three months previously. What Dabbers had told me then, and what Carl would realise soon enough, was that it simply wasn't possible to work any harder. We were on ANA time, and there was nothing we could do about it.

Later that day the two of us took a walk over to the Afghan side of camp, so I could introduce Carl to everyone, say my goodbyes, and see about borrowing some radios for training. We picked up Tariq, the diminutive, hairy interpreter ('Carl, nice to meet you man, you livin' the dream?'), and we walked with him across the huge, cracked helipad for my final time and pitched up at Major Rohullah's office. I pushed back the familiar door, knocking on it as it swung away from me, and walked inside.

'*Salaam alaykum!*' I ventured, with my hand held firmly over my heart.

'*Salaam alaykum,*' Captain Asif replied, standing impishly behind Major Rohullah's desk.

'We need to borrow some radios from you,' I said, 'would that be OK?'

Captain Asif looked at me with his sad eyes. 'Of course,' he said, 'but we must wait for Major Rohullah. He has to sign the paperwork himself.'

It was beyond me why only the man in charge of comms for the entire brigade could authorise us to borrow some radios, but I went along with it. I liked Captain Asif, and I didn't want to give him a hard time.

'Do you know where Major Rohullah is?' I asked.

'He's in a meeting. I think you should come back in half an hour.' said Asif.

'I am sorry,' he added, and he sounded like he meant it. He sounded like he really was pained by our inconvenience. He was too good a man for this sorry old world.

Carl, Tariq and I walked to the Afghans' shop inside a shipping container to get a can of Mirinda. We sipped our drinks, and chatted for twenty minutes, and then trudged back across camp to see if Major Rohullah had returned. I pushed back the door of his office for a second time.

'*Salaam alaykum!*' I said.

'*Salaam alaykum,*' Major Rohullah replied, with a smile breaking out underneath his wispy goatee beard. I looked around the room and saw that Captain Asif had disappeared. Their tag-team was working as efficiently as ever.

'I am leaving,' I announced. 'This is my replacement,' I added, nodding towards Carl.

Major Rohullah behaved exactly as I expected him to. He sized up Carl and shook us both crisply by the hand.

'It has been a very great pleasure working with you,' he told me, with more politeness than enthusiasm, and then turned his attention to Carl. 'It is nice to meet you, and I look forward to us working together for the next six months.' One mentor gone, another one arrived. Significance for Major Rohullah: basically nil.

'Could we borrow some radios?' I asked. 'Carl wants to have a look over them.'

'Of course,' he said. 'I will get you the paperwork.'

He left the room, and came back a few minutes later with a greyish, photocopied sheet of paper.

'I will sign this for you now,' he said, 'and then you must take it to the Combat Service Support kandak, and get their executive officer to sign it as well. Then you must get the radios from Captain Hameed.'

This was getting a bit rich. Even in the ANA I couldn't see why I needed the signatures of two majors, from separate departments, just to borrow a couple of radios.

The three of us – Carl, Tariq and I – upped sticks again. We made our way over the parade ground and past the shipping container that sold Mirinda towards the Combat Service Support kandak buildings. On the way there, we saw the executive officer driving away in a Ford Ranger. Tariq took the initiative. He snatched up the paperwork and sprinted across the gravel, shouting as he ran. He got the vehicle to stop. The executive officer leant his hand out of the window, brandishing a biro, and signed the documents without looking at them. Then he drove on, and Tariq walked back towards us, proudly.

'Nice one,' I said. 'Let's go and see Captain Hameed.'

We turned towards the Combat Service Support billets, and picked our way past the little garden in the desert towards Captain Hameed's office. The door was open, and I leaned my head into the shady room. Hameed was sitting behind his spartan little school desk, listening to the radio.

'Heeeeyy!' he leered at us. His smile spread across his face, reaching backwards to reveal his dirty molars.

'How are you?' I asked, shaking his hand as if I liked him. 'You know I'm leaving, right? This is my replacement. Anyway, before we say our goodbyes, can we get some radios off you? We've got all the paperwork here.'

Captain Hameed looked at our ragged sheet of paper sceptically. He paused for a moment, and then replied.

'Yes, of course, I will send one of my soldiers to get them for you. In the meantime, please sit. Would you like some chai?'

'No, thank you,' I said. It was still Ramadan, and I didn't think it would have been polite. Even though Hameed's waistline was still enormous, he was visibly more tired and subdued than he had been before the start of the fast.

'Are you sure?' he said. 'Just because we cannot drink doesn't mean that you can't either.'

'Thank you,' I said, smiling, 'but I know how hard it must be for you. I don't want to make you any thirstier by drinking in front of you.'

'OK, no problem,' Captain Hameed gave in.

Five minutes later, some chai arrived for us anyway. It would have been ruder to refuse it than to drink it in front of them, and I did fancy a cup of chai, so I gulped it down. Carl did the same, and we all started chatting about nothing in particular. Captain Hameed came up with the usual series of requests for bits and pieces of equipment or trips to the doctor, but I deflected them. After about half an hour, I felt it was time to raise the subject of the radios again.

'How's it going with getting that equipment for us?' I asked, trying not to sound as if I was nagging.

'One of my soldiers is just fetching them,' Hameed said. 'He will be back very soon.'

A few soldiers drifted in and out of the office and spoke to Hameed in Dari. Another half hour elapsed, and then I pressed him again.

'My men lost the key to the storeroom,' he replied this time. 'They have found it now, and the radios will be with us very soon.'

Another half hour rolled by. Eventually the door opened, and a young Afghan private shuffled in, weighed down with different radios. At last.

We stood up, and Captain Hameed rose as well. It was time for me to say my goodbyes. I shook Hameed firmly by the hand, and let the palm of my other hand rest on his shoulder.

'It's been a pleasure to work with you,' I said. I was being fairly dishonest.

'Yes, yes,' he replied, with affection in his eyes. 'And I am sorry for any misunderstandings that have happened between us.' He was referring to an incident three days beforehand, when he had promised twenty of his soldiers for a comms lesson and none had turned up. It had been less of a misunderstanding and more of a refusal on his part to lift a finger for us.

He turned to Carl. 'And I look forward to working with you very much in the future. I hope that we can have a good relationship like I had with Captain Lee, and that you can continue to help us in all the ways that he did.'

We shook hands again, and walked out of Captain Hameed's office into the sandy open air.

'So is it normal to spend three hours trying to get hold of a couple of radios, then?' Carl asked me.

'Yeah, pretty much. That's why nothing ever gets done around here.'

We left Captain Hameed's office and walked back across camp to find Captain Asif, so I could say goodbye to him as well. I needed to do it properly, because I could quite honestly say that Captain Asif was one of the nicest people that I had ever met. He was a peaceful man, with moist, sad eyes and a permanently worried expression, who thought that human beings were strange for inventing the heat-activated sequential rocket launcher. He was a passed-over captain in his forties who should never have been an army officer in the first place, because he was just too gentle.

Nevertheless, he deserved to have lived his life in peace. He was a member of the silent, huddled majority, who should have been allowed a life away from the British Army, and the US Marines, and the Taliban, and the Soviets, and people like me – an unwarlike man, born into a country synonymous with war. He really was a poor old bastard.

We found Asif back in Major Rohulla's office, and he and I said our goodbyes, shook hands and hugged each other warmly. He wished me all the best for my future, and I told him that I very much hoped his country would soon find peace. We exchanged gifts. He gave me a Muslim *kufi* hat, and I gave him an airborne forces scrim scarf, to keep him warm in the approaching winter.

Actually, I gave him half a scrim scarf. I'd already used the other half to stretch over my helmet, as was the fashion in the airborne forces, but he wasn't to know that. We hugged again, and shook hands again, and I walked away with a faint but recognisable lump in my throat. I had enjoyed knowing him.

That goodbye marked the end of my responsibilities as comms mentor. It was now Carl's job and not mine. We stepped out of Asif's office and turned a sharp left towards the great wide helipad. We took a brisk walk back to the British camp, and just like that my job in Afghanistan was over.

15

A few days later, someone else came to take over my role as head of the comms mentoring team. He was a naval lieutenant, and he had absolutely no idea that Carl existed. The two of them had come from different units, in different areas of the country, and had somehow been assigned exactly the same job. The naval lieutenant tracked me down one lunchtime and said, 'Hi, are you the comms mentor?'

'I was,' I replied.

'Well I'm here to take the job over from you.'

'You're too late,' I said, 'I've already given it to someone. You'll have to try and persuade *him* to hand it over to you.'

I told him where he could find Carl, and left them to fight it out between themselves. As professional soldiers they were more than capable of doing so effectively.

I was in Camp Bastion now, waiting for two weeks for flights home and running the occasional firing range for incoming troops. The whole British force in Helmand was changing over and gradually all the radio operators from my squadron began to trickle back to Bastion for flights home. Some of them had had peaceful tours, and some of them had seen more horror than they should ever have had to see. Each time a few more young soldiers returned, from whichever unit they had been providing comms for, we breathed a little communal sigh of relief. These were our last days in Afghanistan and no one wanted to get killed so close the end. The final few patrols and convoys had a habit of throwing up nasty surprises, and people began to get uneasy about their luck running out.

Less than a week before they were due to ship out, we heard that two soldiers from the Parachute Regiment had been shot by an Afghan private. They were relaxing in camp, near Sangin, when he strode towards them with his rifle on automatic. He sprayed the area with bullets and seriously injured them both, then ran off into town to join the Taliban. What a thing to happen, I thought – emerging unscathed from six months of hard fighting and then getting shot by someone on your own side.

Elsewhere in the province, people were finding that their luck was holding out just long enough. A soldier from the Royal Irish took an RPG warhead straight to the chest. It carried an explosive charge that could breach the hull of a tank, but it didn't go off. It bounced off the chest plate of his body armour, fizzed on the ground, and he escaped the Taliban attack with little more than a winding.

Once you were back in Bastion you knew your luck had lasted out. Bar some freak accident you were going to come home alive and in one piece.

I was safe in Bastion now, but there was still one final deployment on offer for me – a resupply convoy up to Sangin. It was being run by the Combat Service Support kandak over in Shorobak, and I knew they were a man short. One of the lads – Stan – had had to drop out when his flights home got changed. I'd been back to Shorobak a few times to run errands, and each time I saw a tantalising blank space on the ops room whiteboard: an unassigned seat on a vehicle.

I still hadn't seen a firefight, and it rankled with me. I nearly put my name down on the whiteboard for Sangin, but something stopped me. Roachy's words were coming back to me now, from all those months previously:

'Never volunteer for anything. When you volunteer for stuff, that's when you fucking die.'

I left the square on the whiteboard blank. The next time I saw it, it was filled with the words:

'Stan's pussied out. Good job I'm here. Airborne! BEN.'

Ben was a sergeant in our mentor company. He'd achieved notoriety by convincing his parents that he wasn't in Afghanistan at all, that he was just on a six-month exercise in Cyprus. Then he ruined it by having his photo taken in Helmand and put on the front page of the *Mirror*.

On that convoy move to Sangin he trod on an IED and blew himself up. Mercifully, he survived with only shrapnel wounds and kept all of his limbs but, if it wasn't for Roachy's advice to me, perhaps I would have gone instead, and he could have gone home without a scratch on his body.

The last of the soldiers from the Signals squadron came back from the FOBs and patrol bases, we packed our bags and we waved goodbye to Camp Bastion. At dawn, one day in early October, we set out from a small hangar near the airstrip towards a waiting Hercules. The sun was beginning to turn the sky a violent orange, and the aircraft propellers were droning in front of us. A single file of brown, skinny, tired-looking bodies walked towards the rear ramp, straining under their bags. A single file of pale, plump new arrivals walked the other way. Each of us looked at least two stone lighter than each of them. Someone in our column shouted out, 'Have a good six months, lads! I'll let you into a little secret – it's shit!' and we laughed quietly at their misfortune.

Nearly thirty of us from the Signals squadron flew to Kandahar on that Hercules, and shuffled into the huge accommodation hangars to wait patiently for thirty-six hours. I was reunited with Jim the operations officer. We killed time together and, four hours into our wait, as we sat about on our camp beds, the rocket alarm went off. Perhaps we weren't safe yet.

In the Kandahar ops room, so the rumour went, they had a map of the camp on the wall. It was divided up into squares, and they took bets on where the next rocket was going to land. If someone got killed then all bets were off out of respect for the dead, because soldiers were sensitive like that.

'Do you think we should put our helmets and body armour on?' I asked Jim.

'Yeah, nice one, mate,' he replied sarcastically. 'You're a dashing young lieutenant, why don't you lead the way? I'll give you twenty quid if you get all your protective gear on and run off and lie down under your bed!'

Great, I thought, *I've survived the whole summer in Helmand, and now I'm going to get killed by a rocket while Jim takes the piss out of me. That would cap my war off just nicely.*

The sirens kept blaring, and I got up from my seat. I was picking my way through the sprawl of camp beds to get a bottle of water, but then I noticed Sig Barrows. He was one of my lads, and I hadn't seen him for months, not since my trip to Gereshk before mid-tour leave.

'How was the rest of the tour then?' I asked him.

'Yeah, not bad, boss,' he replied apathetically. 'We got to go on some good jobs, but I was a bit disappointed by the end. Six months with the infantry doing force protection, and the Taliban didn't engage us once.'

'No,' I said, laughing, 'they never shot at me either, the bastards!'

Three weeks later, in a bar in Colchester, I was angry.

I'd been drinking for ten hours solid. My head was swimming. I was angry and I didn't know why. I was angry at the chubby girls on the wipe-clean sofa who were sipping their Bacardi Breezers through straws. I was angry with the girls because they hadn't been in Afghanistan, and because they would never be in Afghanistan, and because I had. I knew I was being irrational, but I couldn't help it. They didn't look like very good fighting stock anyway. There probably wasn't a size of body armour big enough for them. I walked outside and stood in the cool, dark, autumn night air to have a serious word with myself.

Why are you being such a prick? I asked.

CHAPTER 15

I'd had an easy tour. I had wanted to go to Afghanistan and, now I was back, I was glad that I had gone. To be angry at anyone for not having been there was irrational, and unfair, and weird.

That night was the only time, before or since, that I've felt that way. It was as if some little devil had crept inside my head without me knowing. It had slept there, invisible, until it was doused awake by the booze. Then it was there – irrational and malevolent and alien to me.

If such a thing could crawl inside me, I thought, then what's crawled inside all the people who've seen their friends killed and maimed? What about the lads at FOB Gibraltar, who got shot at every day, all summer? What's crawled inside the soldiers from 2 PARA, who suffered one in five killed or injured? – *one in five!* Whatever it was, it existed, silent and menacing, inside hundreds of men and women coming back from Afghanistan. Perhaps it would creep and claw its way out of them all, slowly and painfully, in the months and years ahead.

A few days later I was sitting on my bed in the officers' mess with my girlfriend. She was one of the citizens of Britain in whose name we were fighting our war, and I was showing her my photos. We got to a shot of me in front of a field gun at FOB Dwyer, and our conversation turned to artillery tactics.

'The big guns stay in our bases,' I said, 'and when someone wants to shell the Taliban, they radio through the coordinates of the enemy to the base. Then the men on the artillery guns fire onto the Taliban position.'

She pursed her lower lip. 'Well then why don't the Taliban just shoot the men who work the artillery guns?' she asked.

'They're in a base,' I said. 'They can shoot the Taliban, but the Taliban can't shoot them, because our artillery guns shoot further than their rifles.'

She looked confused, and adopted the sort of tone someone uses when they think you're incompetent, but aren't sure, and don't want to seem too rude. 'So if you can shoot further than them, then why haven't you won the war already?'

I could sense the start of a long explanation.

'Well, we don't always know where they are,' I tried, as an opening gambit. We took it from there.

Several hours later I walked into the officers' mess bar to meet a friend of mine, and I told him what I'd been up to for the afternoon.

'That's nothing, mate,' he said, smiling. 'Funnily enough, I tried to explain exactly the same thing to my girlfriend once.'

'What ... about artillery?' I asked. Here was another citizen in whose name we were fighting. I wondered what *she*'d had to say.

'Yeah, I explained to her about the guns, and she said, "Yes, but they're not *real* shells that you fire, are they? I mean not like the ones in World War Two and that sort of thing?"

'She gets worried about me, and I think in her head she'd managed to convince herself that Afghanistan was just like a big game of Laser Quest.'

And with that we bought ourselves another beer, and started to talk about something else.